Writing Qualitatively

Writing Qualitatively: The Selected Works of Johnny Saldaña showcases the diverse range of writing styles available to qualitative researchers through the work one of the most internationally cited and referenced methodologists. The traditional academic journal article still holds its place as a convention of published scholarship, but Saldaña illustrates how a variety of approaches to research documentation can evocatively represent social life and one's self in intriguing ways.

Writing Qualitatively assembles journal articles, book chapters, ancillary materials, texts from keynote addresses, and previously unpublished work that illustrate Saldaña's eclectic body of inquiry. Each piece is prefaced with author comments on the selection, and how readers themselves might venture into comparable writing styles. Multiple methodologies and writing examples are included, ranging from case studies to action research; from poetry to ethnodramatic play scripts; from confessional tales to autoethnographies; and from textbook materials to classroom session designs. An introduction to the collection discusses Saldaña's writing processes and how qualitative researchers and educators can extend their own imaginations and creativity to find new forms of scholarly presentation and representation.

Writing Qualitatively serves as a supplemental text for undergraduate and graduate courses in qualitative inquiry, educational research, ethnography, and arts-based research. This unique anthology demonstrates to students, professors, and professional researchers how academic scholarship can be reported through a breadth of literary genres, elements, and styles.

Johnny Saldaña is Professor Emeritus from Arizona State University's School of Film, Dance, and Theatre in the Herberger Institute for Design and the Arts. Saldaña's works have been cited and referenced in over 7,000 research studies conducted in over 130 countries in disciplines such as K-12 and higher education, medicine and health care, technology and social media, business and economics, government and social services, the fine arts, the social sciences, human development, and communication.

World Library of Educationalists series

Learning, Development and Education: From Learning Theory to Education and Practice
The Selected Works of Knud Illeris
Knud Illeris

(Post)Critical Methodologies: The Science Possible After the Critiques
The Selected Works of Patti Lather
Patti Lather

Education, Ethnicity, Society and Global Change in Asia
The Selected Works of Gerard A. Postiglione
Gerard A. Postiglione

Leading Learning/Learning Leading: A Retrospective on a Life's Work
The Selected Works of Robert J. Starratt
Robert J. Starratt

Communicative Competence, Classroom Interaction, and Educational Equity
The Selected Works of Courtney B. Cazden
Courtney B. Cazden

Ideological, Cultural, and Linguistic Roots of Educational Reforms to Address the Ecological Crisis
The Selected Works of C. A. (Chet) Bowers
C. A. Bowers

Writing Qualitatively
The Selected Works of Johnny Saldaña
Johnny Saldaña

For more titles in this series visit www.routledge.com/World-Library-of-Educationalists/book-series/WORLDLIBEDU

Writing Qualitatively
The Selected Works of Johnny Saldaña

Johnny Saldaña

LONDON AND NEW YORK

First published 2018
by Routledge
2 Park Square, Milton Park, Abingdon, Oxon OX14 4RN

and by Routledge
711 Third Avenue, New York, NY 10017

Routledge is an imprint of the Taylor & Francis Group, an informa business

© 2018 Johnny Saldaña

The right of Johnny Saldaña to be identified as author of this work has been asserted by him in accordance with sections 77 and 78 of the Copyright, Designs and Patents Act 1988.

All rights reserved. No part of this book may be reprinted or reproduced or utilised in any form or by any electronic, mechanical, or other means, now known or hereafter invented, including photocopying and recording, or in any information storage or retrieval system, without permission in writing from the publishers.

Trademark notice: Product or corporate names may be trademarks or registered trademarks, and are used only for identification and explanation without intent to infringe.

British Library Cataloguing-in-Publication Data
A catalogue record for this book is available from the British Library

Library of Congress Cataloging-in-Publication Data
Names: Saldāna, Johnny, author.
Title: Writing qualitatively : the selected works of Johnny Saldāna / Johnny Saldāna.
Description: London ; New York : Routledge, [2018] | Includes index.
Identifiers: LCCN 2017057446 | ISBN 9781138486249 (hardcover) | ISBN 9781351046039 (ebook)
Subjects: LCSH: Authorship. | Academic writing. | Social sciences—Authorship. | Humanities literature—Authorship.
Classification: LCC PN146 .S35 2018 | DDC 808.06/6—dc23
LC record available at https://lccn.loc.gov/2017057446

ISBN: 978-1-138-48624-9 (hbk)
ISBN: 978-1-351-04603-9 (ebk)

Typeset in Bembo
by Apex CoVantage, LLC

For the past, Ann Whitehouse

For the present, Harry F. Wolcott

For the future, Matt Omasta

Contents

Republication Credits and Permissions   x
About the Author   xiii
Acknowledgments   xiv

1 Writing Qualitatively   1
Purpose Statement 1
Influences and Affects 1
  Learning About Teaching 2
  Learning About Theatre and English 2
  Teaching About Teaching 3
  Professional Development 3
  Good People, Bad People 4
My Writings, My Writing 5
  Research Studies in Journal Articles and Book Chapters 5
  Books and Textbooks 5
  Other Writings 8
Genres, Elements, and Styles 8
  Stylistic Choices 9
Writing Qualitatively 10
  The Prosaic 10
  The Poetic 12
  The Dramatic 17
  The Technical 20
The Selected Works in This Volume 23
Closure and Transition 25

2 Writing About Action Research   28
Documenting and Analyzing Fieldwork 28
Theatre of the Oppressed with Children: A Field Experiment 31

3 Writing the Case Study 49
Portraits in Miniature 49
Exploring the Stigmatized Child Through Theatre of the Oppressed Techniques 52

4 Writing About Critical Pedagogy 69
The Significance of Moments 69
Social Class and Social Consciousness: Adolescent Perceptions of Oppression in Forum Theatre Workshops 72

5 Writing the Confessional Tale 81
Telling the Truth 81
Ethical Issues in an Ethnographic Performance Text: The "Dramatic Impact" of "Juicy Stuff" 84

6 Writing About Method and Methodology 101
"How To," Not "Talk About" 101
Goodall's Verbal Exchange Coding: An Overview and Example 104
Chapter 10 – "Thinking Narratively": From Thinking Qualitatively: Methods of Mind *111*

7 Writing for the Research Studio 127
The Art of Teaching Research Methods 127
Exercises and Activities for Coding and Qualitative Data Analytic Skill Development: From The Coding Manual for Qualitative Researchers *130*
Group Exercises: From The Coding Manual for Qualitative Researchers *132*

8 Writing Research as Reader's Theatre 140
Presenting Performatively 140
The Reader's Theatre Script for "Lifelong Impact: Adult Perceptions of Their High School Speech and/or Theatre Participation" 143
LAURA A. MCCAMMON, JOHNNY SALDAÑA,
ANGELA HINES, AND MATT OMASTA

9 Writing Autoethnography 156
Telling Your Own Story 156
Gay-Tex-Mex: Autoethnographic Vignettes 159

*Thank You, Mrs. Whitehouse: The Memory Work of One
    Student About His High School English Teacher,
    Forty Years Later   163*

10 Writing Poetry   176
    Poetry as Scholarship   176
    This Is Not a Performance Text   179

11 Writing Ethnodrama   186
    Research as Performance   186
    Becoming a Man   190
    Second Chair: An Autoethnodrama   192
    The Drama and Poetry of Qualitative Method   207
    Street Rat   213
    JOHNNY SALDAÑA, SUSAN FINLEY, AND MACKLIN FINLEY

12 Writing in Role   246
    Character in Qualitative Inquiry   246
    *All I Really Need to Know About Qualitative Research I Learned
        in High School: The 2016 Qualitative High Graduation
        Commencement Address   249*
    Blue-Collar Qualitative Research: A Rant   259

Index   269

Republication Credits and Permissions

The author credits and thanks the following for their permissions to republish selected material:

Chapter 1

For an excerpt from *Finding My Place: The Brad Trilogy*: originally published in Harry F. Wolcott's *Sneaky Kid and Its Aftermath: Ethics and Intimacy in Fieldwork* (pp. 167–210), Walnut Creek, CA: AltaMira Press, 2002; reprinted by permission of AltaMira Press/Rowman & Littlefield.

Chapter 2

For "Theatre of the Oppressed with Children: A Field Experiment": originally published in *Youth Theatre Journal* (a Taylor & Francis Journal), vol. 19, 2005, pp. 117–133; doi 10.1080/08929092.2005.10012580; reprinted by permission of Taylor & Francis Ltd, www.tandfonline.com.

Chapter 3

For "Exploring the Stigmatized Child Through Theatre of the Oppressed Techniques": originally published as Chapter 2 in *Youth and Theatre of the Oppressed*, edited by Peter B. Duffy and Elinor Vettraino, New York: Palgrave Macmillan, 2010, pp. 45–62; reproduced with permission of Palgrave Macmillan.

Chapter 4

For "Social Class and Social Consciousness: Adolescent Perceptions of Oppression in Forum Theatre Workshops": originally published in *Multicultural Perspectives* (a Lawrence Erlbaum Associates Journal), vol. 1, no. 3, 1999, pp. 14–18; reprinted by permission of Taylor & Francis Ltd, www.tandfonline.com.

Chapter 5

For "Ethical Issues in an Ethnographic Performance Text: The 'Dramatic Impact' of 'Juicy Stuff'": originally published in *Research in Drama*

Education (a Taylor & Francis Journal), vol. 3, no. 2, 1998, pp. 181–196; doi 10.1080/1356978980030205; reprinted by permission of Taylor & Francis Ltd, www.tandfonline.com.

Chapter 6

For "Goodall's Verbal Exchange Coding: An Overview and Example": originally published in *Qualitative Inquiry* (Sage Publications Journals), vol. 22, no. 1, 2016, pp. 36–39; doi 10.1177/1077800415603395; reprinted by permission of Sage Publications.

For Chapter 10 "Thinking Narratively" from *Thinking Qualitatively: Methods of Mind*: originally published in Johnny Saldaña's *Thinking Qualitatively: Methods of Mind*, Thousand Oaks, CA: Sage Publications, 2015, pp. 169–183; reprinted by permission of Sage College/Sage Publications.

Chapter 7

For "Exercises and Activities for Coding and Qualitative Data Analytic Skill Development," Appendix D from *The Coding Manual for Qualitative Researchers* (3rd ed.); and "Group Exercises" from the Companion Website for *The Coding Manual for Qualitative Researchers* (3rd ed.), https://study.sagepub.com/node/31740/student-resources/chapter-6: reprinted by permission of Sage Publications.

Chapter 8

For "The Reader's Theatre Script for 'Lifelong Impact: Adult Perceptions of Their High School Speech and/or Theatre Participation'" by Laura A. McCammon, Johnny Saldaña, Angela Hines, and Matt Omasta: originally published in *Youth Theatre Journal* (a Taylor & Francis journal), vol. 26, no. 1, 2012, pp. 26–37; doi 10.1080/08929092.2012.678218; reprinted by permission of Taylor & Francis Ltd, www.tandfonline.com; permission also granted by co-authors Laura A. McCammon, Angela Hines, and Matt Omasta.

Chapter 9

For "Gay-Tex-Mex: Autoethnographic Vignettes": © 2017 by Johnny Saldaña as an unpublished work; reprinted by permission of the author; thanks are extended to Bryant Keith Alexander for commissioning the work for the 2017 International Congress of Qualitative Inquiry conference.

For "Thank You, Mrs. Whitehouse: The Memory Work of One Student About His High School English Teacher, Forty Years Later": originally published as Chapter 1 in Catherine Compton-Lilly and Erica Halverson's (Eds.) *Time and Space in Literacy Research* (pp. 19–32), New York: Routledge, 2014; reprinted by contractual permission from Routledge.

Chapter 10

For "This Is Not a Performance Text": originally published in *Qualitative Inquiry* (© 2006 Sage Publications Journals), vol. 12, no. 6, 2006, pp. 1091–1098, doi 10.1177/1077800406293239; reprinted by contractual permission from Sage Publications.

Chapter 11

For "Becoming a Man": originally published in *Ethnotheatre: Research from Page to Stage*, 2011, pp. 79–80, Walnut Creek, CA: Left Coast Press; reprinted by contractual permission from Left Coast Press.

For "*Second Chair*: An Autoethnodrama": reprinted by contractual permission from Sage Publications; the final definitive version of this paper has been published in *Research Studies in Music Education*, vol. 30, issue 2, pp. 177–191, 2008 by Sage Publications Ltd. All rights reserved. © SEMPRE, 2008. It is available at: http://online.sagepub.com/; doi 10.1177/1321103X08097506.

For "The Drama and Poetry of Qualitative Method": © 2007 by Johnny Saldaña, originally published as Chapter 17 in Melisa Cahnmann-Taylor and Richard Siegesmund's (Eds.) *Arts-Based Research in Education: Foundations for Practice* (pp. 220–227), New York: Routledge, 2008; reprinted by contractual permission from Routledge.

For *Street Rat*: © 2004 by the co-authors as an unpublished work; originally published in Johnny Saldaña's (Ed.), *Ethnodrama: An Anthology of Reality Theatre* (pp. 104–145), Walnut Creek, CA: AltaMira Press, 2005; reprinted by permission of AltaMira Press/Rowman & Littlefield; permission also granted by co-authors Susan Finley and Macklin Finley.

Chapter 12

For "All I Really Need to Know About Qualitative Research I Learned in High School: The 2016 Qualitative High Graduation Commencement Address": © 2017 from *Qualitative Inquiry in Neoliberal Times*, edited by Norman K. Denzin and Michael D. Giardina (pp. 179–189); reproduced by permission of Taylor and Francis Group, LLC, a division of Informa plc.

For "Blue-Collar Qualitative Research: A Rant": originally published in *Qualitative Inquiry* (Sage Publications Journals), vol. 20, no. 8, 2014, pp. 976–980; doi 10.1177/1077800413513739; reprinted by permission of Sage Publications.

About the Author

Johnny Saldaña is Professor Emeritus from Arizona State University's (ASU) School of Film, Dance, and Theatre in the Herberger Institute for Design and the Arts. He received his BFA in drama and English education, and MFA in drama from the University of Texas at Austin.

Saldaña's qualitative methods works have been cited and referenced in more than 7,000 research studies conducted in over 130 countries, in disciplines such as K-12 and higher education, medicine and health care, technology and social media, business and economics, government and social services, the fine arts, the social sciences, human development, sport, journalism, and communication.

Saldaña's research in qualitative inquiry, data analysis, and performance ethnography has received awards from the American Alliance for Theatre & Education, the National Communication Association's Ethnography Division, the American Educational Research Association's Qualitative Research Special Interest Group, New York University's Program in Educational Theatre, and the ASU Herberger Institute for Design and the Arts. He has published a wide range of research articles in journals such as *Research in Drama Education*, *Multicultural Perspectives*, *Youth Theatre Journal*, *Journal of Curriculum and Pedagogy*, *Teaching Theatre*, *Research Studies in Music Education*, and *Qualitative Inquiry*, and has contributed several chapters to research methods books including *The Oxford Handbook of Qualitative Research*, *Handbook of the Arts in Qualitative Research*, and the 5th edition of *The Sage Handbook of Qualitative Research*.

Acknowledgments

I extend my thanks to Hannah Shakespeare, Senior Commissioning Editor of Research Methods, for opening the door and inviting me in to contribute a volume of my selected works for Routledge's *World Library of Educationalists* Series. I also thank Editorial Assistant Matthew Bickerton of Routledge and Jennifer Bonnar of Apex CoVantage for prepublication guidance.

I extend my gratitude to research instructors and colleagues for their inspiration, mentorship, and support: Tom Barone, Mary Lee Smith, Amira De la Garza, Sarah J. Tracy, Ann Whitehouse, Coleman A. Jennings, Lin Wright, Harry F. Wolcott, Norman K. Denzin, Yvonna S. Lincoln, Mitchell Allen, Patrick Brindle, Helen Salmon, Jai Seaman, Ray Maietta, Ronald J. Chenail, Joe Salvatore, Tera R. Jordan, Kip Jones, Duncan Waite, Leo A. Mallette, Linda Essig, Kakali Bhattacharya, Patricia Leavy, Liora Bresler, Joe Norris, Carole Miller, Laura A. McCammon, Angela Hines, and Matt Omasta. Final thanks go to Jim Simpson for his never ending support of my work.

1 Writing Qualitatively

Purpose Statement

The purpose of this book is to anthologize selected writings representing a diversity of qualitative genres and styles by research methodologist Johnny Saldaña.

I begin this volume with a purpose statement because, as a qualitative researcher, it's what I was taught to do. My long-distance mentor, the late educational anthropologist Harry F. Wolcott, advised in his methods writings that all research reports should begin this way. And though this introductory chapter is not a report in the traditional academic sense, the purpose statement frames both the writer and reader for what follows. For the research writer, it forces clarity and focus of intent. For the reader, it establishes an informal contract of understanding between you and me.

Lest you think I adhere slavishly to the traditions and standardized conventions of scholarly writing, know that that is not the case. I both follow the rules and break them. But I had to learn the rules first. One of choreographer Twyla Tharp's most famous quotes is, "Before you can think outside of the box, you have to start with a box." A student once remarked to me that I could "get away with" deviations from the norm in my later writings because I had established myself first as a traditional researcher. I firmly believe the same applies to everyone entering the field of qualitative inquiry: Before you can think outside of the box, you have to start with a box.

Influences and Affects

I developed the phrase *influences and affects* in my methodological writings as the qualitative paradigm's parallel to quantitative research's "cause and effect." In our lives, multiple influences shape who we are and who we are becoming. Every action, reaction, and interaction cannot be attributed to a single, isolated factor. An intricate combination of influences works in tightly interwoven interplay to make something happen. As for affects, the term suggests not just measurable outcomes but internal, emotional responses rooted in belief systems to those influences. Affects are discovered forms of intrapersonal awareness and new interpersonal relationship dynamics as well as the observable consequences of lived experience.

The subsections that follow contribute nothing directly to the purpose of the book, but they present necessary contextual background information about how I became who I am now. If you want to know the writer and his writings, you need to know a few things about his life.

Learning About Teaching

One of the most significant influences on my life and on my career as a qualitative researcher has been education, in its broadest sense. As a child, I loved learning though I may not always have enjoyed schooling. As early as first grade I knew I wanted to be a teacher when I grew up. I was fascinated by the teacher's editions of textbooks that sat on my instructors' desks. The answers to all the questions posed in the teachers' versions were printed in red ink. At school and at home I wrote and designed my own four-page textbooks with all the answers included. Decades later I'm still writing textbooks, but this time for adult researchers.

First through twelfth grade schooling exposed me to a variety of teachers. Most were quite good at their jobs, a few were less than satisfactory, and three in particular were intolerable. Teaching was still my life goal during high school, and in classes I paid attention not only to content but also to pedagogy. I believe that every one of us has had that one special teacher who significantly impacted (influenced and affected) our lives in some way, and Ann Whitehouse – my eleventh-grade high school language arts teacher – was mine. No one to date or since has shown Mrs. Whitehouse's instructional mastery in the classroom. I've replicated her teaching style and methods throughout my university career, and I call upon her spirit to enter me before every class and workshop I facilitate so that I too might teach with the same exceptional quality.

Learning About Theatre and English

My university undergraduate degree is in theatre and English education. Both emphases have served me well as a qualitative researcher. Theatre training taught me how to write plays and detailed character analyses. English education acquainted me with a variety of literary genres and the necessity of effective composition. These skills transferred readily into my scholarly writings, yet there were other unforeseen benefits to a theatre and English education.

Actors are first taught to look at everyday life carefully to observe people's physical and vocal mannerisms in order to create believable characterizations in performance. How relevantly these skills transfer into participant observation fieldwork as I study social life. Directing and theatrical production design training enabled me to look at things in the world conceptually, symbolically, and metaphorically for rich artistic renderings. Those design skills and viewpoints come into play as I analyze and interpret qualitative data as evocative symbol systems of meaning.

Literature courses exposed me to the world's great literary masterpieces in a wide variety of forms ranging from the prosaic to the poetic to the dramatic.

My knowledge of the possible approaches to writing has informed my own eclectic body of work. Teaching English to high school students required that I mastered the fundamentals of grammar and composition principles. And these skills make it so much easier to write – painfully sometimes when at a loss for ideas, but easier when publication deadlines must be met.

Teaching About Teaching

A folk saying among professional educators goes, "To teach is to learn twice." My university teaching assignments consisted primarily of methods courses – teaching future teachers how to teach. The principles of effective classroom pedagogy were not only taught but practiced on my feet. I learned that teachers tend to teach the way they were taught for approximately their first seven years as professional educators. If that is so, then I have a responsibility in the classroom to model the best methods possible. Teaching how to teach reinforced within me the concepts of good pedagogy. Being a teacher educator taught me how best to communicate and how to design instruction in order to maximize learning. I write like I teach. I write as if I'm teaching. To write is to learn twice, too.

Professional Development

I never stopped learning during my 35 years as a professor in higher education. I get bored easily, so I actively seek new opportunities to expand my knowledge base. Conference attendance introduced me to the intriguing work of figures such as theatre artist and activist Augusto Boal, and the figurehead of qualitative inquiry, Norman K. Denzin. I enrolled in graduate level qualitative research methods courses during my sabbaticals and learned the diverse approaches to inquiry from Arizona State University professors Tom Barone and Mary Lee Smith in education, and Saran J. Tracy and Amira De la Garza in communication. Every student I taught, every course I designed, every thesis and dissertation I supervised, and every faculty member I interacted with all taught me something in one way or another.

I keep up to date as much as possible with the academic literature from several disciplines but particularly with books, journal articles, and newsletters about qualitative research methods. I read voraciously, and I yellow highlight on hard copy any passages I deem significant and worth citing in the future. I have never boxed myself into one methodology exclusively. I am fascinated by all approaches to qualitative inquiry. I find a few suspect and I question their legitimacy and trustworthiness, but I acknowledge their place for other scholars intrigued by them.

I also find professional development learning opportunities in the strangest of places. The syndicated television series *Judge Judy* is admittedly one of my favorite programs to watch. Judge Judy herself is certainly engaging when she presides in the courtroom, but my fascination lies with observing the everyday people who appear as plaintiffs, defendants, and witnesses. Their personalities and authentic dialogue exchanges in conflict-laden situations inform me greatly about the human condition. I even use video clips from the program as "data" in my research methods workshops to teach field note and analytic memo writing.

I was trained as a theatre artist that all the world's a stage. Virtually every experience outside my home is a theatrical living laboratory of the social world. Whenever I interact with a restaurant server, retail store sales clerk, a homeless woman asking me for spare change, or the grandchildren I take care of after school one day a week, part of me makes inferences about their lives. Qualitative research training keeps me grounded in reality to prevent implausible conjectures, but there are times when I am too inquisitive and cannot turn off my inquirer's mind. Life to me is one long research study.

Good People, Bad People

No one succeeds alone. I have been remarkably blessed with parents who nurtured my dreams; teachers who inspired me to pursue those dreams; a few faculty colleagues and administrators who enthusiastically supported my work; compassionate professionals in the field who give me opportunities to succeed; an understanding husband who provides me time and space to write at home; and good friends who listen to my woes and celebrate my victories. I have always been amazed at how significantly a single action from just one person can set in motion a new life pathway for a fellow human being. I use the metaphor that, throughout my life, good people have opened doors and invited me in.

Unfortunately, I have also been cursed with hostile actions from bad people who did not want to see me flourish. I identify myself as a gay Hispanic without a PhD. These cultural markers are sometimes perceived by others as stigmas. I have been victimized with: hate mail from a White supremacist; racist graffiti scrawled on my personal property; student refusals to work with me due to my ethnicity or sexual orientation; and condescending dismissal by faculty peers of my qualifications and achievements. Not everyone in the scholarly community finds my writing appealing. A few are even offended by some of my works and, at times, my challenging point of view at professional gatherings. "Haters gonna hate," and those actions have made me feel "lesser than."

Yes, I do indeed feel that throughout my career I've had to work twice as hard to be considered half as good. It wasn't until my research output surpassed those with PhD degrees that I realized working twice as hard made me *twice*, not half, as good. Though I greatly enjoyed teaching and working with students, I retired early from academia due to what I perceived as its microaggressive, elitist, and inequitable work environment. But through time I've learned to find my tribes and affinity groups where collegiality, empathy, and support encourage and motivate me to continue on my professional pathways.

All of the above are the salient influences and affects on my life and career. There are many others but the details are unnecessary. I have yet to address the purpose of this book (to anthologize selected writings representing a diversity of qualitative genres and styles), so let me now transition toward the thematic thread of this volume: writing qualitatively.

My Writings, My Writing

If you want to know who I was and who I am, read what I've written. A writer's works embody his mind at particular stages of his life.

Research Studies in Journal Articles and Book Chapters

Since I bore easily, I try new things constantly. When my early *quantitative research* studies (Saldaña & Otero, 1990) fatigued me, I turned to qualitative inquiry, as had the majority of scholars in the area of theatre education at the time. I conducted a *mixed methods* study comparing Hispanic and White children's responses to the same play production (Saldaña, 1992), and a generic *interview analysis* of artists' and educators' recommendations for working with Hispanic youth (Saldaña, 1991). My first supervised study, as accompanying fieldwork for a qualitative research methods course, was an educational *ethnography* of an inner-city drama teacher (Saldaña, 1997). Now that I was better informed of qualitative data analysis methods, I conducted a *grounded theory* analysis of interviews with child audience participants (Saldaña, 1995b). I then reanalyzed seven years of qualitative data collected as part of a *longitudinal study* (Saldaña, 1996, 2002a, 2008a) in grades K-6 child audience response using *assertion heuristics*.

I next immersed myself in multicultural education, theatre for social change, and performance ethnography, so my research projects delved into *action research* (Saldaña, 2005b), *critical pedagogy* (Hager, Maier, O'Hara, Ott, & Saldaña, 2000; Saldaña, 1999b), and the writing and production of ethnographic performance texts, or *ethnodrama* and *ethnotheatre* (Saldaña, 1998b, 1999a, 2002b, 2003a, 2008b, 2008c, 2010a, 2010c, 2017). Selected participants from these projects also served as *case studies* (Saldaña, 1998a, 2010b). Autoethnography was now cultivating a substantial following, so I too explored writing *autoethnography* (Saldaña, 2014b) and its theatrical presentation as *autoethnodrama* (Saldaña, 2008d). Yet another *mixed methods* study opportunity arose, but this time with a multisite research team with qualitative and quantitative data collected from an *online survey* (McCammon, Saldaña, Hines, & Omasta, 2012). Methodological studies were then conducted in cultural *conversation analysis* (Saldaña, 2016a) and new *coding methods* (Saldaña, 2014a; Saldaña & Mallette, 2017). At the time of this writing, I am working on a *phenomenological study* that explores what it means to be a qualitative researcher.

Books and Textbooks

As you can infer, I've explored several different methodologies of qualitative inquiry throughout my career – deliberately to educate myself on the diversity of approaches in the field. This eclectic body of research experiences, enrollment in qualitative methods courses during sabbaticals, and my own departmental teaching assignment of qualitative research courses for our graduate program, greatly informed my methods textbook writing. My sole theatre education contribution, *Drama of Color: Improvisation with Multiethnic Folklore* (Saldaña, 1995a), was a compilation of session designs for elementary youth, generated from my focused interest in multicultural education. But good people who entered my life cultivated me as a writer of research methods textbooks.

Mitch Allen, former director of AltaMira Press, opened the door and invited me in to publish. I had gained substantial experience in long-term fieldwork projects and illustrated my methodological and analytic principles in *Longitudinal Qualitative Research: Analyzing Change through Time* (Saldaña, 2003b). I then edited for him a collection of research-based play scripts for *Ethnodrama: An Anthology of Reality Theatre* (Saldaña, 2005a). When Mitch later started his own publishing house, Left Coast Press, he again invited me to write a methods book on performance ethnography instead of a second anthology. *Ethnotheatre: Research from Page to Stage* (Saldaña, 2011a) embodied everything I had learned about the genre up to that point.

Earlier, another good person opened the door and invited me in – twice. Patrick Brindle, former research methods acquisitions editor for Sage Publications-UK, noticed I was presenting a short paper on coding at an American Educational Research Association conference, and asked if I might be interested in developing a book on qualitative coding. The idea for writing such a work never crossed my mind, but I was excited by his offer and quickly composed a prospectus and submitted it – which was later rejected by five peer reviewers and Brindle himself.

It hurt to be turned away, especially by a prestigious publishing house, but I graciously thanked Patrick for his time and the invitation to submit. Upon reexamination of the collegial and constructive peer reviews, two noticeable themes emerged. First, I hadn't done my homework. My original prospectus was based on what I knew at that time about coding and qualitative data analysis, which was adequate but not substantive. Second, my chapter organization for the work didn't make sense to reviewers. They couldn't see any logical plotting of the content. I truly did not have a clear vision for what the book was about.

The jurors were right on both counts. So, over the next year I researched the qualitative methods literature and related journal articles and discovered there was indeed a treasure trove of additional coding approaches with which I was unfamiliar. I was overwhelmed by the number of them and needed some way of describing the methods in ways that would make sense to a reader. Serendipitously, a textbook for a theatre education methods course I instructed, *Structuring Drama Work: A Handbook of Available Forms in Drama and Theatre* (Neelands & Goode, 2000), provided the inspiration for reconceptualizing and reorganizing the coding prospectus. First, I discovered that I should not write a conventional textbook; instead, the book needed to function as a *reference manual*. Second, the book should not be divided into chapters but according to *categories of coding methods* with each one illustrated in a standardized *profile format*. I composed a revised prospectus for Brindle and Sage Publications-UK a year later with these new ideas, and *The Coding Manual for Qualitative Researchers* (Saldaña, 2016b) was accepted. It has appeared in three editions to date and is my most cited work by other researchers.

Again, another good person opened the door and invited me in. Patricia Leavy was editing a qualitative research methods series for Oxford University Press. We knew each other's arts-based writings, but she asked me to develop a short textbook on the basics of qualitative research. Since I had been immersed in the subject for over 15 years and considered the offer an easy project, I accepted the commission. But during the initial stages, I learned how extremely difficult it is to write introductory material for novices to qualitative research methods. No assumptions could be made about the reader's previous knowledge base. I could not focus on a particular disciplinary perspective (e.g., education) since the book was to be marketed to people from the social sciences, health care, communication, and other fields. What I had taken for granted as common knowledge by all qualitative inquirers had to be written about and taught to a newcomer as if learning it for the very first time. The result was a slim paperback that truly outlined the *Fundamentals of Qualitative Research* (Saldaña, 2011b).

Helen Salmon of Sage Publications-US was the next to open the door and invite me in. She was seeking someone to update the late Matthew B. Miles and A. Michael Huberman's (1994) classic text, *Qualitative Data Analysis: An Expanded Sourcebook*. Given my writings in research methodology to date, I was charged with not just updating but streamlining the coauthors' massive text. Fortunately, I was very familiar with their work since it was an assigned text in two research methods courses I took during sabbaticals. I revised the book to become what I wish it had been for me when I was a student: better organized, clearer and explicit directions, consistent formatting, easier display references, and describing only those methods most relevant to qualitative researchers in the 21st century. When appropriate, I added content and methods from my own body of work. I never had the opportunity to meet Miles and Huberman personally but I think I would have liked them. It was an honor to revise their rigorous work for a new generation of researchers: *Qualitative Data Analysis: A Methods Sourcebook* (Miles, Huberman & Saldaña, 2014).

Sage Publications continued their relationship with me by publishing a "reader," as I called it, on epistemologies for inquiry: *Thinking Qualitatively: Methods of Mind* (Saldaña, 2015). I was fascinated with a comment I heard from a colleague at a research conference who bemoaned the fact that her students could not extend their data analyses independently beyond a certain level: "I can't teach my students how to think," she complained in frustration. One of my education interests was the movement in grades K-12 brain-based learning, and I reflected how I might apply those concepts and techniques for adult qualitative researchers. An excerpt from the book is included in Chapter 6 of this volume which provides more information on the text.

My most recent textbook is a co-authored work. When Sage Publications asked me to develop a new introduction to qualitative research methods text, I felt I could write one adequately on my own. But by this time in my career my repertoire of examples and methods descriptions had "dried up." I needed new data to illustrate and analyze as samples for readers, a fresher approach to subtopics such as ethics and interviewing, and a better-informed perspective on the current technology available. I opened the door and invited Matt Omasta in – a former doctoral student of mine and a current associate professor.

Qualitative Research: Analyzing Life (Saldaña & Omasta, 2018) brings two theatre artists and educators together for a radically revamped curriculum: teaching data analysis methods *first* and *throughout* the course; and teaching data collection methods *before* methodology and research design. Our rationale is that data analysis is arguably the most difficult yet least emphasized subtopic in the qualitative methods course and deserves daily instruction, not allocation as a latter unit during the semester. Also, research methodology and design make better sense when students have a background in qualitative data collection. Our modus operandi (as theatre training taught us) is: Master your tools before you create; craft precedes art.

Other Writings

Various unpublished writings for workshops, conference presentations, and keynote addresses have been developed, as have published entries for research handbooks and encyclopedias, along with teacher-oriented journal articles, book reviews, and a few forewords. I have also developed PowerPoint presentations I consider quite pedagogically exceptional to accompany some of my research methods workshops, which I willingly share with attendees.

I have ideas and even a few typed notes for a children's chapter book, a folkloric play for young audiences, a collection of short stories for adult readers, a period novel, and a suite of original poetry that may never get written. It occurs to me that these are *fictional* works – a genre with which I have minimal experience writing. I speculate that my career has been so immersed in social reality and truth-seeking that creative literary works cannot be composed, save for a few original yet minor play scripts. How odd that theatre training taught me to act, direct, write, and design for imaginary worlds produced on stage, but I cannot seem to get beyond a few jottings for developing fictive pieces. Perhaps in the future when I'm bored again and need a change....

Genres, Elements, and Styles

Other scholars such as Belcher (2009), Goodall (2008), Van Maanen (2011), Wolcott (1994; 2009), and Woods (2006) have written excellent texts about writing qualitative research. I needn't summarize them here; instead, I refer you to their works for guidance. In the following section I address my own writing processes and principles.

My first research methods textbook, *Fundamentals of Qualitative Research*, focuses on three components of inquiry: genres, elements, and styles. These three components were adapted from literary analysis:

> Genres or forms are literary types, such as short story, biography, poetry, and drama. Elements refer primarily to literary devices incorporated throughout a work, such as protagonist, antagonist, symbolism, foreshadowing, and alliteration. A style suggests the overall tone of the work: for example, tragedy, comedy, satire, romance, or fantasy.
>
> Qualitative research also has genres, elements, and styles.... The genres or forms range from methodologies such as grounded theory to phenomenology to ethnography. The elements of inquiry are not just literary but functional: participant observation field notes, interview transcripts, literature review, and so on. The styles of qualitative research refer to its write-ups and the various approaches to tale-telling: realistically, confessionally, critically, analytically, interpretively, and so on (Van Maanen, 2011; Wolcott, 1994). It is these styles of writing that primarily determine a study's narrative texture.
>
> (Saldaña, 2015, p. 171)

My English education background influenced my classification of qualitative research methodologies and methods. No matter how technical or seemingly mundane, all qualitative research write-ups are literary in nature. Certainly, some writers are better than others at maintaining reader engagement with their prose (or poetry or drama). But my primary focus when I read a journal article or methods textbook, or even when I listen to an oral conference presentation, always attends to the writer's *style*.

Stylistic Choices

Style, in art, can be an elusive concept to grasp. Quite simply, style refers to the consequential and unique result from a particular combination of elements (visual, aural, narrative, etc.), which may or may not work together. As a theatre director, I was always conscious of a production's style when I made specific choices about actor movement, staging, and the design or "look" of costumes, scenery, lighting, and the sound of incidental music, vocal qualities, and special effects. Every choice had to work together and belong together – the artistic principle of *unity* – to ultimately achieve a distinctive production style.

These same artistic principles apply to qualitative reportage. If a researcher makes the methodological or genre choice of a case study, then the constituent elements I expect to see are descriptive passages about the case's physical appearance and general personality, extended yet revealing excerpts from interviews with the case, and representative vignettes culled from participant observation of the case interacting with others in social settings. As for the researcher's write-up – its literary style – multiple choices are available but some may be more effective than others.

The researcher may choose a *descriptive and realistic* style of reportage that presents an unedited "day in the life" of the case without comment or interpretation. Or the researcher might select an *analytic and formal* style that examines unique categories of action or thematic features about the case. Still another option refocuses attention on the researcher's blunders and failings with the project through a *confessional* tale. Or a significant, epiphanic episode from fieldwork might call for exclusive attention in the write-up as an *impressionist* tale.

Another option is to use the case as a stimulus for more *interpretive* renderings about broader social implications, placing focus not on the case but on the issues raised. Perhaps the case lent itself to a participatory action research agenda, and thus a *critical or advocacy* report detailing the changes that occurred when the researcher and case worked together might be written. If the researcher truly wishes to share ownership of the project with the case, a *collaborative or polyvocal* report showcasing both voices and worldviews might be composed.

Traditional literary forms are also available for write-ups. The researcher might decide to portray the case through a *literary narrative* style – "creative non-fiction" as it's been labeled – by writing an evocative representation of the case comparable to a short story. Other arts-based options include *poetic* or *dramatic* write-ups about the case – verse constructions of interview transcripts or dramatization of the case's life in monologic or dialogic forms for the stage or digital screen. Even an exhibit of *photographs* taken by the case and/or the researcher, or other art media such as sketches and portraits, can present and represent fieldwork. Researcher interpretations of the case through *dance* or original *music* composition are not out of the question. The arts are legitimate epistemologies or ways of knowing.

From the diverse range of styles profiled above (and there are more), which one(s) will best represent the research study about the case? These are choices the researcher ultimately makes, but the guiding principle is a selection(s) that will achieve unity – a stylistic writing choice(s) that harmonizes with the genre selected (case study, grounded theory, phenomenology, and so on) and the available elements from fieldwork for analysis (interview transcripts, field notes, written survey responses, statistics, documents, and so on). Ultimately, the style(s) chosen should be the one(s) that will present the most *credible*, *vivid*, and *persuasive* representation of the study.

Writing Qualitatively

My writing methods and techniques for qualitative reportage can be categorized broadly into three traditional literary formats: the *prosaic*, *poetic*, and *dramatic*. And by necessity, writers must also attend to the *technical* matters of composition.

The Prosaic

The compliment I've received most often from students and colleagues about my textbook writing is its clarity. There are several reasons for this. First, the advanced vocabulary used by some qualitative methodologists, particularly those exploring ontological, theoretical, and philosophical matters of inquiry, is just not my style. I am a pragmatist, and thus my word choices tend to be basic for the task at hand. I am also conscious of the fact that my works may be read by newcomers to qualitative research, so I make my narratives as reader friendly as possible to lessen anxiety and maximize comprehension. Even abstract topics such as epistemology and conceptual frameworks are written with as much elegance as I can muster. True analytic revelation, to me, is making the most profound insights using the simplest of words. Perhaps my rudimentary vocabulary use in my writing may also be due to the fact that I frequently taught arts experiences to young children. Teachers must be extremely conscious of their word choices with five- and six-year-olds to offer clear directions and minimize confusion. I told my doctoral students when their dissertation prose became too obtuse, "Write for your *reader's understanding* instead of trying to prove how smart you are."

Second, as I revealed earlier, I write to teach. I write as if I'm teaching. When I speak improvisationally in the classroom or workshop setting, or even when reading from prepared texts, I employ an acting tactic that has served me well: *Think about every single word you're saying.* An actor gives more meaning to his interpretation and performance when he consciously attends to the nuances of dialogic interaction. Rather than delivering lines from rote memory, he immerses himself in the world of the play by listening carefully to other characters, then *reacting* to them by uttering each scripted word as if for the very first time. An observer of my teaching once told me I have a sense of "presence" about me – meaning, an alertness to where I am and what I'm doing at all times. That's because I'm thinking carefully about every single word I'm saying. Whether speaking or writing, I've learned the hard and sometimes embarrassing way that every word choice matters.

Third, my voice has been complimented as melodic and easy to listen to. I am conscious not only of what I'm saying but how I'm saying it. I deliberately inflect and vary my pitch throughout sentences for variety. I emphasize selected words with volume or tempo to give them their due significance. I parse phrases within sentences and in-between longer passages so my students' minds can cognitively process separate meaning units. Imagine a sliver of silence at the slash marks of this narrative: "When you code,/you're transforming longer data units into/condensed/symbol systems of meaning./Methodologists suggest that we're/translating/the data,/giving them/new forms/for later analytic work."

My composition parallel to these vocal qualities and dynamics is making paragraphs short when possible, and using subheadings frequently. I often structure my works to disseminate information in brief units, profiles, or sections. When a publisher or copy editor permits it, I **bold** or *italicize* key words throughout for reader emphasis. Bullet pointing seems to be falling out of favor in some circles, but I have no problem using them for brief lists. I also demand that no gray shaded text appears in my published works. I find it extremely difficult to read narratives with such low printed contrast that I sometimes skip those muddied passages.

Fourth, there is melody and rhythm not only in music, speech, and poetry but also in written prose. When possible, I voice aloud non-stop everything I've written for a first draft to feel how is sounds. (No doubt this is the playwright training in me coming out.) By articulating my text, I assess its narrative textures, ease, and rhythmic flow. Speaking aloud what I've typed helps me revise the prose and gives me embodied ownership of my ideas.

Fifth, I am organized to a fault. My workspaces may not always look neat at first glance, but my materials are properly labeled in filing cabinets and my personal library is carefully shelved according to each book's genre. I manage my classes and workshops with streamlined procedural routines, and I deliver instruction with utmost attention to linear presentation and progression of content. That same work ethic permeates my writing. I may work haphazardly and idiosyncratically on first drafts in the privacy of my office, but the revised drafts and final product are carefully plotted and outlined to make structural sense and hence easier for readers to follow and absorb the ideas.

Sixth, I move my hands frequently when I speak. In my early years, it was a subconscious act. Now, I make gestures (and sometimes facial expressions) deliberately and strategically for visual audience engagement and for supplemental illustration of my speech. I go beyond pointing to a PowerPoint image for eye focus or emphasis. My hands tell stories. They illustrate abstract concepts. They show the processes of qualitative data analysis in three-dimensional space. I'm uncertain how this form of communication influences the initial writing of my work, but it tests the clarity of the final product. If I can gesture (or even pantomime) comfortably the core ideas of a sentence I've typed, then I know I've made my writing vivid and active.

The Poetic

My high school and university courses plus independent reading introduced me to some of the masters of this literary genre. Among my favorite poets are Walt Whitman, Emily Dickinson, Carl Sandburg, and Robert Frost. Special pieces by e. e. cummings, Dylan Thomas, and Anne Sexton stay deep within me. The poetry of Shakespeare's plays and translations of verse playwrights like Molière delight me as a theatre artist. And the contemporary voices of Macklin Finley and Mary E. Weems resonate in my soul for their arresting, angry poems. I love rereading my favorite poets to relive their work. I don't find new meaning – that happened the first time I read their poems. Instead, I get aesthetic enrichment, a warm feeling as if I'm visiting a dear friend whom I have not seen for some time.

I have not written much original poetry. I experimented with it in my mid-twenties and even published two poems in a regional literary journal. But the prosaic and dramatic took up most of my writing energies as my academic career advanced. Nevertheless, I later learned how poetry serves not only as a literary form of expression but as an evocative analytic approach to qualitative data.

Verbatim theatre performer Anna Deavere Smith attests that everyday people speak in forms of "organic poetry." Naturally emergent rhythms, tempos, pauses, and parsing from her participants during audio or video recorded interviews become transformed into poetic format. A prosaic passage such as this,

> I don't know how I got to where I am today. I guess it's because I was just too scared to make better choices when I was younger. I wasn't brave enough, strong enough to say "enough." So now, I'm paying the price of regret.

gets "poeticized" like this,

> I don't know
> how I got to where I am
>   today.
>
> I guess it's because
>   I was just too scared to make better choices when I was younger.
> I wasn't brave enough,
> strong enough
> to say
>   "enough."
>
> So now, I'm
> paying the price of regret.

One of my qualitative data analytic methods is *codeweaving* – the integration of separate codes into a coherent narrative that posits plausible interrelationships between and among the codes. Codeweaving can also be applied to original poetic constructions by the researcher, a method called *found poetry*, when authentic narratives from the participant are adapted into verse form.

In vivo codes are carefully selected verbatim words and phrases from interview transcripts, field notes, or participant writings that symbolically represent larger units of data. The codes are chosen not only for representational purposes but also for their evocative power. As an example, an interview was conducted at a medical center with William (pseudonym), a man with Chronic Obstructive Pulmonary Disease (COPD). He describes his medications, symptoms, and daily life with COPD. *In vivo* codes are set in bold:

[I: What medications are you taking for COPD?]
WILLIAM: I'm on **Montekulast**, **Dulera**, the gray thing, what's it called? **Spiriva**, and the **ProAir** rescue inhaler. And, if it matters, I sleep with a **CPAP machine**, but that was long before I was diagnosed with **COPD**.

[I: How are the medications working for you?]

WILLIAM: OK, I guess. My condition's **constant** but at least it's **not getting worse**.

[I: What's constant?]

WILLIAM: A **shortness of breath**, sometimes climbing upstairs, and sometimes just bending over to pick something up. There's a **mild tightness** in my chest, I have to take some **deep breaths** now and then to catch my breath. Sometimes I feel **tired all day**, but I think that's more my sleep than the COPD. I had a **bout** recently with **atelectasis**, I think it's called, and I had to go on **antibiotics** for that for, for a few weeks, had **x-rays**, it cleared up. No problems since then.

[I: How has COPD affected your daily life?]

WILLIAM: Well, I'm **not exercising** as much as I should, but not because of the COPD, but just because I just tend to **sit around a lot**. I do notice that when I go outside sometimes my breathing gets more **labored**, so I guess that's **stuff in the air** that's affecting me. I try to stay indoors as much as possible. It **hasn't really debilitated me** in any way, but I know I'm not going to be running marathons, so.

[I: Has there . . .]

WILLIAM: Like, right now, there's a **slight tightness** in this part of my chest (*moves hands across upper chest area*), but it's not painful, it's just **noticeable**. And I don't have as much **air power** as I used to have for speaking. My **breath sometimes runs out** at the end of a sentence. I have to **breathe a little more air** in to speak.

[I: How often do you use the rescue inhaler?]

WILLIAM: Not all that often, really, maybe just once every two weeks or so. That's when I feel my chest is **real tight** and I'm having **some difficulty** breathing and I **need some relief**. It really works, the ProAir, it's good.

[I: How does the CPAP machine work for you?]

WILLIAM: It's OK. Sometimes I feel like the **pressure** isn't strong enough, but I know what it's like to have a higher pressure than you need. There's always that **adjusting** when you first turn it on, you have to **sync your breathing** to the pressure, **gasp** in some deep breaths, **get into a rhythm** of breathing through your mouth or nose. I've been using it for years, maybe 15 years now, but it's still **a nightly thing**. I do know what it's like to *not* have the machine, so it works, for sure, and **helps me feel better** when I wake up in the morning.

[I: In what ways?]

WILLIAM: A **clearer head**, like I'm more **alert**. I got the machine for a **snoring** problem originally. I **used to be a smoker** and I snored loud, woke up really **foggy**. My doctor had me go through some **sleep studies** and they felt it best that I go on the machine. It really made a difference in the way I felt when I woke up in the morning. Not as **muddled** or **drowsy**. I used to be on **prescription meds** for sleep, but none of those worked

or had **weird side effects**, so I just use over-the-counter sleep meds now from Walgreen's.
[I: What concerns, if any, do you have about your COPD?]
WILLIAM: Is it going to **get worse**, which from what I understand, it will. So far so good, it's not excellent but **it's good**. **I worry** if I'm ever going to have a really bad attack where I can't breathe at all. **I worry** about whether I'll ever need an **oxygen tank**. I just take it easy now, don't strain myself, but **I can't control** what happens inside **my lungs**. So, I've just gotta **live with that**.

Below are the *in vivo* codes generated from the transcript in the order they appear. As a formatting technique, codes are listed in caps and *in vivo* codes are placed in quotation marks to remind the researcher of their participant-origin:

"MONTEKULAST"
"DULERA"
"SPIRIVA"
"PROAIR"
"CPAP MACHINE"
"COPD"
"CONSTANT"
"NOT GETTING WORSE"
"SHORTNESS OF BREATH"
"MILD TIGHTNESS"
"DEEP BREATHS"
"TIRED ALL DAY"
"BOUT"
"ATELECTASIS"
"ANTIBIOTICS"
"X-RAYS"
"NOT EXERCISING"
"SIT AROUND A LOT"
"LABORED"
"STUFF IN THE AIR"
"HASN'T REALLY DEBILITATED ME"
"SLIGHT TIGHTNESS"
"NOTICEABLE"
"AIR POWER"
"BREATH SOMETIMES RUNS OUT"
"BREATHE A LITTLE MORE AIR"

"REAL TIGHT"
"SOME DIFFICULTY"
"NEED SOME RELIEF"
"PRESSURE"
"ADJUSTING"
"SYNC YOUR BREATHING"
"GASP"
"GET INTO A RHYTHM"
"A NIGHTLY THING"
"HELPS ME FEEL BETTER"
"CLEARER HEAD"
"ALERT"
"SNORING"
"USED TO BE A SMOKER"
"FOGGY"
"SLEEP STUDIES"
"MUDDLED"
"DROWSY"
"PRESCRIPTION MEDS"
"WEIRD SIDE EFFECTS"
"GET WORSE"
"IT'S GOOD"
"I WORRY"
"I WORRY"
"OXYGEN TANK"
"I CAN'T CONTROL"
"MY LUNGS"
"LIVE WITH THAT"

Rather than analytic categorization, the researcher creatively explores how the *in vivo* codes can be adapted into poetic format to capture the essence of the case, story, experience, or phenomenon. When necessary or for intentional effect, codes can be rearranged, repeated, or modified using poetry's available conventions (stanzas, indents, punctuation, and so on). Not all *in vivo* codes from the initial analysis must be used and, when necessary, supplemental verbatim extracts from the interview transcript can be added:

Used to be a smoker . . .

Slight tightness
    shortness of breath
Mild tightness
    deep breaths
Real tight
    labored
        pressure
            GASP

Snoring
    muddled
        drowsy
            foggy
        sleep studies
    CPAP machine
Prescription meds
    Montekulast
        Dulera
            Spiriva
                ProAir
    helps me feel better

COPD
    tired all day
        not exercising
            can't control my lungs

I worry

                                        (I worry)

Writing poetry is an analytic heuristic – a method of discovery. Writing poems with raw data or inspired by them provides new meaning to the experiences we study. It transforms social scientific prosaic data into artistic representations and possible presentational forms. As an artist I find poetry, in its broadest sense, in many things including the visual. I have even found poetry in researcher presentations at conferences, when their analytic prowess and new insights about social life aesthetically arrested me and made me say out loud, "Wow." Good poetry is not just a literary genre; it is profound revelation about the human condition.

The Dramatic

When I first took university courses in qualitative inquiry in the mid-1990s, I was educated in conventional, prosaic forms of qualitative research, fieldwork, data analysis, and writing. But as I read independently the methodological literature of the field, I stumbled upon Norman K. Denzin's (1997) *Interpretive Ethnography: Ethnographic Practices for the 21st Century*. A chapter on performance ethnography in his text appealed to my theatrical interests and broadened my conception of research genres.

I actively searched for published academic literature, play scripts, and video recordings of the genre, and learned that more than 100 terms had been developed by scholars and artists for a family of variants: ethnographic performance texts, verbatim theatre, non-fiction playwriting, conversational dramatism, docudrama, scripted research, theatre of the real, etc., plus my own creation, reality theatre. Ultimately I adopted two umbrella terms coined by anthropologists Joseph Bram and Victor Turner that I felt best represented the forms: *ethnodrama* and *ethnotheatre*:

> An ethno*drama*, a compound word joining ethnography and drama, is a written play script, teleplay, or screenplay consisting of dramatized, significant selections of narrative collected from interview transcripts, participant observation field notes, journal entries, personal memories/experiences, and/or print and digital artifacts such as diaries, social media, email correspondence, television broadcasts, newspaper articles, court proceedings, and historic documents. In some cases, production companies can work improvisationally and collaboratively to devise original and interpretive texts based on authentic sources. This approach dramatizes data.
>
> Ethno*theatre*, a compound word joining ethnography and theatre, employs the traditional craft and artistic techniques of theatrical or media production to mount for an audience a live or mediated performance event of research participants' experiences and/or the researcher's interpretations of empirical materials. The goal is to investigate a particular facet of the human condition for purposes of adapting those observations and insights into a performance medium. Ethnotheatre uses fieldwork for theatrical production work.
>
> (adapted from Saldaña, 2005a, p. 12)

I experimented with the staging of research and learned some things along the way as to the efficacy and aesthetics of playwriting and production. My first venture, "*Maybe someday, if I'm famous . . .*", dramatized my case study research of a talented adolescent with a passion for acting. It was a moderately successful writing attempt, but in retrospect stayed too close to social science to transcend into art. The production quality itself received audience praise, but professional theatre educators questioned the legitimacy of the text (see Chapter 5).

The second project adapted the ethnographic writings of a story that fascinated me: Harry F. Wolcott's case study of Brad, the "sneaky kid" whom Wolcott befriended and later interviewed when the 19-year-old drifter squatted on his property. Wolcott's confessional tales revealed a sexual affair between them and Brad's emergent mental illness, which descended into paranoid schizophrenia, the young man's violent physical assault on Wolcott, and the destruction of his home by arson. The theatre artist in me visualized this gripping story on stage, and I received permission to dramatize the account.

I admired the methods works of Wolcott, and my ethnodrama incorporated multiple selections from his books to "characterize" the anthropologist as he spoke directly to the audience throughout the play. This scene from the opening monologue weaves excerpts from various titles:

(SLIDE: *Finding My Place: The Brad Trilogy*)
(*indicating title slide*)
HARRY: How about my title? Did it reach out and grab you?
(*acknowledges it may have not, for some*)
    I've written with a particular audience in mind: people who engage in fieldwork –
(SLIDE: *book cover for Harry F. Wolcott's* Ethnography: A Way of Seeing)
    ethnography, the rendering of the ongoing social activities of some individual or group from a *cultural* perspective. In fieldwork, you immerse yourself personally – with passion, without apology – for the purposes of research. Fieldwork beckons, even dares you, to become part of what you study.
(SLIDE: *book cover for Wolcott's* The Art of Fieldwork)
    I'd never deny unabashed efforts to approach my work artistically. In its own ways, art is every bit as rigorous and systematic as science. Artists portray. That's also what ethnography is about: to present material in a sufficiently engaging manner to hold the interest of an audience who may not expect to be entertained, but hopes not to be bored.
(SLIDE: *"No two individuals ever get exactly the same message."*)
(*to an audience member*)
    If you fall asleep, I need never know. To hurry through is to miss the point of what both fieldwork and life itself are all about. These are my words, my sentences, my ideas; I stand by them. So, attend to a discussion of *my* problems and solutions and don't remain too preoccupied with your own. I need an audience of others, multiple and complex. No two individuals ever get exactly the same message.

                                               (Saldaña, 2002b, p. 171)

I stayed close to Wolcott's writings, reluctant to freely adapt or imaginatively reconstruct the narrated interactions between Brad and Harry in the original source material. Wolcott offered constructive suggestions for script revisions throughout the process, yet had final word on the performance draft. Chapter 11 of this volume includes additional scenes from the play.

Like my first ethnotheatrical experiment, the production values for *Finding My Place: The Brad Trilogy* were high, especially with a professional actor cast to portray Harry and a dynamic student performer as Brad. The ethnodramatic play script, however, is somewhat verbose and plays it safe. It has a strong plot and storyline but is heavily monologic and, if revised today, I would explore more plausible dialogic exchanges between the two "characters."

The production generated heated audience response during a post-performance discussion session at the Advances in Qualitative Methods conference in 2001. The play seemed to have triggered strong reactions among selected audience members who vehemently objected to what they perceived as the unethical and sexual "abuse of power" perpetrated by Wolcott on his 19-year-old case study. The controversy stirred by his original Brad Trilogy articles resurfaced in their dramatization and performance. The confrontational talk-back session was one of the lowest points in my career, for I did not tactfully respond to the audience's emotional concerns because I could not comprehend their personal perspectives on the issues raised in the play. It was a valuable lesson for me on how powerfully theatre can provoke an unanticipated spectrum of responses, and how artistic defensiveness defeats the necessary understanding of each audience member's worldview.

My third project dramatized Charles Vanover's paper presentation delivered at an American Educational Research Association conference. Charles sat behind a table, as presenters often do at these events, and retold his stories of a White teacher working in Chicago's inner-city, predominantly African American schools. As a teacher educator, I resonated deeply with his moving and poignant account. And as I listened to the gripping tale, I could envision his work on stage as a one-man show with full production staging (set pieces, hand properties, music, etc.). I immediately connected with Charles and proposed that his narrative be transformed into an ethnodramatic play. He agreed but stipulated that he himself and not a different actor must perform it. We collaborated on the venture with me as co-playwright and director of the production which was presented at several venues across the United States as form of "touring research." "Chalkboard Concerto" (Vanover & Saldaña, 2005) was Vanover's first performance experience, and so motivated was he by the pedagogical potential of *inquiry theatre*, as he coined it, that Charles continued using theatre in his own research projects as a modality for exploring teacher education topics.

My fourth ethnotheatrical production, *Street Rat*, an adaptation of fieldwork on and poetry about homeless youth in pre-Katrina New Orleans by Macklin Finley and Susan Finley, holds a place in my 45 years of theatre experience as one of the most successful and artistically rendered play productions I've ever created (see Chapter 11). The original source materials developed by the

Finleys offered dynamic material with which to work. My contribution to the enterprise consisted of transforming their narrative journal articles, Macklin's poetry, and other unpublished data into a dramatic structure. The result was a one-hour script with a strong storyline, three dimensional characters, and a proper balance of monologic, dialogic, and poetic texts.

The production itself was also a culmination of my evolving aesthetic principles for ethnotheatre. I prepared for the project by travelling to New Orleans to conduct short-term fieldwork interviewing homeless youth in the area about their lived experiences. My observations of the sites mentioned in the Finleys' accounts were photographed and documented in field notes for future reference. The scenery and set decoration for the play production consisted of authentic regional artifacts from New Orleans – even the trash scattered on the stage floor. Student actors, on their own initiative, conducted local fieldwork with homeless youth to better inform their characterizations. My direction took a bold traverse staging for the performance with the action occurring in a center track of the venue with audience members seated on either side as if witnessing reality close-up. The company also raised funds for a local homeless youth shelter by soliciting donations from patrons each night after the performances.

When all the constituent elements of a play production work effectively, when the performance achieves a strong sense of unity and style, when the event transcends an evening of entertainment and becomes arresting art, theatre artists label the work "a perfect gem." In school, university, and community theatre productions this accomplishment is somewhat rare. But when it happens, it has the potential to impact an audience, if not the theatre company itself, with a memorable aesthetic experience.

The best written play scripts, whether ethnodramatic or not, achieve in print what live theatre attempts to achieve on stage. The drama conjures strong visual images in the reader's mind. She can "hear" the characters speaking as it's read silently. There's an engagement with the story through a "what happens next?" mindset as scenes and acts progress. The reader feels a sense of significance or magnitude to the work, even if the action portrays the seemingly mundane aspects of human life. This is not only what drama but even prose and poetry about research should accomplish.

The Technical

Writing is an art but it's also a craft. Aside from the prosaic, poetic, and dramatic, research writers must attend to technical matters of composition. Over the years I've developed several pieces of writing advice that I've passed along to others. Just a few of them include:

- Write at least one page a day, and in a year you'll have a book (or a thesis or dissertation).
- You don't need to begin writing the beginning of the work. Write whatever can be written about. If you're motivated to write Chapter 3 before Chapter 1, then write it.

- Subheadings are your friend. Use them often to keep you and your readers on track.
- If you're tired of writing, then edit and proofread what you've already written. Correct any errors in your spelling, grammar, citations, and references.
- If you want to become a better writer of research, then read a lot of it.

All my qualitative research methods textbooks include several more recommendations for writing the final report. These methods range from document formatting to strategies such as searching for "buried treasure" hidden within a paragraph. But the one question I am asked most often by former students and novice researchers is, "How do I get my book published?" Former editor Mitchell Allen's (2016) *Essentials of Publishing Qualitative Research* is the definitive insider's guide for journal article, book chapter, and book publication information. His website's blog (scholarlyroadsideservice.com) offers additional guidance. What I discuss next is introductory knowledge from a writer's perspective based on my own experiences.

Throughout my career, good people – good acquisitions editors and publishers – opened their doors and invited me in. But that didn't mean I could enter their houses empty-handed. A new book idea begins with a well-written proposal that informs and persuades a publishing company why it should invest time and money in your work. Your idea must consider several opposing factors:

- Your personal vision vs. The publisher's market needs
- Revising pre-existing work (such as a dissertation) vs. Developing original material
- Writing from your accumulated expertise vs. Researching and learning about the subject as you write
- Potentially substantial royalty income vs. Minimal royalties but at least a publication credit
- Making a small disciplinary contribution vs. Writing for international, multidisciplinary impact

Book writing and publishing is a combination of initiative, opportunity, networking, time, hard work, and excellent writing skills. Above all, you must be excited and passionate about the subject, or the writing task will be tedious and likely uncompleted. You must also honestly ask yourself whether the book you want to write is a book that others will want to read. But as I was taught by one of my playwriting instructors (modified for monographs instead of plays): "Just write the book you need to write, and let the book find its own readers."

Do your homework with potential publishers. Peruse the websites and catalogs of publishing houses that carry titles comparable to your idea or who may be interested in your work. Send a *short* e-mail to a designated acquisitions editor as an introduction and initial inquiry. If you attend conferences where these companies exhibit, visit their booths and displays, converse with their sales representatives and, if present, their acquisitions editors to learn what types of books they're looking for. Network with previously published authors at these gatherings for mentorship and contacts. Above all, be courteous, professional, and low-maintenance with everyone.

Target just a select number of houses that may be interested in reading your book proposal. Don't neglect lesser-known, niche, or print-on-demand publishers. Electronic self-publishing is certainly an option, but that choice comes with less prestige and potentially fewer readers. Avoid companies that ask *you* to pay *them* to publish your work.

Virtually every publisher has specific guidelines on its website for how book proposals should be written and submitted. Answer their questions succinctly and follow their guidelines exactly. A book proposal is somewhat comparable to a dissertation prospectus, job application and interview, sales pitch, and performance audition. You must demonstrate that you're "humbly qualified" to write a book-length work. The quality of your proposal reflects your quality as a potential author with the publisher and to your book proposal's reviewers. The document exhibits you at your scholarly best; it must be nothing less than perfect.

I have served as a book proposal and manuscript reviewer for several publishing houses, which greatly informed my own proposal writing submissions. I've read both outstanding and poor work, and I recall faults that motivated me to recommend to publishers that they not accept a proposal:

- The proposal appears written in haste
- There are sketchy, unformulated ideas
- The writer is unaware of or makes inaccurate or false statements about the existing literature
- The writer makes grandiose claims about the proposed work and its market
- The prose has a pompous, intellectual tone
- Poor formatting (e.g., small font, minimal white space) makes the proposal difficult to read
- There are excessive, lengthy narratives without subheadings
- The proposal includes an incomplete or messy writing sample
- There are spelling and grammatical errors throughout the document
- There are no page numbers throughout the document
- The writer offers unrealistic proposals for the book's content, length, and delivery schedule

Acknowledge that the majority of acquisition editors know their jobs quite well and know what they're doing. If they reject your proposal, accept it graciously and thank them for their time (remember my story with Sage Publications-UK). Editors are not your enemies – they are genuinely seeking *quality* works to publish. Review the comments offered by proposal reviewers, revise your document accordingly, and resubmit it. If your proposal is accepted, read your contract offer carefully and negotiate any necessary changes. *Strictly* meet all manuscript submission requirements and deadlines.

There is so much more to writing and publishing books, but the first step is to create a well-written proposal. I insist that these documents appear not just thoughtfully composed but technically correct. Just one spelling error jars me. Several grammatical errors annoy me. A document without page numbers frustrates me. If I can't trust the writer to pay attention to details and form, how can I trust the writer to pay attention to content? First impressions matter.

I don't claim to be an excellent or perfect writer. That assessment is for readers and critics to decide, not me. Writing is easy; writing well is hard. Peer reviewers, copy editors, and proofreaders of my published work make me look better than I really am.

I am 63 years old as I compose this sentence, so I have several decades of writing experience behind me. Age is not an automatic qualification for some things, but in this case 63 years of lived experience have greatly informed my life and work. It took me a while to discover, but what I learned eventually was that I didn't need to "find" my voice. All I needed to do was to trust it.

The Selected Works in This Volume

The collection begins with conventional educational research articles then segues into methods and methodological writing. The second half of the book's representative works illustrates arts-based forms and formats. Each chapter includes a brief introduction on the research methodology or writing style employed, along with supplemental background information on the selections.

Chapter 2, "Writing About Action Research," presents the report from a study conducted with fourth and fifth grade children to reduce oppression and to cultivate their conflict resolution strategies at school.

Chapter 3, "Writing the Case Study," profiles one salient class session and one stigmatized girl's experiences during it from the study described in Chapter 2.

Chapter 4, "Writing About Critical Pedagogy," recounts a theatre workshop conducted with two different groups of adolescents and their divergent perceptions of oppression due to their social class.

Chapter 5, "Writing the Confessional Tale," discloses the ethical dilemmas I experienced during the research for and production of an ethnographic performance text about a talented adolescent, his teachers, and parents.

Chapter 6, "Writing About Method and Methodology," includes two selections. The first is a journal article that demonstrates one approach to conversation analysis with an extended example. The second is an excerpt from my textbook, *Thinking Qualitatively: Methods of Mind*, about writing options for qualitative research reportage.

Chapter 7, "Writing for the Research Studio," illustrates supplemental, participatory learning exercises and activities to enhance students' qualitative data analysis skills from the ancillary materials developed for *The Coding Manual for Qualitative Researchers*.

24 *Writing Qualitatively*

The second half of the book showcases arts-based approaches to research writing.

Chapter 8, "Writing Research as Reader's Theatre," demonstrates how the co-authored narrative of a qualitative research report can be transformed into an informal, performative presentation.

Chapter 9, "Writing Autoethnography," includes two selections that illustrate the researcher as a reflexive participant about his own life. The first is a brief narrative on my personal-cultural identities. The second recounts the memories related to an influential high school teacher and her impactful affects on my teaching career.

Chapter 10, "Writing Poetry," includes a poetic response to and manifesto about the misuse of "performance" in qualitative inquiry.

Chapter 11, "Writing Ethnodrama," includes four selections. (Peer reviewers of this book's original proposal recommended expanded content for this chapter since I have written extensively about the genre.) The first selection is a brief, self-standing autoethnodramatic monologue about adolescence. The second is a monologic, autoethnodramatic script about musicianship with background information on the play's development. The third selection includes two scenes adapted from the works of Harry F. Wolcott. The fourth selection is the complete script of *Street Rat*, a co-authored ethnodramatic work about homeless youth in pre-Katrina New Orleans.

Chapter 12, "Writing in Role," an underutilized approach by qualitative researchers, includes two selections. The first is a keynote address written in role as a high school valedictorian for graduates of the fictitious Qualitative High School. The second is a rant on the pretentiousness of scholarship in qualitative inquiry written in role as an angry redneck.

Selections excluded from this volume are pieces either methodologically outdated or written for a narrow interest of researchers in theatre for young audiences. There are a few works I've developed as keynote addresses that received praiseworthy audience response yet cannot be included here. "The Science Fiction of Qualitative Inquiries," delivered at The Qualitative Report conference in 2016, includes an array of film clips from science fiction films woven throughout the presentation. Though the clips' transcripts are not included due to copyright restrictions, the narrative text is available at http://tqr.nova.edu/wp-content/uploads/2016/01/The-Science-Fiction-of-Qualitative-Inquiries-Saldana.pdf.

My most revelatory and emotion-laden autoethnography to date, "Dick and Jane and Johnny: A Childhood Primer," also cannot be included in this volume because my performative reading of the text, audience participation, and accompanying music and PowerPoint slides integrated with the narrative prohibit a print medium. I collect vintage, entry-level, Dick and Jane readers and teaching materials published in the 1950s by Scott, Foresman and Company, and my autoethnography reflects on their meanings for me when I was a child and now as an older adult. The performance was presented at the 2016 ResearchTalk-Odum Institute's Qualitative Research Summer Intensive, and at a departmental graduate student research conference sponsored by Texas State University in 2017. "Dick and Jane and Johnny" is a deeply personal and bittersweet story about aging and mortality, and in my senior years I continue seeking opportunities to present it to live audiences.

I do not like the way I appear in digital video, so recorded documentation of my work is rare. I also dislike guest teaching through online programs such as Skype, for I feel the mediated experience distances me from my audience and prohibits me from truly connecting with others at a human level. I acknowledge that electronic communication is (if not already) the future of research reportage and professional networking, so I will leave it to generations more comfortable with technology and its newer forms of interaction to lead the way.

Closure and Transition

Eclecticism is an essential skill for documenting social inquiry. The more diverse our expressive repertoire, the more each mode informs the others and the more credible, vivid, and persuasive our accounts. I truly believe that being an artist has made me a better researcher, and being a researcher has made me a better artist. My writing ranges from rigorous qualitative data analytic methodology to creative arts-based forms. This has not been an evolutionary change from one extreme to the other, but a palette of genres, elements, and styles I use on an as needed basis for the investigative or compositional task at hand.

I am humbled and honored that my work has been recognized as "accessible," "brave," and "progressive" by individuals and associations across various disciplines. I hope you find some utility in these representative pieces and inspiration for your own ventures in writing qualitatively. Think well and work creatively, but remember: "Before you can think outside of the box, you have to start with a box."

References

Allen, M. (2016). *Essentials of publishing qualitative research*. Walnut Creek, CA: Left Coast Press.

Belcher, W. L. (2009). *Writing your journal article in 12 weeks: A guide to academic publishing success.* Thousand Oaks, CA: Sage.

Denzin, N. K. (1997). *Interpretive ethnography: Ethnographic practices for the 21st century*. Thousand Oaks, CA: Sage.

Goodall, H. L., Jr. (2008). *Writing qualitative inquiry: Self, stories, and academic life*. Walnut Creek, CA: Left Coast Press.

Hager, L. M., Maier, B. J., O'Hara, E., Ott, D., & Saldaña, J. (2000). Theatre teacher's perceptions of Arizona state standards. *Youth Theatre Journal, 14*, 64–77.

McCammon, L. A., Saldaña, J., Hines, A., & Omasta, M. (2012). Lifelong impact: Adult perceptions of their high school speech and/or theatre participation. *Youth Theatre Journal, 26*(1), 2–25.

Miles, M. B., & Huberman, A. M. (1994). *Qualitative data analysis: An expanded sourcebook* (2nd ed.). Thousand Oaks, CA: Sage.

Miles, M. B., Huberman, A. M., & Saldaña, J. (2014). *Qualitative data analysis: A methods sourcebook* (3rd ed.). Thousand Oaks, CA: Sage.

Neelands, J., & Goode, T. (2000). *Structuring drama work: A handbook of available forms in drama and theatre*. Cambridge: Cambridge University Press.

Saldaña, J. (1991). Drama, theatre and Hispanic youth: Interviews with selected teachers and artists. *Youth Theatre Journal, 5*(4), 3–8.

Saldaña, J. (1992). Assessing Anglo and Hispanic children's perceptions and responses to theatre: A cross-ethnic pilot study. *Youth Theatre Journal, 7*(2), 3–14.

Saldaña, J. (1995a). *Drama of color: Improvisation with multiethnic folklore*. Portsmouth, NH: Heinemann.

Saldaña, J. (1995b). "Is theatre necessary?": Final exit interviews with sixth grade participants from the ASU longitudinal study. *Youth Theatre Journal, 9*, 14–30.

Saldaña, J. (1996). "Significant differences" in child audience response: Assertions from the ASU longitudinal study. *Youth Theatre Journal, 10*, 67–83.

Saldaña, J. (1997). "Survival": A white teacher's conception of drama with inner city Hispanic youth. *Youth Theatre Journal, 11*, 25–46.

Saldaña, J. (1998a). Ethical issues in an ethnographic performance text: The 'dramatic impact' of 'juicy stuff'. *Research in Drama Education, 3*(2), 181–196.

Saldaña, J. (1998b) "Maybe someday, if I'm famous . . .": An ethnographic performance text. In J. Saxton & C. Miller (Eds.), *Drama and theatre in education: The research of practice, the practice of research* (pp. 89–109). Brisbane: IDEA Publications.

Saldaña, J. (1999a). Playwriting with data: Ethnographic performance texts. *Youth Theatre Journal, 13*, 60–71.

Saldaña, J. (1999b). Social class and social consciousness: Adolescent perceptions of oppression in forum theatre workshops. *Multicultural Perspectives, 1*(3), 14–18.

Saldaña, J. (2002a). Analyzing change in longitudinal qualitative data. *Youth Theatre Journal, 16*, 1–17.

Saldaña, J. (2002b). Finding my place: The Brad trilogy. In H. F. Wolcott (Ed.), *Sneaky kid and its aftermath: Ethics and intimacy in fieldwork* (pp. 167–210). Walnut Creek, CA: AltaMira Press.

Saldaña, J. (2003a). Dramatizing data: A primer. *Qualitative Inquiry, 9*(2), 218–236.

Saldaña, J. (2003b). *Longitudinal qualitative research: Analyzing change through time*. Walnut Creek, CA: AltaMira Press.

Saldaña, J. (Ed.). (2005a). *Ethnodrama: An anthology of reality theatre*. Walnut Creek, CA: AltaMira Press.

Saldaña, J. (2005b). Theatre of the oppressed with children: A field experiment. *Youth Theatre Journal, 19*, 117–33.

Saldaña, J. (2008a). Analyzing longitudinal qualitative observational data. In S. Menard (Ed.), *Handbook of longitudinal research: Design, measurement, and analysis* (pp. 297–311). Burlington, MA: Academic Press.

Saldaña, J. (2008b). The drama and poetry of qualitative method. In M. Cahnmann-Taylor & R. Siegesmund (Eds.), *Arts-based research in education: Foundations for practice* (pp. 220–227). New York: Routledge.

Saldaña, J. (2008c). Ethnodrama and ethnotheatre. In J. G. Knowles & A. L. Cole (Eds.), *Handbook of the arts in qualitative research: Perspectives, methodologies, examples, and issues* (pp. 195–207). Thousand Oaks, CA: Sage.

Saldaña, J. (2008d). Second chair: An autoethnodrama. *Research Studies in Music Education, 30*(2), 177–191.

Saldaña, J. (2010a). Ethnodramas about health and illness: Staging human vulnerability, fragility, and resiliency. In C. McLean (Ed.), *Creative arts in interdisciplinary practice: Inquiries for hope and change* (pp. 167–184). Calgary: Detselig Enterprises.

Saldaña, J. (2010b). Exploring the stigmatized child through theatre of the oppressed techniques. In P. B. Duffy & E. Vettranio (Eds.), *Youth and theatre of the oppressed* (pp. 45–62). New York: Palgrave Macmillan.

Saldaña, J. (2010c). Writing ethnodrama: A sampler from educational research. In M. Savin-Baden & C. H. Major (Eds.), *New approaches to qualitative research: Wisdom and uncertainty* (pp. 61–79). London: Routledge.

Saldaña, J. (2011a). *Ethnotheatre: Research from page to stage*. Walnut Creek, CA: Left Coast Press.

Saldaña, J. (2011b). *Fundamentals of qualitative research*. New York: Oxford University Press.

Saldaña, J. (2014a). Coding and analysis strategies. In P. Leavy (Ed.), *The Oxford handbook of qualitative research* (pp. 581–605). New York: Oxford.

Saldaña, J. (2014b). Thank you, Mrs. Whitehouse: The memory work of one student about his English teacher, forty years later. In C. Compton-Lilly & E. Halverson (Eds.), *Time and space in literacy research* (pp. 19–32). New York: Routledge.

Saldaña, J. (2015). *Thinking qualitatively: Methods of mind*. Thousand Oaks, CA: Sage.

Saldaña, J. (2016a). Goodall's verbal exchange coding: An overview and example. *Qualitative Inquiry, 22*(1), 36–39.

Saldaña, J. (2016b). *The coding manual for qualitative researchers* (3rd ed.). London: Sage.

Saldaña, J. (2017). Ethnodrama and ethnotheatre: Research as performance. In N. K. Denzin & Y. S. Lincoln (Eds.), *The Sage handbook of qualitative research* (5th ed.) (pp. 377–394). Thousand Oaks, CA: Sage.

Saldaña, J., & Mallette, L. A. (2017). Environmental coding: A new method using the SPELIT environmental analysis matrix. *Qualitative Inquiry, 23*(2), 161–167.

Saldaña, J., & Omasta, M. (2018). *Qualitative research: Analyzing life*. Thousand Oaks, CA: Sage.

Saldaña, J., & Otero, H. D. (1990). Experiments in assessing children's responses to theatre with the semantic differential. *Youth Theatre Journal, 5*(1), 11–19.

Van Maanen, J. (2011). *Tales of the field: On writing ethnography* (2nd ed.). Chicago: University of Chicago Press.

Vanover, C., & Saldaña, J. (2005). Chalkboard concerto: Growing up as a teacher in the Chicago public schools. In J. Saldaña (Ed.), *Ethnodrama: An anthology of reality theatre* (pp. 62–77). Walnut Creek, CA: AltaMira Press.

Wolcott, H. F. (1994). *Transforming qualitative data: Description, analysis, and interpretation*. Thousand Oaks, CA: Sage.

Wolcott, H. F. (2009). *Writing up qualitative research* (3rd ed.). Thousand Oaks, CA: Sage.

Woods, P. (2006). *Successful writing for qualitative researchers* (2nd ed.). London: Routledge.

2 Writing About Action Research

Documenting and Analyzing Fieldwork

Giving readers a vivid sense of "being there" through our writing is a classic ethnographic mandate. Anthropologist Clifford Geertz popularized the term *thick description*, meaning an approach that does not imply lengthy narratives but a selective interpretation of the nuances and complexity of a people's actions. I myself attempt to document in my writing what I call *significant trivia* – rich, telling details about a participant or field site that capture an essence or quality. One of my confessional tales (Saldaña, 2015) outlines a disastrous classroom session with the study represented in this chapter. Below I describe the boy who gave me the most problems as a guest artist during my fieldwork:

> Karl (pseudonym) was the "obnoxious" student [the teacher] spoke of – a blond-haired, slightly overweight but energetic 11-year-old boy with a strong personality and presence. He grinned frequently, as if looking for trouble, and emerged as one of the leaders of the other boys in class. He wasn't labelled "at-risk" or diagnosed with ADHD. He was simply – well, to be honest – obnoxious.
>
> (p. 86)

My first ethnographic educational research study (Saldaña, 1997) took place in an inner-city school neighborhood. Though the school facility was new and well-maintained, the surrounding area was impoverished. Below I describe some significant trivia I observed to take the reader "there." Notice the present tense narrative:

> Most houses around the periphery of the school were originally constructed in the 1930s–1940s. The exteriors now exhibit peeling paint and rotted wood. Chain link fences barricade numerous front yards, while German shepherds growl and bark loudly at passers-by. Layers of spray-painted graffiti cover trash cans, rusty abandoned cars, and the walls of some unoccupied (and occupied) homes. The three modest churches in the five-block

radius appear well-kept, but a few decaying houses in the neighborhood have dirt floors and no indoor plumbing or electricity.

(p. 28)

A popular folk saying goes, "The devil's in the details." I've adapted that adage to read, "The data's in the details." I try as much as possible in my writing to transcend "being there" to create for the reader an immediate and intimate present sense of "being *here*."

Action research studies attempt to solve real world problems and make life better. Unlike conventional ethnographers who document and analyze what currently exists in a sociocultural world, action researchers work collaboratively, cooperatively, and democratically with participants to investigate key sources of conflict and to strategize solutions to improve their personal lives and environmental conditions. It accomplishes these goals through a systematic examination of constituents' values systems, interpersonal relationships, power imbalances, and other aspects that generate conflict, stall progress, and inhibit agency. Collectively, the researcher and participants analyze their situation through data collection, reflection, and dialogue to develop concrete plans that initiate necessary actions to problem-solve and enhance their quality of life.

Action research as a qualitative methodology utilizes several standard data collection methods such as interviews, participant observation, document reviews, and so on. For educational studies, action research also relies on analyzing the intricate interplay between and among administrators, staff, teachers, students, parents, and the neighboring community at large. The action researcher in a school setting listens to many voices, observes many bodies and artifacts, and documents myriad data in explicit detail, for how can problems be solved if their sources are not first discovered? How can conflicts be resolved without a specific set of ideas?

Some problems are solved through trial-and-error, through qualitative field experimentation with an array of tactics and strategies. If one approach doesn't work, then another must be tried. And if the second attempt fails, then a third is explored. Haphazard problem-solving may eventually lead to a positive result – indeed, some discoveries are made entirely by accident or circumstantial happenstance (i.e., luck). But humans learn from experience, and whether those experiments are documented in one's memory or in written form, a record of some kind must be kept.

Action researchers contribute to the literature through meticulous record-keeping of their experiences and reflexive observations. Whether from transcripts, field notes, journals, or video recordings, qualitative data are essential evidence of the trial-and-error experiments we conduct so that others do not make the same mistakes. And even if we report that something didn't work out entirely as planned, that too is valuable knowledge, for it cautions us to be ever-aware of what could possibly go wrong. But the glitches we encounter are not the only things to note. Action researchers should also report the solutions found and the triumphs (hopefully) achieved. Readers need to know that good things are possible with the necessary drive and effort. We need to know that creative solutions to obstinate problems do indeed exist. We need hope, that with good thinking, humane purpose, and constructive action, the world – or at least a small corner of it – can be a better place.

The first qualitative research selection in this volume, "Theatre of the Oppressed with Children: A Field Experiment" from *Youth Theatre Journal*, describes an action research project conducted with fourth and fifth grade children at a local elementary school. The primary purpose of the study was to explore how classroom improvisational drama sessions with young people might reduce conflict (i.e., bullying) between and among children at the school site. The secondary purpose was to document the research team's experiments with adapting and facilitating with youth a repertoire of dramatic activities originally designed for adults.

Theatre of the Oppressed (also known as theatre for social change) is an assemblage of theatrical exercises whose goals are to explore the sources and types of personal and social oppression; to initiate critical dialogic reflection; and to generate possible solutions to activate positive change. The late Brazilian artist and activist Augusto Boal created these theatrical forms which were not intended for actor training but for developing everyday people's critical social consciousness in order to initiate constructive social action.

The article will explain Boal's methods further, but what is important to note here is the application of these theatrical techniques *with children*. Drama educators in the 1990s and 2000s were just beginning to incorporate Theatre of the Oppressed in school classrooms, yet the published literature for teachers was scant. This study documents a field experiment in descriptive detail utilizing a variety of data sources, provides cautionary advice and field-based recommendations for practitioners, and reflects on the efficacy of the residency.

References

Saldaña, J. (1997). "Survival": A White teacher's conception of drama with inner city Hispanic youth. *Youth Theatre Journal, 11*, 25–46.

Saldaña, J. (2015). A *Lord of the Flies* moment: The consequences of wrong gaming directions. In P. Duffy (Ed.), *A reflective practitioner's guide to (mis)adventures in drama education, or, what was I thinking?* (pp. 81–94). Chicago: Intellect.

THEATRE OF THE OPPRESSED WITH CHILDREN: A FIELD EXPERIMENT

Abstract

Boal's Theatre of the Oppressed was facilitated with fourth and fifth grade children to assess any influences and affects on their social interactions with peers.

"Sometimes, you can't be nice to deal with oppression."

(fourth grade girl)

This report shares selected observations and perceived outcomes from instruction of Augusto Boal's Theatre of the Oppressed with fourth and fifth grade children in a southwestern American school.[1] Theatre of the Oppressed (TO) consists of participatory, improvisational, dramatic forms that critically examine power relationships; explore how humans oppress each other in physical and psychological ways; and empower participants for liberating self and others (Boal, 1995, 1998, 2002).

The TO with Children Project employed three Boalian forms: *Games* for exploring concepts such as "power"; tableaux and movement for *Image Theatre*; and verbal improvisation for *Forum Theatre*. Boal's (2002) arsenal of games generally serves as preparatory work for both Image and Forum Theatre. Image Theatre relies on the non-verbal language of the body to explore and express internalized and social oppressions. Forum Theatre relies primarily on interactive dialogue to simulate strategies for combating human oppressors, and provides participants with a sense of personal and social agency.

Research Design

Rationale for the Study

The April 20, 1999 shooting tragedy at Columbine High School in Colorado served as a wake-up call for educators at all levels working with children and youth. Testimony by one teenage girl at a United States congressional hearing investigating violence in schools in the summer of 1999 encouraged curriculum programming and forums to provide "a place to vent anger and teach compassion." Gardner (1999) and Goleman (1995) assert that childhood and adolescence are critical windows of opportunity for such learning experiences and social development. Theatre of the Oppressed sessions I conduct with in-service elementary school teachers to help children cope with bullies and racism are well received and called "important" and "just what we're looking for"

[Originally published in *Youth Theatre Journal*, vol. 19, 2005, pp. 117–133; doi 10.1080/08929092.2005.10012580; edited slightly for this publication.]

by the adult participants. Theatre of the Oppressed serves not only theatre educators but also elementary educators and the children themselves through their exploration of social issues to hopefully create a more positive school and social environment.

Most published materials on TO and related dramatic forms for social change report their applications with and impact on adults (e.g., Schutzman & Cohen-Cruz, 1994; Taylor, 2003), adolescents (e.g., Bagshaw & Halliday, 2000; Banaszewski, 2001; Conrad, 2002; Rohd, 1998; Saldaña, 1999; Whybrow, 1996), and in theoretical/critical contexts with youth (e.g., Doyle, 1993; Wright, 1998). Theatre of the Oppressed naturally finds its way, through selected practitioners, into the elementary school classroom; but reports of these experiences are usually presented as conference workshops.[2] Rarely is TO with young children examined from ethnographic perspectives and published for wider dissemination to other facilitators (e.g., Giffin & Yaffe, 1999; Grady, 2000). Thus, the report of this particular field experiment is a contribution to the qualitative research literature in drama education with elementary school youth.

Participants

Wilson Elementary School (pseudonym) regularly collaborates with Arizona State University (ASU) for educational research projects if the primary investigator secures ASU Human Subjects Review Board permission to conduct the study. Once this permission was obtained, the school principal (female) and six fourth and fifth grade classroom teachers (five female, one male) volunteered to participate. The school's population and community are classified socioeconomically as lower- to lower-middle class and multiculturally diverse.

The ASU research team consisted of myself and four graduate students in our Theatre for Youth program – Gordon Hensley, Doyle Ott, Emily Petkewich, and Michelle White – all of whom had taken advanced improvisation with youth and TO course work before the study began. We labeled ourselves ARTists (*A*rtists-*R*esearchers-*T*eachers) and worked with approximately 125 children ages 9–11 during an eight-week residency in the spring 2000 semester. Due to the six elementary classroom teachers' varying schedules and availability, the number of weekly TO sessions (approximately 60 minutes each) varied from six to twelve within the participating classrooms. Elementary classroom teachers and ARTists received a modest stipend for their participation in the project.

Method

This study was, admittedly, an emergent investigation. I called the project a "field experiment" (a standard term in research design) because the work took place in a naturalistic classroom setting, yet provided participants an experimental TO treatment for the specific purpose of creating positive behavioral change. Quantitative measures were deliberately excluded in favor of qualitative inquiry. The latter is a paradigm in harmony with a social project of this nature, and provides richer descriptive material for analysis.

Preliminary research questions were developed as part of a grant proposal, and they served as initial guidance for fieldwork and data gathering:

1   What oppressions encountered by children (e.g., bullies, teasing and verbal abuse, teachers as oppressors) can serve as content for Image and Forum Theatre work?
2   How can relevant social concepts and terms (e.g., oppression, antagonist, agency) be instructed to children through TO?
3   What adaptations or modifications, if any, of Boal's Image and Forum Theatre techniques are needed for young children?
4   What are the observed and reported influences and affects of TO on children in their school environment and classroom culture?
5   What developmental and gender differences exist when examining the above questions (i.e., differences between boys and girls ages 9–11)?

I will not systematically address in this paper each question in the order they are listed above. Instead, I will use our TO curriculum as the organizing framework for reporting salient observations from this project.

Data Sources

Data sources for the project included audio-taped and transcribed individual pre-and post-field experiment interviews with the school principal and teacher participants; periodic focus group interviews and discussions with ASU ARTists; and pre-and post-whole class interviews with selected fourth and fifth grade participants. The school principal did not permit individual interviews with children due to her concern with what could have been "sensitive" issues raised by the participants. Unfortunately, these types of interviews might have generated richer data and provided children opportunities to privately and confidentially voice genuine concerns about personal oppressions.

ARTists maintained and submitted participant observation field notes and journal reflections of the school and classroom environments, daily classroom routines and special events, playground activities, and all TO sessions. One to two sessions facilitated by each ARTist was video-taped for more extensive analysis. Documents submitted included the ARTists' TO session designs, plus any written artifacts developed by children during TO sessions such as journal reflections, written stories of oppression, and written solutions to a hypothetical oppressive situation.

Data Analysis

I analyzed all data using Strauss and Corbin's (1998) *in vivo* coding – not to construct grounded theory, but to find prominent themes and patterns rooted

34 *Writing About Action Research*

in the participants' own language. Once these codes were organized into categories, Erickson's (1986) assertion heuristics were applied to develop general interpretations from the data corpus. Though some might have adopted critical pedagogical or feminist positions for a research study of this nature, I opted for the educational constructivist paradigm since I was interested in new learnings that would emerge from field experimentation for future classroom applications.

The Field Experiment

Participant Perceptions of Oppression

Before the teaching phase of the project began, I interviewed the school principal, elementary classroom teachers, selected classrooms of children, and ARTists to gather everyone's recommendations for session content and desired outcomes. This strategy harmonizes with the philosophies of constructivist education, critical pedagogy, and liberatory praxis (Freire, 1998; hooks, 1994; Oakes & Lipton, 1999; Shor, 1996), principles interwoven with Boal's theatrical work. Since children were our primary constituents and stakeholders in this project, we prioritized their recommendations above the adults when designing TO sessions.

After the interviews, I reviewed the transcripts, searched for and coded forms of oppression, and organized the categories into a simple taxonomy (McCurdy, Spradley, & Shandy, 2005). Most parents and teachers who work daily with upper elementary school children may find the results compiled in Figure 2.1 common knowledge. The list, in fact, correlates closely with Berk's (2004, pp. 322–327) "textbook" examples of children's social development. But it may

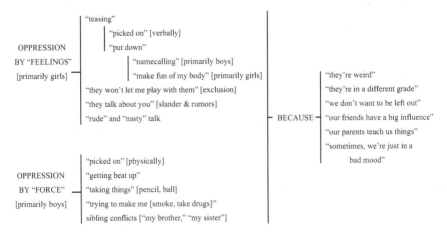

Figure 2.1 Children's perceptions of oppression

also inform us how children themselves perceive the various forms of oppression in their lives.

In this *particular* diverse site, such social constructs as race, ethnicity, and social class were not observed as sources of oppression among ages 9–11 children. Intra-and inter-gender oppression – horizontal and vertical hostility – were the primary sources of conflict. To girls, oppression happens primarily when they are intimidated by "*feelings*" – as one girl said, "When other people make you feel bad, and they're trying to do it on purpose, 'cause maybe they don't like you." To boys, oppression happens primarily when they are intimidated by "*force*" – as one boy said, "forcing you to do something you don't want to." Neither of these two categories are gender exclusive, however; oppression through "*feelings*" is the most prominent form children encounter.

The list of oppressions is fairly self-explanatory, but the reasons why these types of oppressions occur ("because") merits a brief discussion. Children generalize others with physical, behavioral, or cultural differences as "weird," a dynamic confirmed by one of their teachers:

> We've got a little girl in here – she looks different and she acts different, so they'll make up some name that they call her. It seems like every year there's one kid that gets picked on more than somebody else because they're different, because they might look different, they might act different. And out on the playground they do tend to sometimes get pushy-shovy. Like with her *[pointing to a desk]*, I've watched them actually walk by this little girl and purposely bump into her. . . . You know, once they have this idea that something's wrong with them, or they don't like them, then when they start to interact with the kids . . . they're not accepting.

Wilson School's culture includes separate and distinct grade and classroom division, which reinforces social boundaries and hierarchies on the playground ("They're in a different grade"). Children also noted how peers and parents cultivated contagion for oppressive actions: "Our friends have a big influence on how we behave, we don't want to be left out of anything, [and] our parents teach us some things about other people." Finally, children acknowledged that oppression also arises from everyday tension since "Sometimes, we're just in a bad mood."

Teachers felt the primary reason for oppressive behaviors stemmed from children's emerging knowledge of power structures: "A lot of kids are just scared or they're not aggressive, and I think a lot of kids pick up on that." Consequences for the oppressed include "negativity," "withdrawal," "low self-esteem," and boys who "explode" in anger. Teachers, more cognizant of their class's personal situations, acknowledged "parental neglect" and "poverty" as a source of a few children's woes. ARTists initially perceived that teachers themselves may have been significant adult sources of oppression, but children regarded them as the least of their troubles (though some may have been reluctant to identify them as such to the visiting research team).

Emergent Goals

All participants converged on *conflict resolution strategies* as a common theme and goal for the project, yet variations appeared in the suggested pathways toward that goal. Adult participants wanted to achieve a more inclusive classroom climate through community building; children asked for individual problem-solving tactics. Teachers wanted children to exhibit more positive actions ("respect," "graciousness") and self-regulating behaviors ("anger management," "dealing with negativity," "feeling good about themselves"). Children simply wanted to know what to do when they become victims of oppression (discussed later).

While the ARTists were not reluctant to explore the negative emotions that arose during oppressive situations in their classroom sessions, the classroom teachers perceived this as an undesirable reinforcement of the problem rather than a way to cultivate positive, yet compliant, behaviors. Classroom management dynamics established by participating teachers at Wilson School can be illustrated through an amalgam of "Classroom Rules" posted prominently in each room. The ARTists found these rules somewhat antithetical to the principles of TO and our personal ways of working; nevertheless, we adhered to the rules as a courtesy to the participating teachers and to maintain an agreeable collaboration:

1 Raise your hand to speak
2 Keep your hands and feet to yourself
3 Follow directions
4 Line up quietly and quickly
5 Work quietly so you don't disturb others
6 Respect others: No name calling, put downs, or swearing
7 Work and play safely

Consequences if you choose not to follow the rules of the class:

1 Verbal warning
2 Time out (Resource Room or loss of recess)
3 Parents contacted (letter)
4 Sent to office

> Small prizes are awarded at the end of the week for those who show good behavior.
> I will be a great learner and do my personal best!

ARTists found themselves reconciling paradoxical dilemmas as they modeled non-oppressive facilitation behaviors, struggled with typical classroom management issues, and enforced classroom rules.[3] Some children, primarily boys, took advantage of the TO sessions to display obstreperous behavior (i.e., horseplay) among themselves. Ironically, classroom forums to explore oppression became opportunities for a few to exhibit oppressive playing behaviors within simulated dramatic contexts. Image and Forum Theatre gave them "permission" to violate classroom rules with impunity.

As the study progressed, it was interesting to note how initial and ongoing goals from all constituencies conflicted. The school principal saw the opportunity for TO to develop children's literacy more than their social skills: "Emphasize the 'six traits' of good writing. Develop their expressiveness." A school teacher wanted to minimize the negativity of conflict exploration: "Gear it towards more of a positive thing. Give a scenario that is negative and ask them how to solve it in a positive way." Most striking, however, was a parent overheard telling his child: "If someone hits you, you have to hit them back." ARTists attempted to sway children away from reactive toward more proactive responses: "I'd like you to try to come up with other ways aside from insulting back, because anybody can do that. What we're trying to find out are new and different ways of overcoming oppression." In a moment of angst, I felt that the entire project may have been doing more harm than good:

> Maybe we're teaching [children] how to be better oppressors as opposed to rehearsing for resistance. . . . We were giving them a forum for being oppressive. We were saying, "Make an image of oppression." and that was OK, "Say something oppressive," and that was OK.

But one child noted when Forum Theatre scenes generated negative responses: "Sometimes, you can't be nice to deal with oppression."

Terms and Concepts

ARTists instructed children on relevant terms and concepts as sessions progressed to develop a common vocabulary for our work together. These terms reflect the general content we explored and cluster into five major categories:

1 Power and related constructs: oppressor, oppressed, control, resistance, target, agent;
2 Social actions and constructs: inclusion, exclusion, respect, disrespect, stigma, stigmatize, rumor, gossip, slander, difference, uniqueness, mainstream;
3 Emotions: regret, encouragement, jealousy, pride, defensiveness, etc.;
4 Image Theatre: image, sculpting, dynamize, dissociation;
5 Forum Theatre: activating scene, problem solving, protagonist, antagonist, tactic, negotiation, conflict, change, confrontation, lightning forum

Most children could articulate an adequate understanding of oppression once it was explained to them and explored during TO sessions. Boys usually provided a rote definition while girls illustrated the concept through examples. Classroom curricula varied from ARTist to ARTist, yet we all began with Boalian Games and Image Theatre before proceeding to Forum Theatre. Each dramatic form presented us with unique challenges and observations, so they will be discussed separately.

Boalian Games With Children

Boal's repertory of games functioned not only as warm-ups but also as metaphors for enacting and reflecting on power relationships. Games both prepared the group for more advanced work in Image and Forum Theatre, and served as ports of entry for discussions about oppression: "How does this game relate to real life in terms of power?" In some cases, we used games as springboards to discuss a particular class's particular oppressions. The French Telephone demonstrated how rumors spread among fifth graders get more exaggerated with each retelling.[4]

Colombian Hypnosis served as an overt and graphic way to physically illustrate *power* and the difference between two new terms for the group at the introductory session: the *oppressor* and the *oppressed*. One ARTist noted:

> Children were able to describe who had the power as well as verbalize what it felt like to have/not have that power. [They said,] "When you were leading you felt like you could make that person do anything"; "When I was following I felt like, if I didn't do what that person wanted me to, that they would hit me." One boy found his personal understanding in a moment of discovery after playing the game: "Oh, the oppressed is the oppressee!"

Perhaps no other game in Boal's repertory illustrated so perfectly the dynamics of power for these young participants.

ARTists also discovered that the *way* games were played exhibited children's social and cultural dynamics. Selected games served as diagnostic instruments to assess their process and progress as a community. The Space Series (renamed The Grouping Game by ARTists), one of the most easily played games by adults, was difficult for these children. In this game, the facilitator asks, "Get in groups of twos; threes; fours; fives...." Participants then quickly assemble into groups consisting of the number called out. Children's genders and existing friendships prevented them from efficiently achieving the goals of the game. When adults play this activity, they usually group by moving quickly toward each other. Children, however, physically concretized their group through holding, hugging, and expressing "tightness" with "my buddies." Though nothing is wrong with physical contact, the action suggested forthcoming trouble with those the group would later include and exclude. Despite the ARTists' initial efforts to continuously reinforce, "It doesn't matter who you're with," to children, it *did* matter whom they were with.

A fourth grade classroom playing the game, captured on video tape, serves as an example. When the facilitator asked to assemble in twos, most children found a partner quickly, and most often a good friend. For groups of three, children called out for a certain person to join their twosome, usually a mutual friend, and children dashed to them. "Residual" children saw they were too late to join a threesome and were directed by them to look for another group. Gathering in groups of threes and fours took progressively longer for children to negotiate, fours usually taking the longest time to assemble. They not only looked for a cluster of people to form the right number, they verbally (and sometimes physically through a tug-of-war with a child) negotiated and sometimes argued who could be in which group of friends – not just groups, but groups of *friends*. (An ARTist noted: "They all looked frantic and worried that they wouldn't be a part of a group.") On fours, fives, and sixes, children shouted out others' names; some were pulled into a group, others were pushed away if they attempted to join. During this exchange and rearrangement, boys rushed to other boys and girls rushed to other girls. Boys would rather have been "residual" than join a group of girls to help them compose the right number of people in a group. If and when a boy did try to join a girls' group, he was pushed away from it. Occasionally, a girl voluntarily joined a group of boys, if needed, yet she was not accepted willingly or touched.

During reflection, facilitators shared what they observed and asked children to rationalize their ineffective playing. One girl explained:

> It's mostly because some people have certain other friends that they like. There are certain people that don't like other people, and that do like other people, and so they want the people they like to come in their group, and the people that they don't like, they don't want them to. And if the person that they don't like likes them, then that makes people feel bad.

I myself felt it was necessary to share my honest reaction to the dynamics I witnessed:

> If we're going to get over our oppressions, one of the things we need to do is be willing to just accept who comes and not exclude.... You don't have to like everybody, but it is important that you must respect everybody. Liking people is different from respecting people. Respect is simply showing common courtesy and good manners towards someone, you know? I might love some people more than I do others, but I treat everybody the same when it comes to respect.... The important part is to include everybody, regardless of who they are.

Reflections such as these were intended to raise children's consciousness about the dynamics of playing the game. Unfortunately, in not all cases did this consciousness change children's actions or preferences, as one ARTist noted: "The second time they played it they weren't much quicker. There was still a lot of discussion and desire to create the 'right' group." Eventually, we discovered that calling the numbers out randomly rather than successively forced children to think about the *numbers* in a group, not necessarily the composition of them. The Grouping Game became a key diagnostic to assess a class's ability to inclusify and develop as a community. The shorter the amount of time the game took to play (assuming task familiarity was not confounding the assessment), the more the class was lessening their oppressive tendencies among themselves.

Image Theatre With Children

The most salient aspects of Image Theatre in our field experiment were matters of children's physical technique and observations of gender differences.

The majority of children participated actively when ARTists asked for images to be formed individually with each child in his or her own space. Yet many had difficulty physically maintaining a frozen image. For some it may have been due to physical awkwardness, self-consciousness from being looked at by others, or discomfort with the time required to hold the images still. Others broke their frozen images when peer observers commented on them, whether seriously or flippantly. ARTists found themselves frequently prompting "Freeze it" or "Hold it." Video and photo cameras encouraged children to keep their images still; the media devices added a sense of importance to what they created. The physical contact necessary for sculpting and group imaging required ARTists to develop a specific repertory of image theatre guidelines for sculpting others, such as: don't pull on a person's clothing to shape your partner's body; respect the frozen image of another by maintaining some distance from it. ARTists also reminded children that the sculpture has an obligation to hold the image the sculptor created, unless it causes physical discomfort.

Dynamizing an image is to set it in motion. The purpose is to come to a deeper understanding of the dynamics of the oppression portrayed. This concept and its undertaking was, at times, also difficult for children as this ARTist noted: "It just must be that they don't have the focus, or the trust in themselves, to be able to just go with a movement and let it slowly take over and transform into something else." More common phrases such as "setting the image in motion" or "moving in slow motion" didn't necessarily crystallize the concept for participants. Counting as they moved was one tactic to help them get from one point to another. A count of 10 was too long; 5 worked much better. Some perceived the count as a count*down* to move swiftly into the next image, rather than take the time to transition. Finally, asking them to explain the *process* of what was going through their minds during the dynamizing was also difficult for them to articulate.

One successful technique adapted from a non-Boalian source for Image Theatre sessions was a "thought balloon" – a comic-strip convention made into a cardboard cutout, held directly over a child as a strategy for motivating spectator inferences about the image. Children most often identified internalized thoughts in the third person ("He's thinking that nobody will play with him."). ARTists prompted children to rephrase their inferences in the first person ("I feel sad because nobody will play with me.") in hopes of developing not just sympathy but empathy. Though children had a limited emotional vocabulary, they trusted their intuitive and tacit knowledge and showed developmentally appropriate skills at inference making, reading subtextual cues, and interpreting the nuances and intentions of the image creators.

When children selected their own partners for pair and small group work, virtually everyone clustered with same-gender classmates. This provided an opportunity to compare and contrast differences in image compositions between boys and girls. Their independently constructed images of such negative concepts as "disrespect" and "enemies" showed several physical patterns, extracted from field note and video tape analysis of their work. All groups used pointed fingers and multi-leveled arrangements to demonstrate oppressive images. Boys, however, created both realistic and heightened compositions of physical violence, while girls' images were rooted in friendship clusters or cliques. Boys used raised arms and clenched fists; girls used open hands and extended or folded arms. Boys maintained close physical proximity to their same gendered partners, but girls made more physical contact among themselves. In small groups, boys arranged their bodies in nondescript clusters, while girls created circular arrangements. The patterns reinforce what we stereotypically attribute to male and female body images and confirmed the children's own gender-based oppressions: for boys, by *"force"*; for girls, by *"feelings."*

Forum Theatre With Children

Overall, ARTists perceived that children were highly engaged with Forum Theatre's spontaneity, the intrigue of a puzzle to be solved, and the recognition of their own reality dramatized.

Forum Theatre, as described by Boal (2002) and "traditionally" practiced, was considered more successful with fifth graders than with fourth. Verbal improvisation ability (i.e., oral language skills) of older children was attributed as the primary factor for their enhanced work. Variations of Forum Theatre were developed for use with fourth graders, such as teacher-in-role as the antagonist with children as a collective protagonist improvising an initiating scenario – for example, the ARTist as an older sibling bossing around the children as a little brother or sister. Simple non-verbal conflicts were also developed, such as two children moving toward each other, stopping face-to-face, and finding a way of continuing in their respective directions (this is the basic conflict of Dr. Seuss's children's book, *The Zax*). One fourth grade class was asked to write brief activating scenes for Forum Theatre exploration with ARTist guidance. Two examples include:

PROTAGONIST: Can I use that *[a student's pencil]*?
ANTAGONIST: No. I don't want you touching anything of mine.
PROTAGONIST: Wanna work together?
ANTAGONIST: You're so stupid. I'm not working with you.

Fifth graders were able to improvise and write traditional albeit brief Forum Theatre scenarios in small groups and perform as protagonists, antagonists, and spect-actors with the teacher as Joker. Examples of activating scenes constructed by one fifth grade class (required to work in mixed-gender groups by their classroom teacher) include:

"I Got It First" [of all scenes developed by children for one ARTist, this one received majority vote for exploration]
(FIRST BOY and GIRL reach for a ball at the same time)
FIRST BOY: Gimme.
GIRL: I got it first.
FIRST BOY: No you didn't.
GIRL: Yes I did, I got it first.
FIRST BOY: Well, fight for it, then.
GIRL: I don't wanna fight.
(SECOND BOY enters)
SECOND BOY (to GIRL): Wuss.
GIRL: Shut up!
SECOND BOY: Wuss.
(GIRL pushes SECOND BOY)
SECOND BOY: Wuss!
(SECOND BOY grabs the ball; he and the FIRST BOY walk away)

The scene that received the second most votes for exploration was titled "They Do Not Mix":

(A BOY on the floor, reading; a GIRL circles around him)
GIRL: That spiked hair and those shorts do not mix.
BOY: Why do you care?
GIRL: Because I couldn't help noticing that you look like a freak show on ice.
BOY: Bet you have front row tickets.
GIRL: At least I'm allowed into the arena.
BOY: Just back off.
GIRL: No.
BOY: I like my hair and my shorts mixed together.
GIRL: Fine.
(The GIRL walks away)
BOY: Fine!

During replayings, some children called out "Stop!" to replace the protagonist almost as soon as the protagonist began his or her dialogue. The immediacy of whether their ideas would work or not was apparent as children applied their tactics, only to see them stalemate. Children often presented solutions through a limited repertory: name calling (matching verbal taunt for verbal taunt), or walking away to appeal to the adult authority of a teacher (as they had been instructed to do in actual situations). Neither of these two promoted solutions that "worked," though the latter was reinforced as one possible method for solving a problem. ARTists, through critical reflection, encouraged children to go beyond the "fight or flight" options they presented and to find more proactive solutions to the problem.

Evaluation of the Project

Banks and Nieto's (1999) three-stage model of social consciousness development was used to evaluate the TO Project's influences and affects on the child participants. The model was chosen for its elegant, readily identifiable categories for assessment. The three stages progress from awareness (*Knowing and Questioning*), to emotional involvement (*Critiquing and Caring*) to action (*Walking the Talk*).

Knowing and Questioning

The first stage of TO work attempted to cultivate individual and group social consciousness through *Knowing and Questioning*. An ARTist remarked in his journal:

> One student, who is often made fun of due to her slight weight problem, offered that after working in this class she has finally realized just how much they all oppress each other: "I never noticed it before." Many of the students agreed. They then offered specific examples dealing with bullying, exclusion, physical fights, name calling, etc.

One teacher, however, felt that the short length of the residency was insufficient to generate significant results: "The concepts are within reach – practicing them is not. . . . They weren't exposed to it long enough. My concern is that I don't know if we're doing it long enough for it to be a permanent change."

Critiquing and Caring

The second stage cultivates sympathy and empathy among participants through *Critiquing and Caring*. An ARTist entered in her journal:

> The scared look in their eyes clarified something for me. I've been feeling that they were ready to learn some actual tools for dealing with their oppressions. The work that we've done thus far has helped to build a sense of empathy and sympathy for those who are being oppressed – i.e., these students might now think twice about oppressing anybody else.

One teacher affirmed the development of caring in some of her students, but only speculated and hoped that it was making a difference:

> They realize that they hurt somebody or they said something that they shouldn't have said, and they go ahead and try to correct it. And there's a

couple of students who actually – they do this a lot, but I'm wondering if maybe now they're starting to think about it a little bit more before they say it. I mean, that's what I'm hoping is happening.

Action – Walking the Talk

The third stage is behavioral evidence of change, "the opposite of oppression" as ARTists called it or, more formally labeled, *Walking the Talk*. Toward the end of his sessions, one ARTist noted after playing The Grouping Game:

> It seems to me this time that they were more challenged by getting the right numbers in their group than who was in their group. I saw more of helpful behavior between classmates. For example, as a whole they would try to help the "lost" people find a group to join. I only saw one example of bickering this time and I didn't catch anyone banning any other student from his/her group. They might not go out of their way to bring them into their own group but they will help them find another one.

One teacher replied when asked in an interview, "Has the name calling changed?":

> I think it's been better in the classroom, but I really don't know about the playground. I think it will always be a problem because it is part of their lives, and has been for so long. . . . I would say at least a third are getting something out of your activities. It's not always the same third. Some children you will never reach.

Another teacher affirmed that the indoctrination of gender roles may be too entrenched by fifth grade:

> I did see some of the kids who were unaccepting of certain kids look at them in a different light. I found that more with the girls than I did with the boys. They're nicer to somebody else, but the boys are not as into that. Girls try to fix things. They seem to be interested in learning social skills. Boys are just power monsters. They are not willing to compromise.

ARTists and teachers maintained different perspectives on the general outcomes of the TO Project. But we all agreed that precise "measurement" of the field experiment's influences and affects on children was impossible to conduct. There *were* individual success stories, such as the fifth grade scapegoat who appeared more comfortable and self-assured on the last day of the residency, and the Korean fifth grader with limited English skills who spoke confidently before the video camera on feeling good about herself. To the ARTists, what children themselves offered as their learning mattered most to us.

Children's Recommendations to Peers

On the final day of the residency, child participants from two representative class groups were asked to recommend to others in their grade level at other schools how to deal with oppressive actions. Their responses were videotaped, transcribed, and pooled into composite narratives by weaving individual responses into a coherent narrative. Whether their responses are simply "talking the talk" for the research team's benefit, or genuine learning outcomes for "walking the talk" in the immediate future, is difficult to verify. Nevertheless, note how girls' recommendations generally focus on emotional reactions and strategies ("*feelings*"), while boys' recommendations generally focus on behavioral tactics ("*force*").

Girls' Recommendations

Fourth grade girls advised their peers:

> People who are mean to you are, like, just jealous. Say it's a boy being mean to a girl: Don't let the boys make you feel bad because they're just doing that because they either like you or they just want their friends to like them. Boys want to show off to girls to get friends to think that they're cool and stuff, but they're not really cool, they're really mean. I usually fight with my best [girl] friend, and in a couple minutes we'll ask each other if we wanna play. Girls sometimes can't control themselves; like after the fights, they're very, very sad, and they'll, like, apologize to each other.

Fifth grade girls recommended:

> In my opinion, if someone doesn't like you because of what you look like, and a lot of people like you 'cause of what you act like, it's their loss if you're a really friendly person. Nobody should be judged from what they look like, it should be all from the inside. A lot of time people are made fun of because they look different. You're beautiful and unique in your own way; don't listen to anyone who says you're not. Ignore people who mistreat you. Feel good about yourself.

Boys' Recommendations

Fourth graders suggested:

> Just take it to the bathroom after school [or] forget about it. Talk it out [or] walk away. Don't say anything, think of something else, try not to give in to them. [Girls oppress us because] they might be jealous that we're boys and they're girls. Set 'em straight. If you're mad at your brother or sister, don't, like, destroy something of theirs or something they own, because probably

next day you're gonna be really happy with them, then you'll feel sorry that you destroyed something.

Fifth grade boys advised:

> Treat people the way you like to be treated. If you don't like the way they treat you, then you should treat them nice. If people think you're a little different, and you look a little different and you're weird, you should just walk off and go play with someone else; everybody has their own opinion. If someone's being mean to you and calls you names, just back off, walk away, try to ignore them. Don't use self-defense unless you really have to because it can hurt other people really badly. But if someone's really provoking you, and they're hurting you, then you should fight back. Don't take any rap from anybody.

Final Reflections

The ARTists may not have changed the world, but we feel confident asserting that we took some of its young inhabitants at Wilson School through the first stage of social consciousness development. To Boal, TO is "rehearsal for the revolution." With ages 9–11 children, however, TO seems more like an "audition" for preadolescent social interaction. Theatre of the Oppressed overtly reveals the interpersonal social systems and power hierarchies within a classroom microculture. It shows which children are leaders, followers, and resisters; who is influential and who is ignored; which children may continue to assert dominance in later grade levels; and which children may succumb to those with more authority in later grade levels.

One fourth grade boy jokingly called our TO sessions "group therapy," suggesting that TO with children can be both beneficial and, in the wrong hands, dangerous. Creating community through TO is an ideal goal, but – realistically, as teachers noted and ARTists observed – not everyone in the upper elementary classroom will do his or her part to achieve it. Natural child development and individual personality formation, coupled with competitive playground politics and gender socialization embedded within American culture, may inhibit short-term TO experiences from making a permanent, positive impact among some of its participants. But Boal abhors defeatism. These minimal results should not discourage TO facilitators from their continued, valiant attempts to change the world. Children's recommendations to peers for combating oppression may be rhetoric without substance, for not everyone "walked the talk." But children's continuing cognitive and social development will enhance their future ability for critical thought, enabling better analyses of the complexities and ambiguities of oppressive situations, possibly leading to more informed solutions.[5]

What ARTists and teachers hoped for could not be assessed by the end of the field experiment, for it is in the long-term, not short-term, that results may become more evident – a finding supported through comparable research by Giffin and Yaffe (1999, p. 133) and Bagshaw and Halliday (2000, pp. 100–102). As Doyle (1993) asserts, "Transformation . . . usually comes in small doses and usually happens over time" (p. 130). Thus, as Boal advocates, we may have planted seeds in hopes that they would take root. And one cannot tell from a seed just planted whether it will die underground; sprout but then wither; or grow, flourish, and mature.

Notes

1 Funding for this project was provided by Arizona State University's Katherine K. Herberger College of Fine Arts Research Council, J. Robert Wills, Dean.
2 The annual Pedagogy and Theatre of the Oppressed and National Association for Drama Therapy conferences regularly feature such workshops. Recent publications (e.g., O'Toole & Donelan, 1996) have documented TO presentations at international conferences.
3 ARTists found themselves enacting more than just the *facilitator*, *teacher*, and even *joker* role with children. Aside from the traditional dramatic functions such as *storyteller*, *playwright*, *actor*, *director*, and *dramaturg*, ARTists used such descriptors to identify their multiple roles in this project as: *moralist, ethicist, philosopher, confessor, devil's advocate, humanitarian, disciplinarian, counselor, analyst, theorist, big brother/sister, surrogate parent*, and *friend*. Though we understood these multiple roles as responsibilities of any educator of young people, the content of TO heightened our attunement to them in journal reflections.
4 Children's favorite games from Boal's (2002) repertory, based on their responses and requests for replaying, included: The Bear of Portiers, Colombian Hypnosis, One Person We Fear/One Person is Our Protector, The Machine of Rhythms (and variations), Person to Person Quebec-Style, Complete the Image, The Vampire of Strasbourg, Who Said "Ah"?, The Glass Cobra, String Puppet, The French Telephone, and The Great Game of Power.

Games that required a large playing area, such as The President's Bodyguards, were difficult to conduct in the limited space of school classrooms. Two teachers reluctant to move students' desks for our work forced us to think of alternative ways to structure some of the games. For example, The French Telephone, ordinarily played while standing in a large circle, was adapted to accommodate children seated in rows at their desks.
5 Counseling literature suggests that school violence prevention programs succeed when there are comprehensive and collaborative training efforts for teachers, children, and their parents, plus environmental and ecological reorganization within the school and community (O'Toole, Burton, & Plunkett, 2005; Smith & Sandhu, 2004).

References

Bagshaw, D., & Halliday, D. (2000). Handling conflicts at school: Drama as a medium for adolescent leaning. *NJ (Drama Australia Journal)*, *24*(2), 87–103.
Banaszewski, C. (2001). Lunch period drama: An invisible theatre performance with high school students. *Stage of the Art*, *14*(1), 19–25.
Banks, J. A., & Nieto, S. (1999, November). *Town hall meeting*. Discussion at the annual conference of the National Association for Multicultural Education, San Diego, CA.
Berk, L. E. (2004). *Development through the lifespan* (3rd ed.). Boston, MA: Allyn & Bacon.
Boal, A. (1995). *The rainbow of desire* (A. Jackson, Trans.). New York: Routledge.
Boal, A. (1998). *Legislative theatre: Using performance to make politics* (A. Jackson, Trans.). New York: Routledge.

Boal, A. (2002). *Games for actors & non-actors* (2nd ed.) (A Jackson, Trans.). New York: Routledge.

Conrad, D. (2002). Drama, media advertising, and inner-city youth. *Youth Theatre Journal, 16*, 71–87.

Doyle, C. (1993). *Raising curtains on education: Drama as a site for critical pedagogy*. Westport, CT: Bergin & Garvey.

Erickson, F. (1986). Qualitative methods in research on teaching. In M. C. Wittrock (Ed.), *Handbook of research on teaching* (3rd ed.) (pp. 119–161). New York: Palgrave Macmillan.

Freire, P. (1998). *Teachers as cultural workers: Letters to those who dare teach* (D. Macedo, D. Koike, & A Oliveira, Trans.). Boulder, CO: Westview Press.

Gardner, H. (1999). *Intelligence reframed: Multiple intelligences for the 21st century*. New York: Basic Books.

Giffin, H., & Yaffe, K. (1999). Using drama to teach conflict management. In B. J. Wagner (Ed.), *Building moral communities through educational drama* (pp. 113–136). Stamford, CT: Ablex Publishing.

Goleman, D. (1995). *Emotional intelligence*. New York: Bantam.

Grady, S. (2000). *Drama and diversity: A pluralistic perspective for educational drama*. Portsmouth, NH: Heinemann.

hooks, b. (1994). *Teaching to transgress: Education as the practice of freedom*. New York: Routledge.

McCurdy, D. W., Spradley, J. P., & Shandy, D. J. (2005). *The cultural experience: Ethnography in complex society*. Long Grove, IL: Waveland Press.

Oakes, J., & Lipton, M. (1999). *Teaching to change the world*. Boston, MA: McGraw-Hill College.

O'Toole, J., Burton, B., & Plunkett, A. (2005). *Cooling conflict: A new approach to managing bullying and conflict in schools*. Frenchs Forrest, NSW: Pearson/Longman.

O'Toole, J., & Donelan, K. (Eds.). (1996). *Drama, culture and empowerment: The IDEA Dialogues*. Brisbane: IDEA Publications.

Rohd, M. (1998). *Theatre for community, conflict & dialogue: The hope is vital training manual*. Portsmouth, NH: Heinemann.

Saldaña, J. (1999). Social class and social consciousness: Adolescent perceptions of oppression in forum theatre workshops. *Multicultural Perspectives, 1*(3), 14–18.

Schutzman, M., & Cohen-Cruz, J. (1994). *Playing Boal: Theatre, therapy, activism*. New York: Routledge.

Shor, I. (1996). *When students have power: Negotiating authority in a critical pedagogy*. Chicago: University of Chicago Press.

Smith, D. C., & Sandhu, D. S. (2004). Toward a positive perspective on violence prevention in schools: Building connections. *Journal of Counseling & Development, 82*, 287–293.

Strauss, A., & Corbin, J. (1998). *Basics of qualitative research* (2nd ed.). Thousand Oaks. CA: Sage.

Taylor, P. (2003). *Applied theatre: Creating transformative encounters in the community*. Portsmouth, NH: Heinemann.

Whybrow, N. (1996). Turning up the volume at the oasis: Invisible theatre exposed!. *Research in Drama Education, 1*(2), 221–232.

Wright, D. (1998). Embodied learning: Approaching the experience of the body in drama education. *NJ (Drama Australia Journal), 22*(2), 87–95.

3 Writing the Case Study

Portraits in Miniature

Theatre artists label stage monologues *portraits in miniature*. These one-person presentations in print or in performance offer the audience a dimensional rendering of a character in just a few minutes, providing insight into his or her personality, belief system, emotional dynamics, and other facets of dramatic action. The qualitative case study is also a portrait in miniature, for the researcher must represent and present a significant slice of a participant's life in a limited number of pages (assuming a traditional method of reportage other than video documentary). Educational anthropologist Harry F. Wolcott asserts throughout his writings an insightful response when asked by case study skeptics, "What can you learn by studying just one of anything?" His reply: "All you can!"

The case study is a classic research methodology into the focused examination and analysis of a human being and his or her personal lived experiences. (In this chapter, a case refers to one person and not a larger unit such as an organization or major event.) Whether approached from a developmental, psychological, sociological, anthropological, or other disciplinary perspective, the case is more than just about one person. The qualitative researcher thoughtfully reflects on the *implications* of the case – not necessarily as a representative unit of a larger population, but in terms of how the case speaks to broader social meanings. Marisol Clark-Ibáñez's (2008) insightful case study analyses of a "bad boy" and "bad girl" in an inner-city school transcend the local and particular circumstances of the children's behavioral issues to address matters related to gender inequity and discriminatory educational policy. Michael V. Angrosino's (1994) classic case study of Vonnie Lee, a developmentally disabled adult, is another example of an artfully rendered profile that, in its conclusion, rises above the case to address matters of research methodology, worldview, and human aspiration.

In my own case study write-ups, I try to include several elements that provide a portrait in miniature for the reader. First, I develop a representative description of the individual's physical appearance, particularly the face, and clothing that might be worn on any typically given day. I describe how he or she moves through space and if there are any distinguishing gestural habits.

I certainly include key monologic and dialogic excerpts of the case's speech, yet I also attend to the tone of voice and any unique spoken language qualities.

The case's actions, reactions, and interactions are portrayed through a series of short vignettes that can stand on their own yet cumulatively develop into a composite portrait. I especially look for and document *moments* in the person's life – significant trivia that are inference-laden and rich with meaning. In one of my case studies, I describe how a young man's seated posture was relaxed and open when he spoke about his beloved mother, yet gradually transformed into a fetal position as he gnawed on a small crucifix hanging around his neck when he spoke about his alcoholic father.

All cases are contextual, so it is difficult to prescribe specific guidance or formulaic outlines for representing an individual's life (that is, a portion of it). But the best case studies I've read went beyond seeing people as research "participants." These write-ups portrayed their cases as *people in some kind of trouble*. The best case studies are those that readers can connect and empathize with in some way. The best case study write-ups are those with a strong story-line that has a conventional beginning, middle, and end; with people who have goals to achieve yet obstacles to overcome; with occasional humor and bittersweet irony; and with a conclusion that reveals how the researcher was personally affected by the life observed and followed.

The case study selection in this chapter, "Exploring the Stigmatized Child through Theatre of the Oppressed Techniques," emerged from the larger action research study profiled in Chapter 2 of this volume. Many qualitative studies with moderate to large participant samples hold the opportunity for an ancillary case study report. This piece was commissioned by *Youth and Theatre of the Oppressed* co-editors Peter B. Duffy and Elinor Vettraino, who assembled a collection of chapters about Brazilian theatre artist and activist Augusto Boal's Theatre of the Oppressed, facilitated by educators with children and adolescents.

Sarah (pseudonym) is a young case profiled within the case of a one-hour classroom drama session. The event was videotaped, permitting repeated viewings for in-depth analyses of dialogue and movement. The video also enabled a detailed transcription to be prepared so that dialogic excerpts could be analyzed further and included in a written report. Certainly, the entire classroom of children was considered a case group of participants, but Sarah was given particular focus in this session since its thematic content was inspired by her personal plight.

In this report, I provide contextual background information on Sarah at the beginning, but the ending addresses the implications of the case through the social concept of *stigma*, as profiled by sociologist Erving Goffman. I also provide, as a researcher, my own honest responses on how the case affected me personally – a move that is not a self-indulgent act but a necessary component of case study reportage. For who can intimately study another person's life and not be touched in some way by it?

References

Angrosino, M. V. (1994). On the bus with Vonnie Lee: Explorations in life history and metaphor. *Journal of Contemporary Ethnography, 23*(1), 14–28.

Clark-Ibáñez, M. (2008). Gender and being "bad": Inner-city students' photographs. In P. Thomson (Ed.), *Doing visual research with children and young people* (pp. 95–113). London: Routledge.

EXPLORING THE STIGMATIZED CHILD THROUGH THEATRE OF THE OPPRESSED TECHNIQUES

The purpose of this chapter is to profile a case study experience from a larger fieldwork project in Theatre of the Oppressed (TO) with fourth and fifth-grade children (Saldaña, 2005). One primary goal of the study was to explore how young people at the upper-elementary school levels responded to session content with Boal's Games, Image Theatre, and Forum Theatre – techniques often described in print for adult participants but rarely for youth. The most important goal of the project, however, was to provide children opportunities through TO to explore how their personal oppressions, such as victimization from bullying, could be recognized and dealt with in the classroom and on the playground.

A team of five adult facilitators from Arizona State University worked in a neighborhood elementary school's classrooms over an eight-week period in 2000 to facilitate and document their experiences and children's responses to selected Boalian theatrical forms. Before the study began, I interviewed participating fourth- and fifth-grade teachers to explain the goals of the project, to describe the nature and purposes of TO, and to gather ideas from them for session content. One story in particular from a fifth-grade teacher struck me, not just as an idea for a Forum Theatre event, but as a story hauntingly similar to my own childhood experiences with stigmatization from peers:

TEACHER: We've got a little girl in here – she looks different and she acts different, so they'll make up some name that they call her.... It seems like every year there's one kid that gets picked on more than somebody else, because they're different, because they might look different, they might act different.... Like with her (*pointing to a child's desk*). I've watched them actually walk by this little girl and purposely bump into her or something like that, but then, even though you're watching them, the kid'll turn around and say, "Well, I didn't do that," after you confront him.

JOHNNY: What kinds of differences do kids tend to target?

TEACHER: With this one student, the kids seem to zero in because she did look different.... You know, once they have this idea that something's wrong with them, or they don't like them, then when they start to interact with the kid ... they're not accepting.... But most of the other kids in this room have been together for years, so she's brand new ... and so it's the [new] ones. They're kind of not fitting in because they weren't with this group as they moved on through school.

JOHNNY: Like a newcomer?

TEACHER: Uh-huh, I think it *is* like a newcomer thing.... It's basically the new ones.

[Originally published as Chapter 2 in *Youth and Theatre of the Oppressed*, edited by Peter B. Duffy and Elinor Vettraino, New York: Palgrave Macmillan, 2010, pp. 45–62; edited slightly for this publication.]

I resonated with this story because, like the young girl, I too was a newcomer to one particular school during my childhood and felt lonely and isolated from brand-new classmates. I was also grossly overweight as a child and frequently teased and cruelly taunted by others for my physical appearance. Bullies intimidated and threatened me on the playground and in the classroom. There were many days I pretended to be sick so I would not have to go to school to face the humiliating verbal abuse from my peers.

Sarah's Stigmatization

In the teacher's account above, the young girl – whom I'll name Sarah (pseudonym) – had no distinguishing physical differences from others. She was of average height and weight for her grade level, wore glasses (as did a few others in her classroom), had long brown hair and plain facial features, and was, from my interactions with her, a pleasant young girl. The ostracizing Sarah received from peers was most likely due to her outsider status as a newcomer to the school and classroom cultures, her academic intelligence, and perhaps what might be attributed as, from children's perceptions, her mildly "nerdy" physical appearance.

A few weeks before the TO study began, I conducted ethnographic fieldwork at the school site to acquaint myself with its staff, students, and ways of working. I observed a schoolwide talent show assembly presented in the elementary school's cafeteria. The dancing, singing, and other acts performed by children varied in quality and most received enthusiastic applause. But one particularly poor presentation was a karate demonstration by three boys, choreographed to the Village People's *Macho Man*. Their work appeared as if it had been under-rehearsed, and their discomfort, nervousness, and embarrassment performing in front of others led them to laugh and "goof around" onstage throughout the song. Their work received mild applause accompanied by "boos" from older child audience members, whom teachers quickly admonished.

Sarah was one of the few children at the talent show who performed solo with a new-age folk dance performance set to recorded music. I myself found her work to be of exceptional quality with good energy and presence. But despite the excellent work, she too received "boos" from her classmates. Again, teachers verbally admonished children for their inappropriate response. At the time, I was unable to rationalize why Sarah received disapproval until I later interviewed Sarah's teacher, who told me the story included at the beginning of this chapter. Even though Sarah exhibited what I perceived as natural talent, she received undeserved negative response from peers.

Young participants in this study frequently labeled their perceptions of non-average appearances and behaviors in others as "weird" – the childhood equivalent of stigmatization. The stigmas attributed to Sarah inspired a particular TO session with her fifth-grade class: to examine oppression toward the newcomer. Certainly I was not going to explore with these children in just one hour the sociological complexities and dynamics of stigma meticulously described by Erving Goffman in his classic text (1963), but instead I focused on one of his operational definitions: "the situation of the individual who is disqualified from full social acceptance . . . reduced in our minds from a whole and usual person to a tainted, discounted one" (pp. i, 3).

The TO project received both the host school's permission and our university's approval through its Institutional Review Board to conduct the study. However, we approached our work and this particular session cautiously. I did not state in Sarah's classroom that the Image and Forum Theatre work was inspired by or exclusively about her own plight. Instead, we designed the session to explore *fictional others* who have been stigmatized to provide a sense of comfortable distance for child participants. Banaszewski (2006) asserts that adult TO facilitators introduce and examine their personal yet hidden social agendas covertly and subtextually in the public school classroom. This particular session would be no exception.

The Session Design

Session Preparation

I had already been working with Sarah's fifth-grade class once a week for approximately four weeks before the session on stigma was conducted. The TO curriculum thus far consisted of selected Boalian Games and introductory Image Theatre work to acquaint students with basic terms and concepts such as *power* and *oppression*. Forum Theatre would be the next technique explored, but I wanted children to observe adults facilitate and participate in this relatively complex improvisational form before they attempted it themselves. *Demonstration*, *modeling*, and *example* are common pedagogical methods for instructing new learning. Therefore, I asked two of the other four university facilitators working on the TO project, Michelle White and Emily Petkewich, to participate and serve as a Forum Theatre protagonist and antagonist, respectively, with myself as the Joker.

Sarah's story as the stigmatized newcomer, recounted by her teacher, lent itself to Forum Theatre scenario construction – particularly the passage, "I've watched [students] actually walk by this little girl and purposely bump into her." I recalled Augusto Boal, at a Pedagogy and Theatre of the Oppressed plenary session, illustrate an elegant activating scene. He portrayed the antagonist who turned away from and folded his arms in indignation in response to the protagonist, who had approached him with a smile and an extended hand to greet him. Our Forum Theatre work would begin with the female adults portraying two elementary school students, one as the antagonist who would deliberately bump into the protagonist as they walked past each other. Emily was encouraged to portray the antagonist as "savvy" and slightly bullyish. Michelle was asked to portray the protagonist as a nice girl but reluctant to stand up for herself.

Midway through the study at the host elementary school, the university facilitators felt restricted adhering solely to Boalian theatrical techniques during our TO sessions. As drama educators, we were also acquainted with such dramatic structures (Neelands & Goode, 2000) as "hot-seating," "teacher-in-role," "critical events," "role-reversal," and other improvisational forms that lent themselves readily to the praxis of TO. We modified our original charge to focus exclusively on Boal's techniques by integrating more developmentally appropriate dramatic methods for children. This was not perceived as "watering down" Boal, but rather enriching TO with a supplemental "arsenal" of tactics to employ when appropriate. For example, one of my own devices was a medium-sized cardboard cutout of a "thought balloon," commonly seen in print cartoons to reveal the inner monologue of a character. This visual aid had been used previously with Sarah's class to help children articulate the unspoken thoughts of people in sculpted images.

The activating scene, coupled with a variety of dramatic structures described above for more detailed examination of the issue, would eventually evolve into a one-hour session reminiscent of theatre-in-education, a hybrid form of performative content by adults, interspersed with child audience improvisational participation. The protagonist and antagonist actors were informed beforehand of the session's basic content and goals but knew that their in-class contributions would be truly improvisational as the children and I explored the issues surrounding stigma. As you'll read below in the "Instant Forum Theatre" section, there were several opportunities (or, in educational parlance, "teachable moments") in which new Forum Theatre scenarios were spontaneously constructed, based on ideas contributed by children.

It is difficult to prescribe or recommend to others "how" TO work with youth gets designed. The predetermined plotting of this lesson, coupled with the spontaneous, in-class choices from the instructor's "mental rolodex" of dramatic structures, were the heuristics employed before and during the case study session described later in this chapter. In one sense, elementary school classroom drama educators already possess, by the nature of their training, the requisite facilitation skills of Boalian Jokers. Like a Forum Theatre event, we enter the space with a prepared script or scenario but must keep ourselves open to the unexpected and sometimes creative directions our class of young spect-actors takes us.

Documentation of the Session

Selected sessions of the TO project were videotaped to gather more detailed qualitative data for analysis. This particular session was recorded, since it would be the children's first experience with Forum Theatre. The single-camera placement provided an excellent visual record of the events, but children's soft voices were not always captured audibly on tape. Nevertheless, the recording enabled me to transcribe and thus quote most children's comments and to identify Sarah's specific contributions as a participant and spect-actor during the Forum Theatre scenes inspired by her classmates' oppression.

Narratives of TO with children are rare (and even rarer on video), so the extended description of our work in this chapter, written in the present tense, provides artists and educators a case study with selected details to vicariously experience this session on stigmatization.

Term Review and Warm-up

Since I had not worked with Sarah's class for two weeks, I begin the session with a review of terms we previously explored, and I ask children for definitions or examples:

- *Oppression*: "Like, when someone gives you a hard time, does something bad"; "put-downs"
- *Power*: "Like, you're the ruler of something"; "You have control"; "You act like you're the best"
- *Images*: "Pictures of us sculpting"

We then review our sculpting techniques such as asking the person for permission first to touch and sculpt her, moving the person's body gently, mirroring an image for her to copy (especially for facial expressions), verbally telling her how to shape herself, and not pulling on a person's clothing to sculpt.

Afterward, I facilitate a physical warm-up with a grouping game from "The Space Series" (Boal, 2002, p. 128). I tell children I do not want to explain why they will play the game but that they simply play as I observe. I direct them to group together by twos, then by threes, then fours, fives, and sixes. For the most part, they assemble and reassemble fairly quickly, but there is noticeable gender division since boys cluster primarily with boys and girls with girls. Sarah does not appear to have any difficulties participating in the game or finding a group. Afterward, I ask them to describe what went through their minds that influenced and affected their choices for who would be in which group: "Why did you decide to go with some people and not with others?" Children offer the following responses:

BOY: Some people that were being mean to me and stuff.
GIRL: They're our friends.

I remark that factors such as these play an important role in deciding whom we choose to work and be friends with.

I then introduce them to the terms and their modified definitions that will serve as the focus for our session:

- *stigma*: "Something about the person that other people have decided isn't right" (*I use the example of my own overweight childhood*); "But a stigma might also be for other reasons; maybe a stigma is something you *do* that other people may not like, and have decided 'You're not going to be a part of us anymore.'"
- *stigmatized*: "Someone who has a stigma."

Michelle and Emily, the adults who will portray the protagonist and antagonist, respectively, are introduced to the class as actors and teachers who will work with us today. (Michelle was asked beforehand to wear her reading glasses to the session since eyewear is sometimes a stigma among youth. Coincidentally, Michelle's clothing choices are light and soft textures, appropriate for the protagonist's character, while Emily, as the antagonist, wears a dark-colored wardrobe.)

Images of the Newcomer's Oppression

I ask for three volunteers to sculpt Michelle into someone who looks as if it is her first day in class at a new school in the middle of the academic year. Three girls are chosen, one of them Sarah, who not only raises her hand to volunteer but also waves it energetically for selection. I ask whether Michelle should stand or sit; Sarah says she should sit and gets a chair for her. Then, three other volunteers (all girls) are chosen to sculpt Emily as if she is a "regular" in this school who has attended it from the beginning. They, too, seat Emily, but sitting next to her is one of the volunteer girls as a classmate/friend.

Now that Michelle has been sculpted to look as if it is her first day at a new school (slouched, looking downward and downcast, with one arm crossed in front of her), the thought balloon is placed over her head, and I ask children to voice what she might be thinking or feeling. One example from a girl is "I don't have any friends, and I'm sad."

I direct just Emily and her classmate friend's heads to look toward Michelle. The cardboard thought balloon cutout is placed over Michelle, and children contribute the following as her thoughts:

GIRL: I wonder what they're thinking about?
GIRL: They're looking at me weird.
BOY: Maybe I should get to know them.
GIRL: Why are they staring at me?

Sarah offers, "I wonder if they're thinking about being my friend?"

I place the thought balloon over Emily staring at Michelle, and I ask children a series of questions:

JOHNNY: What if Emily looked at Michelle and wanted to stigmatize her? What if Emily got an immediate dislike of Michelle because of something? What might Emily say about Michelle that says, "I don't like her"? What *about* Michelle does Emily not like?

Children respond with the following:

BOY: I don't like your hair.
GIRL: I don't like your glasses.

GIRL: She looks very quiet; she might not be an interesting person.
BOY: I think she has "four eyes."

Sarah does not raise her hand to offer any ideas for Emily's image.

Emily and Michelle are prompted by me to stand and face each other approximately ten feet apart. Both are asked to voice a brief, inner monologue:

MICHELLE: I'm so nervous, it's hard to be new and not have any friends and kinda scary.
EMILY: I don't think I wanna be friends with her; she has "four eyes."

The Activating Scene

I then ask the two women to dynamize their images by walking toward each other to see what will happen. Emily passes by Michelle and deliberately bumps into her, which draws gasps and giggles from the child spect-actors. I instinctively call out "Freeze," place the thought bubble over Michelle, and ask, "What is Michelle thinking or feeling?" Sarah is the first to raise her hand, and I call on her to respond: "Why in the world did she do that?" The thought balloon is then placed over Emily, and children are asked to voice her thoughts:

GIRL: That was funny.
GIRL: That was fun, let's do it again.
GIRL: She looked very funny.

As before, Sarah does not raise her hand to volunteer any ideas about Emily's thoughts.

JOHNNY: Emily has stigmatized Michelle. But was there any good reason, I wonder?
A FEW CHILDREN: No.
JOHNNY: Not to me. I don't know about you . . . Emily, in character, why did you stigmatize Michelle?
EMILY: 'Cause she's new, and she wears glasses, and I don't like her clothes.

The two actors then sit apart from each other yet stay in character for a brief "hot-seating" exchange. Children are invited to ask questions of the two characters, and Sarah raises her hand to ask Emily, with a slight tone of admonishment:

SARAH: Why in the world are you judging someone like that? You should judge them by their attitude and not how they look – that wasn't right.
EMILY: I know, but I already have friends, and I don't need any more, so I really don't care.

Examples of questions for Michelle include the following:

GIRL: Were you thinking, "Why did she do that?"
MICHELLE: Yeah, I smiled at her and she bumped into me. I don't know why.
GIRL: Is this someone you think you should avoid?
MICHELLE: Um, maybe, I don't know. We're in the same class, but I don't know how much I can avoid her.
BOY: Why didn't you stand up for yourself?
MICHELLE: I was afraid. I don't know. She looks mean. She's kind of tough.

Sarah raises her hand periodically throughout the exchange above. I call on her to speak. Rather than ask a question of Michelle, though, she makes a statement:

SARAH: You really shouldn't really mind much about how people think you look, as long you feel good about yourself.
JOHNNY: (to Michelle) But do you think you'd have the courage to do it?
MICHELLE: Not right now. I move around a lot, so, I don't know …

The class and I briefly discuss the problems encountered by someone who moves frequently, such as readjustment to a new climate and the inability to make long-term friendships. I then walk toward Emily and ask the following:

JOHNNY: Emily, do you care about Michelle?
EMILY: I don't even know her.
JOHNNY: So I guess it's kind of hard to care about somebody if you don't know them. I guess I still don't understand why you hate her.
EMILY: Well, I don't "hate her," I just don't wanna be friends with her.
JOHNNY: But you bumped into her. What was the reason for that?
EMILY: It was fun; it was funny. It made my other friends laugh.
JOHNNY: (to the class) We're going to have to find some ways to help Michelle. One of the things when we face oppression is that we can't always change the person who's giving us a hard time. We have to work sometimes, when we feel oppressed, on overcoming it and try to make *ourselves* feel better.

Simultaneous Dramaturgy

We replay the activating scene – Emily deliberately bumps into Michelle as they walk past each other. I solicit ideas from children to explore through Boal's simultaneous dramaturgy technique, which will later segue into Forum Theatre scenarios: "We're going to take the ideas that you've got and play them out and see if they work." A noticeable surge of excited talk and energy emerges from children with this proposal. One child recommends that Michelle push Emily back when Emily deliberately bumps into her. The idea is played out, but it escalates into a shoving match and verbal confrontation between the two women. I stop the fight saying, "Pushing back might not be the best idea."

Sarah has been waving her hand energetically before I ask if there is another idea to try out. When I call on her, she offers, "What if Michelle had somebody with her? After that happened, she would have someone to help her." Since an additional "character" for the activating scene is suggested by this idea, and since my way of working in Forum Theatre is to encourage the contributor to enact her own suggestion, I ask Sarah, "Can you volunteer to be that person?" Sarah nods then moves to take her place in the action. The activating scene is replayed. Emily deliberately bumps into Michelle, and Michelle walks toward Sarah:

MICHELLE: Uh, hi. (*pointing to Emily*) See that girl over there? She's kind of unfriendly, and I really don't know how to handle it myself. Could you help me?
SARAH: Sure!
MICHELLE: OK, what do we do? (*they walk toward Emily*)
SARAH: You just tell her you didn't like it; that's all.
MICHELLE: And you'll come with me?
SARAH: Uh-huh.

(There is a visually stunning moment on videotape when both Michelle and Sarah simultaneously brush their hair back behind their ears as they dialogue. It is as if, for one fleeting moment, they are mirror images of each other.)

The two reach Emily. Michelle looks at Sarah for help. Sarah smiles at Michelle and nods as if to encourage her to speak:

MICHELLE: (*to Emily*) Um, why did you push me? I didn't like it.
EMILY: I don't know. I just thought it was funny.
SARAH: It wasn't very funny, 'cause if you do it a lot harder, you could really hurt her.
EMILY: But I didn't push very hard.
MICHELLE: You could have.
EMILY: It was an accident.

I stop the action at this point (in retrospect, a bit too early; I should have let the scene continue) and ask the group, "How did that idea work?" Children collectively respond with "Good," yet one girl rightly observes, "But there's still some problems," since Emily denied that her bumping was deliberate. I offer that Sarah's idea was a start to reconciling the problem and one possible solution to Michelle's oppression. When I ask children if there are any other ideas to try out, children now take the problem to other settings in their school milieu: the cafeteria and the playground.

Instant Forum Theatre

A girl suggests that Michelle join Emily at lunch and try to start a conversation. My original plan was to forum only the activating scene, but the new idea and its setting sound inspiring so I accept the scenario. Chairs are arranged to suggest a lunch table, and the suggestion is played out. Emily and a child cast as her friend chat with each other about boys during lunch. Michelle asks if she can sit at the table with them. The friends half-heartedly say, "Yes," but both ignore Michelle afterward. Emily offers to her friend that they play four-square after school. Michelle asks if she can join the game – she was quite good at it at her previous school – but Emily coolly remarks that they already have enough people.

I stop the scene noting that Michelle made a concerted effort to become friends with Emily, but I ask the children what else happened. The children observe that the rejection continued. One girl suggests that Michelle get contact lenses so she won't be a "four eyes," but I counter with, "I wonder if her family can afford that?" Michelle, in-role, says that her family just moved here and her father got a new job, so there is probably not enough money to make that happen. Then, the following dialogue occurs:

GIRL: She should maybe look for someone else to be friends with.
JOHNNY: So just avoid Emily altogether?
GIRL: Well, not avoid her, but you know, if it's not working out, then she should find someone that it does work out with. She shouldn't be mean to her; she should just be friendly still.

Another girl suggests, "Maybe, when they're playing four-square, she can just go up and play or ask different people if they want to play."

A new Forum Theatre scenario has been proposed. I seek two volunteers to set up the space with Emily and her friend to play four-square. Several children, including Sarah, eagerly wave their hands and call out "Me, me!" I select two boys closest to the presentation space. When the area is established, the four friends play as Michelle comes by to ask if she can join. Emily replies that they already have four players. Michelle then asks if she can play with them tomorrow, but Emily seems reluctant to commit to her request. Michelle acknowledges the rejection and ends the scene by saying meekly that she will find others to play with.

After a brief discussion of the oppression, I ask children to replace Michelle and try out their ideas in this scenario. Sarah raises her hand for selection, but I feel the need to call on others to maximize participation. I ask a girl to replace Michelle and select three other girls to join Emily as her fellow four-square players:

PROTAGONIST GIRL: Hi, can I play ball?
EMILY: Well, we're in the middle of a game. (*to her four-square friends*) This girl wants to play with us.
ANTAGONIST GIRL 1: I don't know. She's funny looking.
ANTAGONIST GIRL 2: I don't know if she can play.
JOHNNY: Why? Let me stop you.

The interruption is an instinctive act on my part to examine the rejection from the antagonist's perspective through "hot-seating":

JOHNNY: Why can't she play? Why won't you let her play?
ANTAGONIST GIRL 2: I don't know her or anything. She shouldn't be playing this game. We don't know her.
JOHNNY: Aren't you supposed to be working together, to help people make friends? Why all of a sudden are you stigmatizing her?
ANTAGONIST GIRL 2: I don't know.
JOHNNY: If you don't know, then why are you doing it? (*silence*) You don't have an answer for me, do you? If you don't know why you're doing it, then why are you doing it?
ANTAGONIST GIRL 1: What if she's different?
JOHNNY: *So what* if she's different?

A boy is then selected to replace the protagonist's role (and the gender of the character is changed to "Mike"):

MIKE: Do you think I could join in your game?
EMILY: No, I don't know, we're right in the middle of the game right now. But maybe you could have a turn.
ANTAGONIST GIRL 1: When somebody gets out.
EMILY: Yeah, after somebody gets out.
MIKE: OK.
(*The girls look at each other and wickedly smile, suggesting that it's not going to happen.*)

We examine the outcome and infer from the female antagonists' nonverbal communication that the acceptance was insincere. Sarah is then chosen to explore her idea, and three different girls are selected to join Emily as antagonists:

SARAH: Can I play?
EMILY: No, this is our court. Go find another one.
SARAH: What's your favorite game?
EMILY: This *is* our favorite game.
SARAH: Do you have any others you like?
EMILY: (*pause*) I like basketball.
SARAH: Hmm.

I ask Sarah, "What did you try to do?" Sarah explains that her next idea is to see if Emily will join her and her friends in a game of basketball. Though Sarah, in one way, veers into a "that's magic" direction from Forum Theatre (in which the solution proposed is improbable because the circumstances are radically altered by the spect-actor), I nevertheless accept Sarah's proposal. I inquire if she needs additional people to complete her scene. Sarah says, "Yes," so I ask her to choose her teammates. Many children raise their hands asking Sarah to select them. She assembles six others to join her and gives them directions before the scene begins:

SARAH: OK, we've been playing a basketball game, but we're short some people, so we're gonna go ask them if they wanna play with us.
(*Sarah and her group approach the four-square players*)
SARAH: You guys wanna play basketball with us?
ANTAGONIST GIRL 1: No, we're playing.
SARAH: Are you sure?
ANTAGONIST GIRL 2: Yeah, we're kind of busy right now.
SARAH: How long do you think you're gonna be? (*pause*) You guys wanna play after you're finished?
EMILY: How many people do you need?
SARAH: We only need four. 'Cause, everybody else is playing soccer and all those other sorts of things.
EMILY: (*to the antagonists*) You guys wanna play after we're done with our game? (*they reply "Yeah," "Sure"*) OK, we'll come when our game is over.
SARAH: OK. Do you know how long it's gonna be?
EMILY: (*shrugging her shoulders, asking her friends*) How long? (*brief pause; to Sarah*) Just a few minutes, OK?

I bring the scene to a close, and we gather for whole group discussion. When I ask what just happened in the forum, one girl remarks, "They created conversation." I also observe how Emily seemed different: "She was willing to listen this time."

Attitude Adjustment

The original activating scene – Emily deliberately bumping into Michelle – is replayed. I then ask children to recommend solutions to Michelle on what she can do this time to overcome this particular oppressive action. After Michelle hears their ideas, she employs several of them. Emily deliberately bumps into Michelle, yet Michelle responds politely with, "Excuse me," and initiates a friendly conversation, noting that she saw Emily playing four-square and offers to teach Emily a special four-square maneuver she learned at her previous school. Emily says that would be nice. I interpret that Michelle had opened the door to a new friendship, but some children infer that Emily's acceptance was a trick to learn the new maneuver then shut Michelle out of the game. I suggest the following to the children:

JOHNNY: There are times you can do some things to help you overcome your oppressions . . .
BOY: Maybe Michelle should invite Emily to do something.
JOHNNY: But you know what? Michelle can do all of those things, and Emily still won't be her friend. Isn't that kind of realistic? (*children agree*) So, we can

do our best to try to stop being stigmatized, but ultimately we also gotta work on it ourselves. It seems as if we've been spending so much time on trying to change Michelle and what she could do, that we really haven't been putting enough focus on where the problem really is: the person who stigmatizes. This is what we need to work on. (*to Emily*) You need to adjust your attitude.

The next portion of our work incorporates an Image Theatre technique demonstrated by Chris Vine of New York City's Creative Arts Team at a Pedagogy and Theatre of the Oppressed conference session. I borrowed but relabeled the technique "Attitude Adjustment."

Emily sculpts herself into a position that shows she accepts Michelle as a friend by sitting next to her, smiling, with her hand around Michelle's shoulder (the ideal image), then creates an antagonistic image by sitting away from, pointing at, and defiantly giggling at Michelle (the realistic image). I encourage children to stand behind Emily and say things that might persuade her to transform herself incrementally out of the realistic image and move closer toward the accepting and ideal image. I prompt children to "Change the way she thinks and feels." I also caution them that there might be statements they make that will have no effect on Emily and statements that could even motivate her to retreat back toward the realistic or stigmatizing image. As I give these directions, Sarah raises and waves her hand briskly throughout, but I select two other children to go first.

One girl's initial idea stimulates a subtle change in one of Emily's gestures: "What you like about her. Look for something that you like about her." A second statement from a boy initiates no change in Emily's image: "Just be her friend." Sarah is then chosen to speak to Emily:

SARAH: I think you need another friend. Michelle, she's really very nice. You should get to know her; she's really nice.

Sarah's idea motivates Emily to drop her taunting gestures and to move her chair three feet closer to Michelle.

The following sample ideas bring Emily incrementally closer to Michelle and the ideal image:

BOY: Maybe you should think about how you felt when you first came.
GIRL: She's very smart. She could help you with your homework.
GIRL: When you're learning Spanish, she could help you learn Spanish.

Emily makes no change when a girl says, "She could keep your secrets," and even retreats back slightly toward the realistic image when another girl offers, "She can help you find a boyfriend."

Lightning Forum

Due to limited remaining time for the session, I initiate Boal's "Lightning Forum" technique. I ask children to line up directly behind Emily, who by this time has moved two-thirds the distance toward the accepting image, and speak their ideas quickly to get Emily to the final ideal image. Nine children assemble themselves behind her, and Sarah moves quickly to be first in line. (Due to the distance of the camera's microphone from the final unit of action, I was unable to document what children said exactly.) With less than a minute remaining for the session because the class has to leave for lunch, I ask the nine children (Sarah among them) clustered around Emily to simultaneously whisper their ideas to get Emily to move. Several mention that there would be access to a car if they were friends. Their ideas eventually work, and Emily shifts into the final ideal image and places her arm around Michelle's shoulder. I enthusiastically praise the class with "You did it!" The children applaud and shout, "Yay!" but Sarah is the only child who raises both arms in triumph and jumps up and down enthusiastically. Time does not remain for us to process the climax of the unit, but I close our work with, "Thanks for helping Emily realize there's no reason to stigmatize, that it's just stupid to begin with."

Reflections on the Session

Sarah, whose real-life oppression generated the day's TO work, contributed the most ideas, initiated the Forum Theatre scenes that required additional casting, and played the role of spect-actor protagonist with fairly fluent dialogue. After the session, she came up to Emily and Michelle and confessed that she had experienced the same problems we explored today. As TO sessions progressed with this group, Sarah became one of the most engaged and active participants in the fifth-grade class.

Self-esteem is one of the most critical psychological foundations for human beings. How we each feel about ourselves impacts our identity and shapes our functioning and ability at daily living, particularly with interpersonal relationships. When we think less of ourselves, when we feel we have a "spoiled identity," as Erving Goffman phrases it, our social interactions with others become ineffective. We assume a subordinate role and make ourselves vulnerable to oppression. We become easy prey and the target of a dominant individual's or group's stigmatization. Sarah's perceived similarities with the protagonist made the session "high stakes" for her. There was resonance, investment, and ownership because Michelle's problems, their stigmas, were identical.

During "Attitude Adjustment," Sarah said to Emily – who represented the classroom antagonists in her own life – "I think you need another friend. Michelle, she's really very nice. You should get to know her; she's really nice." Sarah now had a public forum, situated in a simulated dramatic context, to express her inner desire to peers. "Attitude Adjustment" suggests that the goal of the spect-actor is to change the attitude, value, and/or belief systems of the antagonist (or protagonist). But Sarah was not only trying to persuade Emily to stop stigmatizing Michelle. *Sarah was also searching for acceptance from Emily.* The triumphant moment for her, when Emily accepted Michelle as a friend, fulfilled her own need to belong to the classroom community, to no longer be ostracized as an outsider, to no longer be stigmatized for misperceived differences.

There was also acceptance of Sarah in other ways during the session. By dramatizing the daily reality of her life, there was acceptance of her problem as a legitimate concern and worthy of examination. By selecting her – accepting her – to shape Michelle's image, there was transference of her unspoken feelings into Michelle's own body, which Michelle accepted. And when her suggestions were played out in the role of spect-actor, not just once but several times, there was acceptance of her ideas because they generally "worked" to stop the oppression. Sarah's status was elevated from stigmatized student to expert player and problem solver.

One fourth-grade girl in the TO study poignantly told me, "Sometimes, you can't be nice to deal with oppression," after I expressed concern that the children's Forum Theatre solutions were mostly combative. But Sarah took the high road in this session. When needed, she admonished Emily gently but confidently. Her Forum Theatre tactics were neither deceptive nor diversionary – they were sincere attempts to communicate, sincere attempts to create community, sincere attempts to make friends with those who unfairly stigmatized her. Goffman (1963) speaks primarily of individuals with physical disabilities when he offers the following advice, but it so readily applies to Sarah's peacemaking efforts:

> The nondisabled, when they stigmatize, should be tactfully helped to act nicely. Slights, snubs, and untactful remarks should not be answered in kind. Either no notice should be taken or the stigmatized individual should make an effort at sympathetic re-education of the normal [sic], showing him, point for point, quietly, and with delicacy, that in spite of appearances the stigmatized individual is, underneath it all, a fully-human being.
>
> (p. 116)

Children who label peers "weird" have stigmatized them. Jokers have the opportunity to examine stigma through Boal's theatrical forms with young people. Not only can we explore how the protagonist might respond to oppression or stigmatization, but we also can examine the antagonist's often-irrational reasons for labeling and thus oppressing. TO facilitators have the potential to become supportive allies for the stigmatized. Goffman further reminds us that

> the first set of sympathetic others is of course those who share [her] stigma. Knowing from their own experience what it is like to have this particular stigma, some of them can provide the individual with instruction in the tricks of the trade and with a circle of lament to which [she] can withdraw

for moral support and for the comfort of feeling at home, at ease, accepted as a person who really is like any other normal [sic] person.

(p. 20)

I admit to having a soft spot in my heart for those mistreated unfairly by others. Given my own stigmatized past (and by some, my own stigmatized present), I can't help but empathize. When I see that one of my students, regardless of age level, has been oppressed and needs a mentor – or an ally, a friend, a rescuer, and so on – I take him or her under my wing, as the cliché goes. Most times the relationship strengthens the stigmatized student – and me. Only on rare occasions have I been disappointed or burned from trusting too much or too easily.

I cited earlier that adult TO facilitators introduce and examine their personal yet hidden social agendas covertly and subtextually in the public school classroom. So, could this session have been designed and driven by my subconscious need to exorcise my own personal demons? Did I step onto precarious shaky ground or venture into some ethical conundrum by dramatizing and scrutinizing a real person's story in front of her peers? Was Sarah's engaged participation and dramatic victory some form of emotional catharsis for my own troubled childhood memories? I would prefer that readers themselves reflect on those questions and develop their own answers. As for me, I was simply trying to do my best as an elementary educator to "change the world" – one child at a time.

Closure

At the time of this writing – fall 2008 – Sarah should already have graduated from high school and may now be a sophomore in college.

I have heard from my adult female university students how adolescent girls can sometimes act "viciously" toward each other during their young adult years. Popular media stereotypically portray high school girls as cliquish rivals, vying for popularity, and insulting of each other's appearance if it does not conform to current fashion trends and standards of beauty. I wonder if Sarah was still taunted by her peers, still stigmatized, and whether those TO sessions during fifth grade empowered her to stand up to oppression as she grew. School privacy acts and my originally approved research protocol do not permit me to track down Sarah's whereabouts, yet I really do want to know how she's fared with her adolescent life course. I hope she has not experienced the same type of peer abuse I encountered in junior and senior high school.

The TO project with children produced observable but sporadic outcomes from teachers' perspectives, due primarily to the relatively short amount of time we spent in their classrooms. One teacher both quantified and qualified the results by suggesting we had influenced and affected perhaps only one-third of the children and that there were some – mostly boys – whom we would "never be able to reach." Nevertheless, seeds of social consciousness and strategies for dealing with oppression were planted back then through TO. I can only hope that they fell on good soil in Sarah, took root, and grew deep within her.

Acknowledgments

Funding for the Theatre of the Oppressed with Children project was provided by a grant from the Research Council of the Katherine K. Herberger College of the Arts at Arizona State University. The research team included Emily Petkewich, Gordon Hensley, Doyle Ott, Johnny Saldaña, and Michelle White. Thanks are extended to Sally Dorothy Bailey, RDT, who introduced me to Erving Goffman's *Stigma*, and to Jim Simpson, psychotherapist, for analytic consultation.

References

Banaszewski, C. (2006). *Adult theatre of the oppressed facilitators' questions, roles, and rules when using theatre of the oppressed with adolescent participants*. Unpublished doctoral dissertation, Arizona State University.

Boal, A. (2002). *Games for actors and non-actors* (2nd ed.) (Trans. A. Jackson). New York: Routledge.

Goffman, E. (1963). *Stigma: Notes on the management of spoiled identity*. Englewood Cliffs, NJ: Prentice Hall.

Neelands, J., & Goode, T. (2000). *Structuring drama work: A handbook of available forms in theatre and drama* (2nd ed.). New York: Cambridge University Press.

Saldaña, J. (2005). Theatre of the oppressed with children: A field experiment. *Youth Theatre Journal, 19*, 117–133.

4 Writing About Critical Pedagogy

The Significance of Moments

A *moment* as it is used in several disciplines today does not imply the passage of one or two seconds of time, but instead connotes a significant, self-contained unit of interpersonal social interaction or intrapersonal reflection. Moments can range in length from one minute to an entire day. Their content varies from mundane actions to life-altering epiphanies. Washing, drying, folding, and ironing clothes is a moment. A high-speed amusement ride at Disneyland is a moment. Giving birth to a child is a moment. Myriad moments occur in our lives that become documented as strong memories in the mind. Whether routine or ritual, the actions have made an impression of some kind – either to those who experience them directly or for those who witness them happen to others.

Multicultural education and critical pedagogy examine moments of *encounter*. Conflict-laden interactions rooted in sexism, homophobia, ethnic discrimination, the inequitable distribution of resources, and other forms of power imbalance, provide opportunities for deep reflection and initiating positive policy change to right the wrongs:

> Critical inquiry examines inequality and injustices through sound investigation of social conditions. An openly political and moral agenda drives the research to uncover and document evidence of social ills and to critique their origins and effects on human life. By raising awareness of problematic issues, researchers take the first step advocating for productive solutions and emancipatory action.
>
> (Saldaña & Omasta, 2018, p. 292)

Moments of encounter in education documented in qualitative research include titles such as C.J. Pascoe's (2007) study of high school heteronormativity in *Dude, You're a Fag*, and Jonathan Kozol's (1991) blistering investigation of inner-city schools in *Savage Inequalities*.

My readings of the multicultural education literature and attendance at organizational events sponsored by Pedagogy and Theatre of the Oppressed, and the National Association for Multicultural Education, have acquainted me with the seminal work of Paulo Freire, James A. Banks, Christine E. Sleeter, Sonia Nieto, and other writers. They address theory, pedagogy, praxis, and policy in the field with expertise and humanity. But what remains in my memory after all the books, journal articles, conferences, and workshops are the stories – the moments – of children, teachers, parents, and the social world at large all facing encounters at school and at home.

I remember the story about a young African American boy who suffered through school for days with a toothache, but who thought the pain was normal for the poor. I remember the story about a tough, overweight Latina who frequently got into trouble at school for physically fighting with others, yet cried when the interviewer asked about her family. I remember reading about the bravado of a group of working-class teenage boys disrespecting their teachers as the researcher foreshadowed their limited working-class futures. I remember the story about a young gay teen who dropped out of school and became a victim of sex trafficking and drug abuse. And I remember the story about a young girl gender transitioning to male and the ridicule he received from classmates, forcing him to attend an alternative school.

These are just a few of the moments that have stayed in my memory. The researchers who documented them wrote the stories but elaborated on them as well. Small encounters provide opportunities for scrutiny of their larger social implications. They enable if not strongly motivate us to comment on and critique the current conditions of schooling, parenting, social welfare, and the factors leading to inequality – arguably the greatest cause of most human misery (Charon, 2013, pp. 157–158). The critical researcher investigating the world makes no apologies for a values-driven perspective and agenda. Certainly, the study should be solidly grounded in evidence and the results not knee-jerk assertions. Moments of encounter witnessed by the researcher can become moments of written responsive resistance to the injustices observed.

"Social Class and Social Consciousness: Adolescent Perceptions of Oppression in Forum Theatre Workshops" continues the thematic thread of works about August Boal's Theatre of the Oppressed profiled in Chapters 2 and 3. I did not preconceive this article as a planned research study. Two workshops I facilitated on the same day became an "accidental" or opportunistic event – a moment – for deep reflection. What happened between me and a group of high schoolers struck me so personally that I felt the need to write about it for my colleagues in the National Association for Multicultural Education's journal, *Multicultural Perspectives*.

There are times when the convergence of multiple subject interests in our professional careers synthesizes in a unique way. At the time of the workshops described below, my various studies in multicultural education, critical pedagogy, secondary school theatre, adolescent development, theatre for social change, and emotional intelligence all blended into my thought and practice. The article selection can be considered a case study of an event, but the lens, filter, and angle of my writing took a critical pedagogical slant.

References

Charon, J. M. (2013). *Ten questions: A sociological perspective* (8th ed.). Belmont, CA: Cengage Learning.

Kozol, J. (1991). *Savage inequalities: Children in America's schools*. New York: Crown.

Pascoe, C. J. (2007). *Dude, you're a fag: Masculinity and sexuality in high school*. Berkeley, CA: University of California Press.

Saldaña, J., & Omasta, M. (2018). *Qualitative research: Analyzing life*. Thousand Oaks, CA: Sage.

SOCIAL CLASS AND SOCIAL CONSCIOUSNESS: ADOLESCENT PERCEPTIONS OF OPPRESSION IN FORUM THEATRE WORKSHOPS

Abstract

Two workshops on Augusto Boal's Forum Theatre were conducted with two high school student groups coincidentally divided by class: one lower to lower-middle, and one upper-middle to upper. Students created oppression scenarios for improvisation that focused primarily on horizontal hostility: the group versus the stigmatized individual. The two workshop environments, however, differed in quality due to the facilitator's perception of *class* as an influential variable. Students in the upper-middle class to upper-class group made choices and exhibited actions characteristic of those living in the culture of affluence and privilege. I reflect critically on the event's implications for multicultural educators.

The annual High School Theatre Day at Arizona State University (ASU) brings students and theatre teachers from more than 25 Phoenix area schools to campus for a series of workshops and performances. ASU faculty and graduate students conduct numerous concurrent sessions, and two to three school groups are assigned to each instructor for a 1-hour session in various theatre topics. In February 1998, approximately 60 students from five high schools participated in two improvisation workshops I conducted – 25 in the first, and 35 in the second. Student participants in the first workshop attended two schools located in Phoenix's inner-city area, and represented a diversity of ethnic backgrounds from lower- to lower-middle class families. Three schools assigned to the second workshop were located in affluent Phoenix suburbs, and the vast majority of students were upper-middle to upper-class white residents. These assigned groupings were coincidental and unintentional by the event coordinator.[1]

Both workshops were an introduction to Augusto Boal's improvisational Forum Theatre (FT) from his repertory of *Theatre of the Oppressed* (1985):

> Forum Theatre is a theatrical game in which a problem is shown in an unsolved form, to which the audience ... is invited to suggest and enact solutions. The problem is always the symptom of an oppression, and generally involves visible oppressors and a protagonist who is oppressed.... After one showing of the scene, which is known as "the model" ... it is shown again slightly speeded up, and follows exactly the same course until a member of the audience shouts "Stop!", takes the place of the protagonist and tries to defeat the oppressors.
>
> (Boal, 1992, p. xxi)

To Boal (1995), audience members in FT are not spectators but "spect-actors," because the essence of theatre resides in the human being observing

[Originally published in *Multicultural Perspectives*, vol. 1, no. 3, 1999, pp. 14–18; edited slightly for this publication.]

itself. He or she "not only 'makes' theatre: it 'is' theatre" (p. 13). The FT facilitator is referred to as the "Joker" because, like the face card, he or she can play multiple roles: director, discussion leader, devil's advocate, and so forth. The function of FT is not entertainment but pedagogical exploration. FT is rehearsal for reality – opportunities to find solutions to our oppressions, change our actions, and thus change the world. The philosophies of Boal harmonize with those of his fellow Brazilian, Paulo Freire (1993).

Two warm-up activities from Boal's *Games for Actors and Non-actors* (1992) were played to break the ice quickly among participants. The first was an introductory handshaking game that encourages continuous physical contact. The second functioned as both a physical warm-up and segue into the dynamics of power. One person places his or her hand 12 inches away from a partner's face. The hand is moved slowly across space while the partner follows, keeping the exact distance between the head and the hand. The follower may be led across the room, onto the floor, or in any position forced by the leader. After 1 minute, roles are exchanged. This activity physicalizes the symbolic characteristics of the oppressor and the oppressed.

Next, the origin and basic purpose of FT were briefly described, and two ASU students demonstrated an FT model. The actors improvised a scene in which a man asks a woman for a date. The protagonist was unable to assert herself by stating directly that she did not want to go out with him. She offered excuses such as rehearsal commitments, homework, and studying for a test. The male antagonist took advantage of her weakness, negated the woman's excuses, and coerced her physically through proximity and sexually suggestive postures. The female actor reacted non-verbally to his presence through hesitant gestures and inference-laden facial expressions. This 2-minute improvisation ended without resolution.

Next, high schoolers participated as spect-actors in a replay of the improvisation. When students felt alternative solutions to the woman's oppression came to mind, she (or he, because cross-gender participation was encouraged) raised her hand, called out "Stop," and replaced the protagonist. The antagonist responded as the new situations suggested, but did not acquiesce to the spect-actor unless a solution left him speechless – a clue that the student's idea "worked." I emphasized that this was not a contest to determine the best solution, but an exploration of multiple and plausible resolutions to the conflict. Students participated well, and approximately four spect-actors from each group volunteered ideas. As the Joker, I facilitated brief discussions and reinforced how FT was structured. After this cursory introduction to FT, students then developed their own oppression scenarios.

The FT Scenarios: Horizontal Hostility

Each student wrote a one to two sentence description of an oppression or power imbalance to explore in a second round of FT. Unfortunately, I did not separate the scenarios developed by each of the two workshop groups. I did not foresee the contrast of each group's engagement with FT (discussed later). I could analyze only the collected body of scenarios, but that in itself was most revealing. Of course, the results do not represent all high school students, nor do they necessarily profile their utmost concerns because limited time prohibited prewriting reflection. Generalizability and transferability to other settings are left to the reader. The 71 scenarios (some students wrote more than one) were coded and categorized, and the results both informed and surprised me of their perceptions.

I anticipated that adults would be the most oppressive antagonists in these young people's lives. But scenarios that portrayed oppressions *by* adolescents *toward* adolescents, primarily in the school setting, totaled 80%. Exclusion, intimidation, and ridicule by *groups* perpetrated on *individuals* perceived as different was the most prominent subcategory (62%). One term for this phenomenon is *horizontal hostility* – this is, teenagers are their own worst oppressors. Examples, as students wrote them, include:

> The 'cool' group picking on one person, trying to draw that person into a fight. The cool group knows it's going to win, then making fun of them while fighting, uterly [sic] humiliating the person.

> New person sucked in by certain group who happen to be stuck up to others, but he/she doesn't agree, but also doesn't want to be the target

> Pregnant teenage high school girl sitting in class and having people call her names

Sources for their ideas were not solicited, but I inferred that examples such as these originated from their own painful experiences:

> When you're short, people will make fun of you, use you as an arm stand . . .

> A kid who has been home schooled all of his life comes to high school with other people and he has no social skills. A group of boy [sic] pick on him and shove him into lockers. He never does anything to stop them. He's powerless around them.

> Why are you so stupid? Having your little club was something you did in 3rd grade. You think that's something hip now. It's lame, Vanessa, get it into your head that *your* [sic] lame, *your* club is lame & everything about you is *lame*.

The second subcategory, totaling 18%, was inequitable boyfriend-girlfriend relationships, but this may have been influenced by the FT model presented at the beginning of the workshop. Examples include:

> Two people, a boy and a girl. They have been in a relationship and maybe gone a little farther sexually than they intended. They are discussing the situation and what they should do next. One of them could be making all the decisions while the other one goes along w/ it.

The Boy is a player and the Girl isn't strong enough to stand up to him. Like, for example, he kisses her, and the next day, he's kissing another girl, but the 1st girl won't talk to him about it. She lets him control her.

In the next major category, oppressions by *adults* toward adolescents totaled 15%.[2] Most scenarios were parent-child conflicts and portrayed fathers as oppressive, dominant figures, particularly toward daughters:

Father/Daughter Father has high standards that daughter feels she can't meet/or has difficulty meeting them.

Father (very strong – dominant male type) and *daughter* (naïve and young – wants more than anything to please her father & be loved). They are sitting alone talking & she expresses her desire to perform. He wants her to stop dreaming & face reality.

Minor categories include racism (5%), classism (4%), heterosexism (1%), and ableism (1%).[3] Examples include:

A poor student being made fun of by a rich student

Not me, but others at school. Monkey, slave references, never use "N" word, but work around it.

Most adolescent-to-adolescent scenarios portrayed oppression by a "group," "club," "class," "crowd," "people," "others," and so on – the collective force attacking the stigmatized individual. In gender-related scenarios (boyfriend-girlfriend, father-daughter), the oppressions were one-on-one with power manifesting itself through antagonist coercion, manipulation, and negation of the protagonist's desires. Not surprisingly, the man was the primary oppressor.

Analyzing why racism, classism, and other "isms" receded to the background may also answer why horizontal hostility was prominent. Most adolescents focus on individual, personal needs rather than larger sociological issues. What we label as teenage self-absorption is *adolescentrism*.[4] Boal observes that oppressions in western countries focus on "themes of loneliness and alienation" (Schutzman and Cohen-Cruz, 1994, p. 4), attributes we also assign to angst-ridden high schoolers. Theatre teacher Grote (1997) speaks from decades of experience with secondary school students and shared this from his personal-practical knowledge:

Teenagers live in constant, daily terror that revolves around one single idea: No one must ever find out I'm different from everybody else. When they talk about "just being themselves," they never mean "being themselves." Almost always, they really mean "being accepted by others," which is not quite the same thing. They are terrified that if their "true self"...should be exposed to public view, it will automatically be exposed to public ridicule.
(p. 159)

For this group of workshop participants, *equity* is not a matter of race or class. *Equity* means freedom from stigma and inclusion in peer group membership – the status of belonging. *Social justice* applies not to the social world around them, but to their immediate social circle of peers and the fulfillment of their personal desires. Oppression surfaces when the individual adolescent, whose needs or characteristics vary from adult expectations or group cultural norms, becomes targeted for "terrorism": exclusion, intimidation, ridicule, coercion, manipulation, negation of desires, and – at its worse – physical violence. Blumberg and Blumberg (1994), in *The Unwritten Curriculum: Things Learned But Not Taught in School*, noted the importance of an adolescent "simply to be accepted as a valued, or at least not a devalued, member of one's peer group. . . . [Peer] life in school is one of the social crucibles through which a young person begins to learn what the interpersonal and group world is all about and how best to make his or her way in it" (p. 76).

Race and class may also have receded to the background because these constructs are "givens" in the workshop participants' respective school cultures. The inner-city schools' diverse student bodies (not predominantly students of color but an average of 45%), with their shared lower to lower-middle class status, makes them level on the playing field, if you will. In the affluent suburban schools, the predominantly upper-middle to upper-class white student bodies are part of the everyday environment and thus are perceived as the norm. To adolescents *at these particular sites*, racial and class tensions are not visible oppressions and hence not of immediate concern.[5] But because these oppressions are invisible to affluent suburbanites, this may have affected how they responded to FT in unexpected ways.

Social Class and FT Choices

Students were grouped in twos or threes to share with partners what they wrote, and to choose one scenario as an FT model to present to the whole group. Participants had only 10 minutes to negotiate and prepare, and only a few scenarios could be seen. Here is where unique differences between each workshop group emerged.

The first group – participants from inner-city areas – chose and improvised scenes based on adolescent-to-adolescent hostility. Through majority vote, the students elected to explore the "new kid at school" theme with the entire workshop group. As the Joker, I recall feeling satisfied after the first session because focused, substantial improvisation and discussion occurred among students in a cooperative and supportive environment.

In the second workshop – students from the affluent, predominantly white suburbs – scenarios shared were not adolescent-to-adolescent themes, but material reminiscent of television sketch comedy and theatre sports.[6] One scene by two boys portrayed the President of the United States coercing a Secret Service Agent to cover-up a sexual indiscretion for him. (This idea obviously emerged from news stories about the Clinton scandals current at that time.) A second scene portrayed an aggressive, door-to-door, vacuum cleaner salesperson pitching her product to a homeowner. The latter idea received the majority vote for whole group FT exploration. One scenario voted down included the clique intimidating a newcomer to school. As the Joker, I felt frustrated that the group made this choice, but I was bound by FT guidelines for democratic use of the aesthetic space.

When the two boys shared their President-Secret Service scene, I inferred from their exaggerated characterizations and satiric commentary that the intent was not to examine an oppression seriously, but to showcase their own perceived comedic talents and to entertain the group through material similar to the TV show *Saturday Night Live*. To me, the vacuum cleaner scenario was not a reality-based oppression relevant to their own lives, but an amusing framework for competitive improvisation: Who can most cleverly oust the salesperson through FT? In some cases, students who replaced the homeowner did not speak more than one sentence before another spect-actor called out "Stop!" I intervened as the Joker and asked them to allow the protagonists a bit more time to explore their strategies.

The actions by these upper-class adolescents consisted of: denying the existence of more serious social issues in their world; subverting the facilitator's "authority" to control their own desires; suppressing others' ideas in favor of one's own; and contemptuously treating the working-class salesperson as an annoyance to be expunged. To me, these actions and the entire workshop environment reflected stereotypical attributes about the privileged class: conservative tastes; competitive; capitalist; political controllers who denigrate Democratic leaders; and aggressive show-offs.

Adams, Bell, & Griffin (1997) commented on the penalties of privilege, but their assertions also apply to the adolescent group oppressing the stigmatized individual:

> Members of dominant or privileged groups . . . internalize the system of oppression and through their collusion with the system operate as agents in perpetuating it. Internalized domination is the incorporation and acceptance by individuals within the dominant group of prejudices against others and the assumption that the status quo is normal and correct. It includes feelings of superiority, and often self-consciousness, guilt, fear, projection, and denial.
>
> (p. 12)

Like a targeted adolescent, I became the victim of group ridicule. This socially self-conscious, upper-class group excluded me from their cultures of adolescentrism and privilege. They denied my agenda for social issues exploration by transforming theatre from an art form that examines the human condition, into shallow entertaining diversion. My pedagogical desires were negated; like the broad brush we apply to those with wealth and power, their needs came first. The framework for their preferred FT model was not the fearful reality of life around them, but improvisational stand-up comedy. Their need to maintain superiority and status manifested itself by projecting the role of antagonist onto a working-class character. The young and affluent, perhaps out of guilt, can afford to ignore and laugh at injustices of the world that do not directly affect them. But am I stereotyping and distorting this analysis? Was it just this particular group?

One of my student teachers placed in a different affluent suburban school attempted sociodrama with his beginning acting class.[7] He shared that the teenagers rejected these issues-oriented topics, telling him the content was "too *After-School Special*" for them. When I asked the student teacher what they wanted to do, he replied wearily, "Stand-up comedy, Monty Python stuff." A second student teacher, placed at one of the affluent schools participating in the second workshop, conducted a sociodramatic session on homophobia. The university supervisor observing the lesson felt the approach was too cerebral rather than emotional, and commented afterward that the young people seemed arrogantly proud, rather than socially conscious, that they were able to discuss this "grown-up" issue in their classroom.

Discussion

I was raised in a lower-class Mexican-American neighborhood, and my personal experiences and parental teachings ("Don't ever trust the white man") have linked wealthy whites with discrimination. I also have disturbing memories of working in affluent, predominantly white settings. One of my student teaching experiences in Texas in the mid-1970s placed me in "the rich kids' school," where one white boy told me he would not audition for my play production because he didn't want to "work with a Mexican." Scars remain, and some wounds never heal. I tell my student teachers that if I were to return to public school service, I would seek a position at a lower- or lower-middle class school. I find the students in those settings more diverse and *genuine*. Affluent schools, with their predominantly white populations, intimidate me the moment I enter them because I anticipate exclusion ("What is *he* doing here?"). I perceive they think less of me – perhaps because they think more of themselves.

My research in multicultural education has focused on inner-city schools, students of color, and marginalized youth such as lesbians and gays. I have immersed myself in "oppressed" people but neglected the position of the affluent, except in the most contemptuous of ways. So often when multicultural educators and writers focus on *class*, most prioritize the culture of poverty and its effects on classroom learning.[8] I now realize I must also educate pre-service teachers on gaining entry to the perspectives and ethos of young people living in the culture of privilege. Otherwise, pedagogical agendas for raising social consciousness through drama could become adolescent targets for devaluation and ridicule. In addition, my students as well as myself might continue to unfairly and unwisely overlook the diversity in temperament and social consciousness that will most likely be found in this group, as well as the inner-city groups that were discussed earlier.

In *Emotional Intelligence*, Goleman (1995) asserted:

> the present generation of children [is] more troubled emotionally than the last: more lonely and depressed, more angry and unruly, more nervous and prone to worry, more impulsive and aggressive. . . . [Childhood] and adolescence are critical windows of opportunity for setting down the essential emotional habits that will govern our lives.
>
> (p. xiii)

Emotional intelligence's outcome, "decent human beings – is more critical to our future than ever" (Goleman, 1995, p. 263). "Kids are cruel" and "It's just part of growing up" are phrases we sometimes use to validate the horizontal and emotional hostility adolescents perpetrate on each other. I reflect on the physical and verbal abuse from peers I suffered as a teenager for being overweight (*fatso*), Hispanic (*wetback*), and gay (*faggot*). Throughout my embarrassment, anger, depression, and contemplation of suicide, one central question ran through my mind: "*Why* are they doing this?"

I feel that examining *why* adolescents "do this," and what young people can do when they encounter peer oppression, are two important goals in today's multicultural classroom – more than a counseling office, more than peer mediation, and especially more than a suicide hotline. Some teachers fear opening doors they may be unable to close when it comes to dramatic simulation and improvisational role-play. But as Spry observed, FT is not intended as a psycho-dramatic, therapeutic tool, but as a forum for social critique (as cited in Schutzman, 1994, p. 224). I believe that drama can help develop "decent" teenagers, particularly to help heighten their awareness of horizontal hostility, adolescentrism, and – with affluent youth – the penalties of privilege.

Notes

1 I did not intend to write an article about my workshop experiences, but what occurred during those sessions prompted me to reflect on and document the work. I must rely on admittedly sketchy memories to reconstruct what happened. One of three graduate students who attended the workshop offered feedback on article drafts. I extend thanks to Heather Drastal for her corrections and comments.
2 Only one scenario illustrated an oppressive teacher, perhaps due to students' positive relationships with them or a greater concern with peers. One ASU student (and former educator) speculated cynically, "Students don't feel that teachers are a threat these days. These kids know they can walk all over them." This perception may hold some validity because two scenarios generated by theatre teachers at the workshops stated:

Freedom of speech – wanting to speak my mind, but not being able to because of the confines of school
Students who want to tell me off (think I'm a bitch, etc.)

3 The total of all categories is 106%. A few scenarios overlapped into more than one category (e.g., a female adolescent sexually harassing a male adult).

80 *Writing About Critical Pedagogy*

4 This term emerged during my own reflection, but it has probably been used by other writers.
5 Recent racial conflicts in Phoenix high schools emerged from a few middle-class schools in suburbs with prominent Mormon and White populations. Rural and urban students are brought together into environments where students of color are indeed the minority.
6 *Theatre sports* are judged, competitive activities in which opposing student teams or individuals improvise with scenarios suggested by the audience or selected by random drawing. Students are judged on such criteria as concentration, characterization, creativity, humor, and so forth.
7 *Sociodrama* is a genre of educational theatre that examines social issues through improvisation. Its goals include problem solving, perspective taking, values clarification, and training for real-life encounters (Sternberg and Garcia, 1989, p. 4)
8 See Banks (1994), hooks (1994), Sleeter (1995), and Adams, Bell, and Griffin (1997) for theories and strategies for working with dominant and privileged groups.

References

Adams, M., Bell, L. A., & Griffin, P. (Eds.). (1997). *Teaching for diversity and social justice: A sourcebook*. New York: Routledge.

Banks, J. A. (1994). *Multiethnic education: Theory and practice* (3rd ed.). Needham Heights: Allyn and Bacon.

Blumberg, A., & Blumberg, P. (1994). *The unwritten curriculum: Things learned but not taught in school*. Thousand Oaks, CA: Corwin.

Boal, A. (1985). *Theatre of the oppressed*. (C. A. McBride, & M. L. McBride, Trans.). New York: Theatre Communications Group.

Boal, A. (1992). *Games for actors and non-actors*. (A. Jackson, Trans.). New York: Routledge.

Boal, A. (1995). *The rainbow of desire*. (A. Jackson, Trans.). New York: Routledge.

Freire, P. (1993). *Pedagogy of the oppressed* (Rev. ed.). (M. B. Ramos, Trans.). New York: Continuum.

Goleman, D. (1995). *Emotional intelligence*. New York: Bantam.

Grote, D. (1997). *Play directing in the school*. Colorado Springs, CO: Meriwether.

hooks, b. (1994). *Teaching to transgress*. New York: Routledge.

Schutzman, M. (1994). Canadian roundtable: An interview. In M. Schutzman & J. Cohen-Cruz (Eds.), *Playing Boal: Theatre, therapy, activism* (pp. 198–226). New York: Routledge.

Schutzman, M., & Cohen-Cruz, J. (1994). Introduction. In M. Schutzman & J. Cohen-Cruz (Eds.), *Playing Boal: Theatre, therapy, activism* (pp. 1–16). New York: Routledge.

Sleeter, C. (1995). Reflections on my use of multicultural and critical pedagogy when students are white. In C. Sleeter & P. L. McLaren (Eds.), *Multicultural education, critical pedagogy, and the politics of difference* (pp. 415–437). Albany: State University of New York Press.

Sternberg, P., & Garcia, A. (1989). *Sociodrama: Who's in your shoes?* New York: Praeger.

5 Writing the Confessional Tale

Telling the Truth

John Van Maanen's (2011) classic treatise, *Tales of the Field: On Writing Ethnography*, profiles major tale types or styles of research writing: the realist, impressionist, and confessional, among others. Harry F. Wolcott (1994) classifies three levels of writing in *Transforming Qualitative Data: Description, Analysis, and Interpretation*. The tales thus far in Chapters 2, 3, and 4 can all be classified generally as *realist* due to their *descriptive* content. But there are also tints of the *analytic or formal* tale types whenever categories and percentages are noted; and shades of *critical or advocacy* tales when social issues are openly addressed in the researcher's commentary. Chapter 2 includes a brief *collaborative and polyvocal* passage when children themselves offer recommendations for overcoming oppression, while Chapters 3 and 4's examples attempt to transcend toward the *interpretive* level in their concluding reflections.

Most qualitative research reports are rarely one distinct tale type, though they may feature one predominant writing style. The example in this chapter is also *descriptive and realistic*, by necessity, to explain a unique project to its readers, but it does so through a *confessional* filter. The confessional tale

> is the researcher's first-person account of the subjective experiences she encountered throughout the project. This style departs from the supposed objectivity of analytic, formal, descriptive, and realistic writing to admit to readers the researcher's own emotions, vulnerabilities, uncertainties, fieldwork problems, ethical dilemmas, and data collection or analytic blunders. It is a reflexive, prosaic self-portrait of sorts that reveals the investigator's inner thoughts. Virtually no research project is conducted perfectly; thus, the confessional tale also serves as a cautionary tale for readers to consider before venturing into comparable projects.
>
> (Saldaña & Omasta, 2018, p. 287)

The representative article in this chapter, "Ethical Issues in an Ethnographic Performance Text: The 'Dramatic Impact' of 'Juicy Stuff'," describes the dilemmas I encountered with my first ethnotheatrical research project: the staging of a young teenage actor's life, with the actual case study participant portraying himself in the play. Barry (the pseudonym I assigned to the case, which he later told me he hated) had been followed by me and other research team members since he was five years old as part of a longitudinal study in theatre education. The study concluded when he was 12 years old, but I initiated a follow-up study when the participants were in high school to assess any residual effects from their elementary school treatment of classroom drama and theatre-viewing experiences. Out of 30 child participants, Barry was the only one who chose to pursue secondary school theatre. He thus became an intriguing case study from his sophomore through senior years. The article will describe the contexts of the case and the ethnographic performance text we created. Here, I wish to discuss the origin and evolution of the article.

Virtually all researchers wish to look competent and professional, if not brilliant, in the reports they compose, and I was no exception. My original write-up of the project, like the ethnographic play itself, presented everyone in their best light. The article draft addressed in glowing prose the success of the venture and its beneficial outcomes for all concerned. The editor and peer reviewers of the journal *Research in Drama Education* reviewed my initial manuscript but rejected it for publication. Most juror comments focused on how the project seemed *too* perfect. One reviewer responded, "It seems as if the author is not being truthful with the reader, as if he's hiding something."

I was.

I reflected deeply on that sole comment and decided to tell the truth. And even if the complete truth could not be told due to Institutional Review Board restrictions, I would explain how and why I felt stuck between a rock and a hard place, especially when writing the play script: "Had I been able to present Barry's story uncensored and with impunity, the possible effects on an audience would have been compelling and heart-wrenching. But the results for Barry and his parents might have been devastating and irreversibly damaging."

I was familiar with Van Maanen's *Tales of the Field* but my previous writings to date had all fallen under the realist category of reportage. I revised my report as a confessional tale, focusing on matters that had been problematic rather than successful with the study. It wasn't until months later that I realized I had read but forgotten an important principle about research writing espoused by educational anthropologist Harry F. Wolcott (himself a controversial figure among research ethicists): "When in doubt, tell the truth." Wolcott boldly told the truth in his own confessional tales and was chastised for it by the academic community. I worried the same might happen to me.

A good peer reviewer will sometimes make that one comment that crystallizes the major problem with an article. "He's hiding something" resounded within me as a call to come clean. *Tension* is a dramatic concept that keeps the audience engaged with a "what happens next?" mindset as they watch the characters' conflicts unfold. Tension also refers to the levels of anxiety that may be experienced during an actor's dramatic enactment during an improvisational simulation. "Ethical Issues in an Ethnographic Performance Text" reveals my tensions as a researcher throughout the process, from writing the script (and what I could and could not include), to casting the actors (and how they were misinterpreted in performance), to audience reactions (ranging from complimentary to condescending). The culture of theatre implicitly demands that its artists perform — literally and figuratively — at their personal best at all times. Failure is devastating to people with fragile egos trained to feel deeply. Yet, truth is what theatre tries to capture. Truth is what qualitative research tries to capture. And so, I told the truth.

This article was the first I published that was later cited by researchers from disciplines other than theatre education. "Ethical Issues" in the title seemed to have led to several hits of the piece through keyword searches by those interested in the topic. And "juicy stuff" became a catchphrase I occasionally heard at conferences when researchers referred to the intriguing, secretive goings-on about their participants.

This was a difficult piece to write because I exposed myself as an imperfect novice qualitative researcher who made some glaring mistakes with the participants' welfare. (That is, after all, one of the defining features of a confessional tale.) But the good news is that all's well with "Barry" and his life twenty years after this article was first published. He's now married, has a child, received a Masters of Divinity degree, pastors at a community church, and engages in political activism and social justice issues. To this day he remains a Facebook friend of mine. Fortunately, a few confessional tales do have happy endings.

References

Saldaña, J., & Omasta, M. (2018). *Qualitative research: Analyzing life*. Thousand Oaks, CA: Sage.

Van Maanen, J. (2011) *Tales of the field: On writing ethnography* (2nd ed.). Chicago: University of Chicago Press.

Wolcott, H. F. (1994). *Transforming qualitative data: Description, analysis, and interpretation*. Thousand Oaks, CA: Sage.

ETHICAL ISSUES IN AN ETHNOGRAPHIC PERFORMANCE TEXT: THE "DRAMATIC IMPACT" OF "JUICY STUFF"

Abstract

This confessional tale describes the author's first time venture with producing an ethnographic performance text, an alternative mode of research presentation. In ethnotheatre, significant selections from a qualitative study's field notes and interview transcripts are carefully arranged, scripted, and staged for an audience to enhance their understanding of the participants' lives. This particular project dramatized the story of Barry, an adolescent who dreams of becoming a professional actor. Barry participated in a longitudinal study of drama and theatre as he progressed from kindergarten through sixth grade. A follow-up study from his sophomore (tenth) through senior (twelfth) years in high school observed his continued and exemplary participation in the art forms. Barry, his mother, and his two high school theatre teachers were interviewed to assess the social influences on his career goals and to gain multiple perspectives on his ways of working. Unknowingly, the researcher was to grapple with several ethical issues as the study progressed. Immediately before and during the initial fieldwork period, Barry and his parents underwent and eventually recovered from difficult conflicts, inhibiting complete researcher investigation. Several casting choices for the ethnographic performance text raised audience concern over the representation of participants' lives and their welfare. Finally, the confessions and revelations of personal history by participants during one-on-one interviews challenged the ethnographer to reconcile his obligation to respect each member's privacy with his desire to write a play script containing "juicy stuff" for "dramatic impact."

Introduction

This report is a "confessional tale" (Van Maanen, 1988) of post-production reflections on personal experiences with an alternative research report format, an "ethnographic performance text," sometimes labelled "ethnotheatre" or "ethnodrama," terms used interchangeably in this article. Generally, ethnotheatre employs traditional techniques of formal theatre production to mount a performance event whose characters are actual research participants portrayed by actors (though in some variations, the research participants themselves may be used). Significant selections from interview transcripts and field notes of a particular study are carefully arranged, scripted, and dramatized for an audience to enhance their understanding of the participants' lives through visual representation and emotional engagement. Many aspects of my experimentation with this genre could be addressed, but after a discussion of the production I will focus on the most prominent issue raised throughout the process – ethics.

[Originally published in *Research in Drama Education*, vol. 3, no. 2, 1998, pp. 181–196; doi 10.1080/1356978980030205; edited slightly for this publication.]

Evolution of the Project

In January 1997 I completed my fieldwork on a case study participant from Arizona State University's (ASU) 7-year longitudinal study of drama with and theatre for children (Saldaña, 1987, 1989, 1995, 1996; Saldaña & Otero, 1990). From 1984 to 1991, Barry (pseudonym) was one of 30 treatment group children who received continuous classroom drama and theatre viewing experiences from kindergarten through sixth grade[1]. In August 1995 I searched for the original 30 participants – in tenth grade at that time – for a follow-up study to assess any residual effects from their elementary school treatment. Of those I could locate, Barry was one of two participants enrolled in theatre courses at a local high school, but the only one involved with extra-curricular theatre productions on a regular basis. Barry was considered the most exceptional longitudinal participant during his elementary school years, and his continued interest in theatre as an adolescent was worthy of examination. My fieldwork progressed on a part-time basis from Barry's tenth through twelfth grade years and consisted of periodic interviews, participant observation of classes, rehearsals and performances, plus interviews with Barry's mother and two of his theatre teachers. All necessary approvals and consent for this study were obtained from ASU's Human Subjects Review Board and the participants themselves.

I began writing my report in the traditional method for journal submission and adjudication: 30 pages double spaced; adherence to MLA (Modern Language Association of America) guidelines for research reports; outline of methods, analysis, discussion, etc. But also at that time I had just completed Norman K. Denzin's new book, *Interpretive Ethnography: ethnographic practices for the 21st century* (1997). One of the chapters, "Performance texts," intrigued me as both a researcher and theatre artist. This genre, in various forms, had been presented at sociology, anthropology, and education conferences for approximately 15 years. But, ironically, ethnographic performance texts were rare at theatre conferences in the USA. I myself had never seen one, and was intrigued by Denzin's assertion that "The performance text is the single, most powerful way for ethnography to recover yet interrogate the meanings of lived experience" (pp. 94–95).

Qualitative research is contextual, and so are its methods of representation and modes of presentation. Written reports can be slippery mediators of participants' life experiences, particularly if they involve artistic enterprises such as visual art or dance (Blumenfeld-Jones, 1995; Barry, 1996; Eisner, 1998). Barry's story is that of an aspiring performer, a young man whose "passion" for theatre plays a central role in his life. Barry's personal beliefs about the art form, and social influences (parents, peers, theatre teachers, educational experiences) that shaped this perception of himself, could readily be described in a written article. But the representation of his development as an actor – researcher observations of his classroom work ethic, rehearsal process, characterization, voice and movement, performance quality – would be reconstructed synthetically through text. Any success at capturing and portraying in an article Barry's ways of working is substantially dependent on joint efforts: the writer's descriptive flair with fidelity, and the reader's ability to image. A written report would suffice as a mediator of Barry's personal meanings documented through our interviews, but not of his working process interpreted from my participant observation of him in the field.

Photography, video, and film are not merely data gathering instruments for fieldwork, but alternative, non-print modes of research presentation (Harper, 1994). These documentary forms and formats enhance fidelity through image reproduction and display the ethnographer's on-site work to an audience through aural and/or visual representation. But the camera lens focuses on specific and limited parameters of the field. Cropping and editing are based on researcher interpretations of what is salient to the study. Viewers do not receive the entire "picture" and, obviously, media data are costly. Radio dramas (Walker, Pick, & MacDonald, 1991) and minimally staged reader's theatre (Donmoyer & Yennie-Donmoyer, 1995) as research rely on the evocative power of voices and text, and may be appropriate choices when visual representation is inconsequential to the topic – "teacher talk," for example. The obvious sacrifice of visual images in these modes (or other audio products such as cassette tapes) further limits their applicability and utility as modes of research presentation.

Mienczakowski (1995; 1996; 1997), Mienczakowski, Morgan, and Rolfe (1993), and Mienczakowski, Smith, and Sinclair (1996) have published work on their ethnodrama projects and discuss the theoretical underpinnings and aesthetic complexities of the genre, which I will not reiterate in this report. Their profiles of performance works dealing with health issues such as detoxification offer conceptual templates for those interested in mounting ethnotheatre, particularly if forum theatre components are included as part of the event. Only a few complete scripts in the literature are accessible as models (Blumenfeld-Jones, 1995; Ellis & Bochner, 1992; Walker, Pick, & MacDonald, 1991), leaving researchers interested in producing such works to learn by doing while reflecting on the dual roles of ethnographer and playwright (or, in some cases, multiple roles including director, designer, and actor).

An ethnographic performance text is certainly not an appropriate presentation mode for all qualitative research studies in drama or theatre. Performance critic Sylvia Drake challenges a playwright to consider the appropriateness of a story for the stage by asking whether it would be best told for an audience through live theatre, television, or film. A comparable question might be asked to discern the most appropriate mode of presentation for qualitative research: will the participant's story be best – i.e., validly – told for an audience through a written report, poetry, video documentary, photographic portfolio, radio drama, reader's theatre, ethnotheatre, etc.? The evolution of my case study into an ethnographic performance text was both serendipitous and a conscious choice to explore *research as art* (Barone, 1997). The convergence of fieldwork completion, exposure to Denzin's new work and the writings of ethnodramatists, an invitation to deliver a keynote presentation at the Second International Drama in Education Research Institute (IDIERI), and receipt of a university grant to experiment with ethnotheatre was, to me, similar to how Barry perceived his future as a professional actor: "destiny." Besides, what could be more compatible than employing the art form to exhibit research about a participant's relationship *with* the art form?

Development of the Performance Text

Next I address how the play script and its staging emerged. Both, I feel, embody my personal ethos about qualitative research and theatre production.

I was educated in qualitative inquiry by Thomas E. Barone and Mary Lee Smith, two prominent Americans in their field yet each with a different approach to research. Some of Barone's course readings were from Elliot Eisner and the emotion-laden works of Jonathan Kozol. Smith's readings were the data analytic strategies of grounded theory and Miles and Huberman. Barone challenged my perceptions of research authority, while Smith demanded evidentiary rigor in my field notes. He is art and she is science. Barone's spirit floats over my left shoulder, gently prodding me to compose evocative narratives. Smith's spirit sits firmly on the right and scrutinizes my coding system. Barone encourages me to fly; Smith tells me to keep both feet on the ground. Hence, I am a schizophrenic researcher still searching for my own voice but, in the meantime, writing to appease the jurors – too frightened to fall, too frightened to lose my footing.

Wishing to remain on safe ground for my first venture with ethnotheatre, I followed Denzin's key suggestions closely for text development: construct an "evocative" rather than explanatory text; create on-stage verisimilitude; and search for participant "epiphanies" in the data. But woven with these threads of advice was Smith's influence on my work. Hence, the playwriting phase began not as an artistic vision but as a data analytic process.

Excerpts chosen from over 150 pages of transcripts and field notes were influenced by my eclectic, collective methods of analysis gleaned from various texts and experiences. For example, Seidman (1991) influenced my reduction of the data corpus to what was essential and salient. Miles and Huberman's (1994) influence led me to search for triangulation among participants' versions of their stories. Anselm Strauss's (1987) *in vivo* coding method determined the number and content of specific scenes. Even the play's title, *Maybe someday, if I'm famous . . .*, is an *in vivo* code and core category because it crystallizes Barry's life ambition. This quotation originated during one of my latter interviews with him when he referred to my micro-cassette tape recorder: "Maybe someday, if I'm famous, you'll be able to pull these tapes out and see what went into making a famous person, a successful person." Though Barry is not (yet) a celebrity, this is what his story is "about."

Once the technical approaches to data reduction and analysis were completed, I was left with an array of selected field notes and participant monologues pooled by categories needing a specific framework suitable for theatrical presentation. My analytic lens for the next phase of text development changed to that of a storyteller to arrange the data sensibly into monologue and dialogue

88 Writing the Confessional Tale

for a coherent play script. Ellis and Bochner's (1992; 1996) realistic, episodic plot in their script served as a model for my own. The structure of *Maybe Someday* is a linear collage, framed loosely by chronology and progressive reflexivity. It begins with Barry's past and ends with his projected future. In between is a series of scenes that advance from Barry's public performances to his more personal, private thoughts. The interplay of participants in the text includes Barry's mother, Sandy; his primary theatre teacher, Derek; a second theatre teacher, Diane; and myself as the interviewer and participant observer.

Including myself as a "character" – and a primary one at that, since my field note descriptions compose a quarter of the script – suggests that this project was perhaps my story as much as Barry's. But the primary intent was to function as a narrator, a trite yet essential device to place the participant narratives in context. A few IDIERI audience members wished I had offered more analytic and interpretive commentary on the case study. In retrospect, I wished I had done so as well but I was too frightened to fall, too frightened to lose my footing. My prologue framed what I perceived would be a different research presentation experience for an audience. It also illustrated Mary Lee Smith's strong hold on my work since I felt compelled to explain my methods:

JOHNNY: *[slide: "Johnny"]* I am experimenting with this case study report of a high school actor by constructing an interpretive, ethnographic performance text. *[Barry turns and looks at Johnny; slide: "Barry"]* Barry's life is immersed in theatre, so this format for presenting his story seems most appropriate, *[slide: transcribed interview excerpt]* All participant quotes are extracted verbatim from the transcripts of 12 separate, one-on-one interviews, but *[slide: handwritten field note page]* field notes from approximately 40 clock hours of participant observation have been revised slightly for clarity, *[slide: rough draft page of play script with handwritten coding memos]* Each scene represents a major, emergent analytic category from over 17 months of part-time fieldwork and data analysis. The vignettes of these multiple voices have been carefully edited, ordered, linked, and juxtaposed for purposes of story progression, triangulation, disconfirming evidence, irony, or *[pause]* dramatic impact. Since each audience member brings his or her own personal experiences to this work, each one will interpret the performance text differently. I deliberately withhold overt theoretical commentary to make this text evocative rather than explanatory. This entire enterprise is a departure from my traditional research report formats *[slide: book cover of Denzin's* Interpretive Ethnography*]* and tests Norman K. Denzin's assertion that "The performance text is the single, most powerful way for ethnography to recover yet interrogate the meanings of lived experience."

Theatrical artistry, research rigor, and personal fear merged to shape the production. The prologue suggested that this was not a traditional work of theatre intended solely for the entertainment of a general audience, but a research project employing theatre production techniques for an audience of peer researchers and drama/theatre artists. In performance I deliberately parsed "experimenting" for emphasis, as if to negotiate a contractual understanding between me and my colleagues that I was taking a risk. Projected slides of *in vivo* codes, fieldwork settings, production and research artifacts, and family photographs appeared throughout the event to accompany the spoken text. One IDIERI audience member interpreted the *in vivo* codes as a Brechtian device to reinforce the themes. But their purpose simply was visually to compensate for what I feared was a heavily verbal play script. I myself am easily bored as an audience member unless a theatrical production offers visual variety. Hence, projecting 120 slides during a 45-minute performance was one tactic to maintain spectator engagement.

As playwright and director of this production, I was worried about losing the audience's interest with the case study. This was a success story, a play about an exceptionally talented young man with a positive attitude, value, and belief system. With the exception of one scene about Barry's drug use in adolescence, and another scene on his failure in a specific play production, there were no major crises, obstacles, or conflicts to maintain what I perceived as a suitable flow of tension. This performance text would not have the emotionally-charged content of Ellis and Bochner's two-person play on abortion (1992), or the social significance of detoxification issues explored critically in Mienczakowski's work (1995; 1996). I took minimal comfort in Ellis and Bochner's statement that "Most of life is commonplace, so a lot of [ethnography] will focus on details of everyday life that won't provoke . . . raw emotions" (1996, p. 23). As a playwright, my anxiety motivated me to include lengthy "monologues" sparingly, and to interweave the participants' voices frequently for variety. As a director, I asked actors to vary their points of view by addressing their monologues to me as an interviewer, to another character as an involved listener, and directly to the audience.

Barry's story consists of eight scenes of varying length, each depicting a different facet of his life and work. The first three scenes ("I Developed My Passion," "I Was Completely Empty," and "I Never Found It in Sports") examine Barry's childhood, early adolescence, and possible influences on his current "passion" for theatre.

From scene 1, "I Developed My Passion":

[two slides of Childsplay, Inc. productions are projected; Barry crosses to the screen and talks to the audience]
BARRY: And I remember going to see the shows . . . a lot of Childsplay stuff. . . . I remember them coming out and taking their bows and then talking to us after the show. And the energy they had! . . . They were answering questions and they seemed to be having so much fun just being there. And I think that's when I first decided *[slide: "I wanted to be an actor"]* I wanted to be an actor. . . . It was an amazing feeling. That was when I first started thinking, "Hm, this is something I want to look into."

From scene 2, "I Was Completely Empty":

BARRY: *[to audience]* There was a period during junior high when I had no theatre in my life, didn't have any exposure to it, and I got really heavy into *[slide: "drugs"]* drugs. I was hanging out with the wrong crowd.

SANDY: *[to audience; slide: photo of Barry with long hair in early adolescence]* He was never anti-social, but making the statement – the way he dressed, the way he looked. . . . In fact, some of his junior high teachers would call me and say, "I noticed that he's hanging out with some unsavory characters and I think . . .," you know, that kind of stuff. . . . It was kind of like teaching the dog not to run in the street by getting hit by a car. *[looks at Barry]* It was a horrible, painful, awful time. And yet, *[slide: "If it doesn't kill you, it'll make you stronger"]* if it doesn't kill you, it'll make you stronger. That's what happened to Barry.

DEREK: *[to audience; slide: "Derek"]* When Barry came to University High School he was on the point of either being a doper or doing something. And I worked really hard with him to get him to stop smoking . . . to develop a sense of, *[to Barry]* "Hey, you've got something to work *with* instead of working *against*" *[Derek posts a cast list; slide: University High School campus]*

BARRY: When I came to University High I saw theatre was something that I knew, something that I was interested in. *[slide: University High auditorium]* So I came and I got cast in my first show, *[he glances at the cast list]* I got a lead for my first show which made me think, "Whoa – maybe there's something I'm good at here." And I was in the position where . . . there wasn't anything standing in between me and theatre because there wasn't anything in my life. Drugs had taken up my whole life. And so as soon as I was ready to get out of that, I mean – Theatre helped draw me out of drugs, and drugs helped draw me *[slide: "into theatre"]* into theatre, in that they voided my life of everything else so I was completely empty – completely open towards picking up on theatre.

Scenes four and five ("I Think a Good Actor . . ." and "Love the Art in Yourself") demonstrate Barry's artistic process through vignettes of his rehearsal and performance work on stage and in the theatre classroom:

[slide: "develop a character"]

JOHNNY: Derek directs at a *[Glass] Menagerie* rehearsal, *[sits at side, watches rehearsal, writes field notes]*

DEREK: *[to Barry]* Can you give me the idea that you're creating the scene, not just recalling? . . . When you recall and create, this is where we're talking about him transforming it – he's elevating it to something else.

JOHNNY: Derek asks for a line to be . . .

DEREK AND JOHNNY: "stronger."

JOHNNY: Barry says it louder.

DEREK: Wake up your mom.
BARRY: *[as Tom, forcefully]* "Goody, goody! Pay her back for all those rise and shines!"
JOHNNY: After Barry asks why he's blocked to stay on the sofa, Derek responds,
DEREK: You have to find some reason for staying there. You have to make some decisions.
JOHNNY: Derek directs *[slide: "constructivistly"]* constructivistly. He asks actors,
DEREK: *[to audience]* Why an upward inflection? What's the color of the verb? *[to Barry]* How do you feel about that?
BARRY: *[to audience]* I love working with Mr. Smith because he and I kind of have an unspoken understanding. . . . He never gives me character insights or anything, that's me – I get to do that. But one thing that he does is, he'll tell me all these things that he wants me to do, and then up to production week . . . I gotta remember, "Do this, do this, do this," and get everything engrained in my mind. And then production week I let go of all that, and whatever falls away wasn't part of my character, and whatever stays, stays.

Scenes six and seven ("The Support of People" and "Theatre's a Very Spiritual Thing") are more introspective and reveal Barry's spiritual philosophy and feelings toward the adults and church in his life:

JOHNNY: *[to audience]* Barry occasionally wears a small crucifix on a chain around his neck.
BARRY: I've been doing a lot of *[slide: "soul searching"]* soul searching since my drug use, and most of my values have come from drama. . . . Like I said, I'm a romantic, and I see theatre as being romantic. And theatre has instilled me with a very chivalrous attitude towards life.
SANDY: *[to Johnny]* He's very sensitive to other people's feelings, *[to audience]* I've seen him give his last five bucks – I'm telling you, he's grown up a poor kid and that's a lot of money – his last five bucks to someone on the street. He's a very compassionate person.
JOHNNY: *[to Barry]* What do you get out of theatre? *[slide: "What's the payoff?"]* What's the payoff? *[he holds the micro-cassette tape recorder closer to Barry]*.
BARRY: *[to audience]* The theatre is some place that I feel so comfortable in. . . . When those lights go down, and I'm sitting out in the house, it's like I lose all self, and I become one with the show, and it becomes almost a *[slide: "spiritual"]* spiritual thing. I think theatre is very spiritual for me.

Since the play begins with an examination of Barry's past, the final scene ("I Want This"), presents participant reflections on his future:

[Barry sits at the side and skims through college catalogs; slide: a university campus]
SANDY: *[to audience]* I would never step on his dreams or anything. His grandma's been after him, "What college are you going to?" For a long time it was,

BARRY AND SANDY: "I'm not going to college."
SANDY: I didn't say a word, *[to Johnny, holding the micro-cassette tape recorder]* Barry's a very, very smart person. It would not bother me at all if Barry did not go to college right out of high school. Now, *yeah*, if I had *my* first choice, you bet! But *[slide: "life is a wonderful teacher"]* life is a wonderful teacher.
DIANE: *[to Sandy, then audience]* Barry wants to move to New York City, live on the streets, and be an actor.

Later in the scene, Barry contemplates:

JOHNNY: What do you want to do after high school?
BARRY: Well, *[to Johnny; slide: "I'm struggling"]* I'm struggling with that right now. College is a very scary thing for me to think about. . . . *[to audience]* The thing that scares me the most about that is my parents both had big dreams. My mom wanted to be an actress, my dad wanted to be a politician – you know, they both had big dreams. Both went to college, got a degree, and they're both teachers now. They teach about what it was that they wanted to do, and I don't want to do that. . . . I don't wanna be able to give up *[slide: "my dream"]* my dream that easily. What I would love to do is to get out of high school, work around the valley for a bit, like – I don't know, just some crap job to get the money, *[slide:* Playbill *theatre programs; Barry crosses to screen]* go to New York or Chicago, and try to make it big. *[slides: scenes from Broadway's* The Phantom of the Opera, Les Miserables*]* You know, every actor's dream: to go to one of the big towns and try to be famous, try to get my big break, *[to Johnny]* And I know that it's not likely that it will ever happen, but there's a part of me – I guess it's the romantic side of me again – that says, if *[slide: "I want"]* I want it bad enough I'll get it. And that's what separates me from other people who are out there – starving artists – is that drive, is that I want it more than anything, more than life itself, *I want*, I want this.

During rehearsals, revisions of the text's first draft focused primarily on reducing the final performance length to 45 minutes (the time limit of the IDIERI keynote address). Rewriting and rewording a participant's grammar or vocabulary were not permitted in order to maintain the authenticity and integrity of the voices, but editing extraneous sentences from lengthy interview passages was allowed.

This personal need for clarity and elegance seems to have been influenced by my readings of educational anthropologist Harry F. Wolcott (1994). I admire the descriptive directness of his storytelling, the style that emerged in the ethnodramatic play script and, as I later connected, a style comparable to my own directing products. I attempt to create productions that are minimalist and clean, yet laden with nuance. I de-emphasize massive scenery to emphasize the actors. Costumes and numerous hand properties, frequent movement, and detailed gestures receive more attention since they are most immediate to the performer's space and audience's focus. Well-acted realism and naturalism in particular are genres I enjoy as both an audience member and director. Hence, I collaborated with the *Maybe Someday* company to create honest, believable "characters" in a story told simply and directly.

The performances at ASU and IDIERI generated diverse reactions from the audience, but I will address the most prominent theme of their responses next.

Ethics

It is not until the end of *Maybe Someday* that the 18-year-old actor cast to portray the primary participant admits openly that he *is* "the real Barry." (Audible "ahs" were heard from a few ASU and IDIERI audience members at that point.) Some IDIERI participants shared they did not know until the conclusion of the play that the actor was portraying himself. Others suspected he *was* the actual participant, deduced from family photographs of Barry at a young age projected on-screen early in the play. Withholding his true identity until the end of the text was a playwriting choice for dramatic impact, and a directorial tactic to engage audience members' reflexivity throughout the performance (e.g., "I wonder if that's the real kid?"). No one shared with me any feelings of deception generated from this action. But Barry's actual presence during the post-performance discussion may have hindered questions of utmost concern from the audience. Revealing his true identity was essential at some point. If discussion had progressed with "the real Barry" in a covert role, deception would have been operative, with the results potentially embarrassing for the participant and those in attendance.

By casting the actual case study participant to portray himself, I felt a high level of fidelity had been achieved in the performance text. No other actor, no matter how talented, would have *truly* understood Barry's feelings and meanings attached to the epiphanies in his life. This was the primary reason I asked "the real Barry" to participate in this event. Barry seized the opportunity because it would be his first "paid gig" in the acting profession, as he put it, and an opportunity to bring a sense of closure to his high school experiences. In fact, during the pre-production process I considered inviting all the adult participants (Barry's mother and his two theatre teachers) to portray themselves in this project since they were all "theatre people" and could act. However, personal issues shared by them during interviews were, at times, extremely sensitive. Compounding the problem were confessions and personal revelations by Barry and Derek which were then unknown to Sandy (e.g., Barry's drug use), and family history raised by Barry and his mother who did not want it documented as data. I feared that bringing all of them together for dramatizing their own lives might have generated awkwardness, tension, and possible confrontations. All four participants portraying themselves and revealing their true identities at the end of the performance would have been intended as "dramatic impact." But to some audience members, the effect might have been interpreted as self-indulgence, exploitation, or betrayal.

I did not anticipate the impact that casting Barry would make on selected audience members and on the participants themselves. For example, concern was expressed the next day from one parent in the IDIERI audience over the depiction of personal lives on stage. Though I cannot recall her exact words, they were something to the effect of: "If that had been my son on stage, I would have felt horrified at the violation of privacy." I explained that the young actor and his mother were made aware at all times of the research protocol, and they each had final word on how they were portrayed on stage. I did not feel this audience member was overreacting; her concern, in fact, was similar to the real mother's anxiety. When Sandy attended the performance at ASU, I could see her in the front row of the audience with her arms folded tightly around herself. Afterwards, Sandy shared with me how she attended the event with grave reluctance but felt relieved that everything had been depicted favorably – even though she had read and approved the play script months before rehearsals began.

Perhaps Sandy's discomfort stemmed from one line she asked me to delete from the script's initial draft for the ASU performance. In *Maybe Someday* there are continuous references to, but the physical absence of, Barry's father. A particular dialogue exchange was noted by some IDIERI audience members as "intriguing":

JOHNNY: What does Barry's dad think of his son?
SANDY: His father loves him. *[pause]* Could you turn off the tape recorder?
BARRY: Mr. Smith, without even knowing it, has always been *[slide: "like a father"]* like a father to me.

"Could you turn off the tape recorder?" implies there were personal family stories Sandy did not want as part of the official, transcribed data corpus. Barry also states that his theatre teacher is "like a father" to him. When IDIERI audience members questioned me about this moment in post-performance discussion, I said there was some "juicy stuff" to this case (regrettably, a tactless comment on my part), but I could not include it in the final performance text at the request of Barry and Sandy. During the primary fieldwork period from August 1995 to December 1996, I hesitated about contacting the father for an interview due to the way Barry described their dysfunctional relationship. At one interview, Barry shifted into a semi-fetal position in his chair and chewed on his crucifix as he described his father – actions I wanted to replicate in performance but which, in rehearsal, appeared stylistically inappropriate. There were sensitive family issues at the time that made it intriguing yet unwise for me to probe as a researcher. These were resolved eventually after the fieldwork period, but by then my reluctance to interview the father was still present. "Could you turn off the tape recorder?" was deleted from the Arizona performance because Barry's father attended the production. Permission was granted, however, to include this line at the IDIERI presentation in Canada.

Especially problematic was my temptation to include the more revelatory passages from interview transcripts in the performance text, hoping that participants would approve their inclusion after an initial review of the play script. Though these passages were peripheral to Barry's development as an actor, they were central to his personal life and, quite frankly, potentially engaging for an audience. But had I included this material and distributed play script drafts simultaneously to the four participants involved, the results would have been a breach of researcher ethics to protect them and respect their privacy. I censored myself as a playwright because I did not want to damage further a family relationship that was, *at the time*, unstable. Hence, the story maintained its primary focus on Barry's acting skills with occasional references to how his personal relationships interacted with his development. As for participant reviews of the play script, I resolved that since this was Barry's story he would have first read-through and approval of the text before it proceeded to his mother and teachers. For example, his drug use in early adolescence was a critical period and related to his entry into high school theatre. Had I excluded this epiphany from the text, an important link in the chain of events leading to his "dream" would be missing. Barry kept this part of his life secret from Sandy, but he permitted inclusion of this story since he felt "She's probably suspected it all along." When Sandy read the first play script draft, Barry's suspicion was verified and, fortunately, it promoted "a good, long talk" between them.

Bolton (1996) renounced Jardine's dissertation on his life and work because it included biographical inaccuracies and misrepresented his relationship with his wife, despite attempts to negotiate with the author who, according to Bolton, stood by her feminist interpretations. I myself have been interviewed as a participant in a doctoral student's study and felt at all times – from fieldwork to publication – that I was offered opportunities to review and validate the researcher's interpretations. Most important, I felt that respect for me had been maintained. Nevertheless, I was worried about self-image and my representation in his study throughout the project. I have also been interviewed and mistreated by a journal editor in the USA: tape-recorded without my knowledge and consent; offered no opportunity to verify his published written report which was laden with factual inaccuracies; and publicly embarrassed by his profile of me and my university program. Thus, I feel I have comparable understandings of what the participants in this ethnographic performance text may have experienced when it came to issues of confidentiality, privacy, and how they were portrayed in print and on stage.

On one hand, I am legally and morally bound as a researcher to protect the participants and respect their wishes for how they are represented. On the other hand, I am concerned as a playwright and director with telling and staging an engaging story for an audience. By depicting Barry as a young man with few faults or negative characteristics, he became a model adolescent, the ideal actor in a secondary school theatre program. Had I been able to present Barry's story uncensored and with impunity, the possible effects on an audience would have been compelling and heart-wrenching. But the results for Barry and his parents might have been devastating and irreversibly damaging. As a result of what I was permitted to represent, some audience members – as I feared – said the resulting story was "weak" and "sanitized." I probed for feedback from someone whom I admired at IDIERI, who merely glanced downward and said, "Well, you took a risk." My personal desire to include "juicy stuff" to enhance the dramatic impact of the event was non-negotiable and moot. The participants' welfare came first, and they were given final word on what was included and excluded from the performance text. To do anything less would have been unscrupulous.

Another ethical issue focused on my responsibility as director of an ethnographic performance text to represent the actual participants in a reasonably comparable manner through my casting choices. For example, the actor who portrayed Sandy was not in her mid-forties, like the mother, but in her late twenties. Appropriate costume and hairstyle choices suggested an older woman. The audience suspends their disbelief – a standard convention of theatre – and accepts that a younger actor is portraying a parent. The casting choice for Derek, however, led to inferences made by selected audience members on participant relationships with each other as portrayed by the actor and represented in the text.

A few IDIERI participants – privately and hesitantly – questioned me about the "true" relationship between Barry and Derek Smith. Some inferred a more than professional or platonic interest on Derek's part for his protégé. The actor who portrayed Derek is openly gay and possesses what some may interpret as stereotypically gay qualities in voice and movement. His acting choices to make physical contact with Barry at selected moments (hands on shoulders, primarily), coupled with praise both men expressed towards each other, may have led to the erroneous inference that a homosexual attraction from the teacher towards his student existed:

BARRY: Derek Smith's given me so much of.... Whenever I'm feeling kind of dry, I come to theatre just not inspired, *[slide: "I feed off of him"]* I feed off of him, I feed off his energy. He's given me more than I can ever explain.
DEREK: He *is* *[slide: "special"]* special, and he *is* different. He's one of the few.

The real Derek is married with children and does not possess stereotypically gay mannerisms. His relationship with Barry is professional, yet also exhibits the tight bond a theatre teacher might feel with a student after a close working relationship of 4 years. But the actor portraying Derek inferred that there may have been more affection than articulated by the mentor:

BARRY: He cares about me. He has never told me but he does. He's not somebody who gives out compliments easily. He's not someone who talks a lot. He's very introspective, and yet he's a very brilliant, dynamic man.

The actor chosen to portray Derek was an ASU faculty member and selected from those who auditioned for his age-appropriateness, professional theatre background, and collegiality. Sexual orientation was not a factor in casting, but the actor's own characteristics and interpretation of Derek in performance may have generated subtext within audience members who inferred a different kind of relationship. Did I have an ethical responsibility to represent Derek's persona on stage as it appears in "real life"? Or was I permitted artistic freedom in casting like any production project might allow? Perhaps my own gay identity and politics did not motivate me to authenticate the portrayal of the real Derek and Barry's relationship on stage. This is an example of how artistic choices, influenced by personal identity issues, can skew performance text data, reduce the fidelity and, thus, its interpretation by individual audience members. Barry, despite the high regard he holds for his mentor, chose not to invite the real Derek to attend the event at ASU. Barry did not state why.

The final ethical issue is the possible detrimental effect this experience might have on Barry himself. A few IDIERI participants pondered whether I had "set Barry up for a fall." The performance was perceived by one audience member as an "ego trip" for the young man since it showcased his acting abilities and his positive outlook on life. Barry was portrayed as a "hero" according to Madeline Grumet, IDIERI's outside eye for presentation commentary. The adults in his life (and in this performance) called him "special," "smart," "talented," and other accolades. After the IDIERI performance I observed six audience members huddled around him asking questions, and a friend of mine said Barry was "strutting like a peacock" the next day. Would the low probability that he would actually achieve success as a professional actor be damaging to him after being part of this project? Now that the production is over, Barry will not be abandoned. I have told him that I am available to process anything he wants or needs to discuss. He also acknowledged that the personal contacts he developed through ASU and IDIERI may be helpful to him in the future. Sandy speculates in the final scene of *Maybe Someday*:

SANDY: He's got it up here *[points to forehead]*, but he's *[slide: "not motivated"]* not motivated to go through the hoops yet. I don't know if he would do very well in college right out of high school. It might take making $4.25 an hour for a while before he becomes motivated to do something else.... He's smart enough and talented enough that I'm not worried about him. I don't think he'll be content to flip burgers his whole life. So if he has to do that for a while, fine. Because of his people skills, he could very well end up being one of those people who makes it.

The culture of theatre includes gossip and rumor among its practitioners – slanderous backbiting, folklore of production failures and mishaps, "Where are they now?" stories, etc. In January 1998 I reunited with Diane, one of Barry's former teachers, at a local theatre conference. "Did you hear about Barry?" she asked. "No," I replied, inferring that some type of tragedy had occurred, "I haven't seen him for about five months." My last contact with Barry was a month after the IDIERI presentation. He was working as a cashier at a bagel and coffee shop near the ASU campus. I was delightfully surprised to meet him there, and Barry told me he was auditioning for a role in a community theatre production later that week. I felt a twinge of irony that Sandy's prediction of minimum wage jobs for him had come to fruition. When I visited the shop a few days later he was no longer working there.

Diane updated me on the "juicy stuff" – what she had heard as *rumor*: Barry, still living at home with his parents, was despondent over the break-up between himself and his girlfriend. He was also in flux about his life and future. A suicide attempt was made followed by extensive hospitalization. Diane also told me that this was his second attempt (if this was indeed reliable information), the first having occurred during his early adolescence – something Barry and his mother never shared with me. His involvement with the performance text and concerns expressed by the IDIERI audience reverberated in my mind. I was reluctant to telephone him – I have difficulty with awkward situations such as this – but I did mail a greeting card the next day with a message of concern and outreach. I wrote, "I heard you may have been going through a rough time lately," but did not reveal my source. "If this is so, and you'd like to talk, give me a call." At the time of this writing I have not heard back from Barry.

Also ironic was a statement I heard a week later, made by the chairman of the ASU Human Subjects Review Board at their monthly business meeting: "I'm happy to report that there have been no incidents of adverse effects on participants as a result of research from any studies we approved." Most qualitative methods texts relegate a chapter on ethics to the end of the book, as if it were an obligatory chapter, yet irrelevant to the author's primary discussion on data gathering and analysis. Like those texts, ethical issues in this project did not emerge prominently until the latter stages, but they had been waiting in the wings all along to make their entrance.

Concluding Remarks

One of my colleagues mused after seeing the ASU performance, "Is this art? Is this research? Is this artful research or research-oriented art?" Admittedly, I do not have immediate answers. Admittedly, I do not care. I will leave academic elitists for whom these questions hold importance to formulate their own theories. Denzin calls the ethnodrama genre "messy," and that, to me, makes sense. The performance event, unlike the published research report, is temporal and ephemeral. All that remains of *Maybe Someday* is a videotape of the production, a few slides and photographs, and the written text – artifacts of the event *but not the event itself*. *Maybe Someday* can never be accessed again unless the production company remounts it. It would have been less troublesome, less expensive, and perhaps less ethically problematic, to write a traditional research report on Barry and make it available to a wider body of interested scholars. Yet part of me believes that the same amount of time devoted to play script development, rehearsals, production matters, and performances, would have been comparable to the time needed to write a substantive, traditional report. And I would not have grown as a researcher had I chosen the latter.

Jonathan Neelands, in his IDIERI keynote address, noted that the thrust stage venue (in which we performed *Maybe Someday*) shapes an audience into "silent witnesses" of a theatre event. But I anticipated that this particular, academic, critical audience with its high standards for drama would enter the performance text, not as "witnesses" of an experiment with research presentation, but as curious "voyeurs," framed with expectations of rigorous but engaging storytelling through art rather than lecture. The novelty of such an event, accompanied with its directorial and visual tactics to maintain audience interest, can only go so far. In other words, we *want* to hear "juicy stuff" and we *want* "dramatic impact." That is, after all, what makes theatre exciting and probably why several people probed me afterwards to learn more about Barry's unspoken autobiography. Though it would have been a breach of confidence and unethical of me to answer their questions, these individuals did not seem to consider *themselves* unethical for asking those questions in the first place.

Denzin's assertion that "The performance text is the single, most powerful way for ethnography to recover yet interrogate the meanings of lived experience" applies during both ethnodramatic process and product; for the researcher, participants, and audience members; and regardless of what is and is not represented on stage. I hope that the rumor of Barry's suicide attempt is false. But if it is true, I hope his participation in this project was not linked to that tragedy. I do want to hear from him soon, but if I don't, I pray he is in good health and motivated to achieve his dream. Maybe someday, if he *is* famous, the approximately 150 people at ASU and IDIERI who witnessed his performance and validated his life story will have played a significant role in "making a famous person, a successful person."

Permit me to end this confessional tale with dramatic impact. In the final scene of the play, Barry predicts:

BARRY: I'm looking towards a *[slide: "bright future"]* bright future. I really have a feeling of security when I look in the future, that no matter what comes, I'll be able to deal with it. And without even trying to sound pompous or anything or full of myself, I really do believe that no matter what the future holds I will be able to deal with it, and that I will be successful to some extent. At least I will be happy.

Note

1 In the United States, children generally enter kindergarten when they are 5 years old. By the end of their elementary school education in sixth grade, children generally range from 11 to 12 years in age. A follow-up study with Barry from his tenth (sophomore) through twelfth (senior) grades of high school means he participated from age 16 to 18.

References

Barone, T. (1997). "Seen and heard": The place of the child in arts-based research in theatre education. *Youth Theatre Journal, 11*, 113–127.

Barry, D. (1996). Artful inquiry: A symbolic constructivist approach to social science research. *Qualitative Inquiry, 2,* 411–438.

Blumenfeld-Jones, D. S. (1995). Dance as a mode of research representation. *Qualitative Inquiry, 1,* 391–401.

Bolton, G. (1996). Letter to the editor: A betrayal of feminism. *NADIE Journal, 20,* 4–5.

Denzin, N. K. (1997). *Interpretive ethnography: Ethnographic practices for the 21st century.* Thousand Oaks, CA: Sage.

Donmoyer, R., & Yennie-Donmoyer, J. (1995). Data as drama: Reflections on the use of reader's theatre as a mode of qualitative data display. *Qualitative Inquiry, 1,* 402–428.

Eisner, E. (1998). *What the arts teach: A cognitive perspective.* Arizona State University guest lecture series.

Ellis, C., & Bochner, A. P. (1992). Telling and performing personal stories: The constraints of choice in abortion. In C. Ellis & M. G. Flaherty (Eds.), *Investigating subjectivity: Research on lived experience* (pp. 79–101). Newbury Park, CA, Sage.

Ellis, C., & Bochner, A. P. (1996). Talking over ethnography. In C. Ellis & A. P. Bochner (Eds.), *Composing ethnography: Alternative forms of qualitative writing* (pp. 13–45). Walnut Creek, CA: AltaMira Press.

Harper, D. (1994). On the authority of the image: Visual methods at the crossroad. In N. K. Denzin & Y. S. Lincoln (Eds.), *Handbook of qualitative research.* Thousand Oaks, CA: Sage.

Mienczakowski, J. (1995). The theatre of ethnography: The reconstruction of ethnography into theatre with emancipatory potential. *Qualitative Inquiry, 1,* 360–375.

Mienczakowski, J. (1996). An ethnographic act: The construction of consensual theatre. In: C. Ellis & A. P. Bochner (Eds.), *Composing ethnography: Alternative forms of qualitative writing* (pp. 244–264). Walnut Creek, CA: AltaMira Press.

Mienczakowski, J. (1997). Theatre of change. *Research in Drama Education, 2,* 159–172.

Mienczakowski, J., Morgan, S., & Rolfe, A. (1993). Ethnography or drama? *National Association for Drama in Education Journal, 17,* 8–15.

Mienczakowski, J., Smith, R., & Sinclair, M. (1996). On the road to catharsis: A theoretical framework for change. *Qualitative Inquiry, 2,* 439–462.

Miles, M. B., & Huberman, A. M. (1994). *Qualitative data analysis: A sourcebook of new methods* (2nd ed.). Thousand Oaks, CA: Sage.

Saldaña, J. (1987). Statistical results in progress for the theatre for children component of the ASU longitudinal study. *Youth Theatre Journal, 2,* 14–27.

Saldaña, J. (1989). A quantitative analysis of children's responses to theatre from probing questions: A pilot study. *Youth Theatre Journal, 3,* 7–17.

Saldaña, J. (1995). "Is theatre necessary?": Final exit interviews with sixth grade participants from the ASU longitudinal study. *Youth Theatre Journal, 9,* 14–30.

Saldaña, J. (1996). "Significant differences" in child audience response: Assertions from the ASU longitudinal study. *Youth Theatre Journal, 10,* 67–83.

Saldaña, J., & Otero, H. D. (1990). Experiments in assessing children's responses to theatre with the semantic differential. *Youth Theatre Journal, 5,* 11–19.

Seidman, I. E. (1991). *Interviewing as qualitative research.* New York: Teachers College Press.

Strauss, A. L. (1987). *Qualitative analysis for social scientists.* New York: Cambridge University Press.

Van Maanen, J. (1988). *Tales of the field.* Chicago: University of Chicago Press.

Walker, R., Pick, C., & MacDonald, B. (1991). "Other rooms: other voices": A dramatized report. In C. Pick & B. MacDonald (Eds.), *Biography, identity and schooling: Episodes in educational research* (pp. 80–93). Washington, DC: Falmer Press.

Wolcott, H. F. (1994). *Transforming qualitative data: Description, analysis, and interpretation.* Thousand Oaks, CA: Sage.

6 Writing About Method and Methodology

"How To," Not "Talk About"

Mitch Allen, former owner and acquisitions editor of Left Coast Press, gave me a valuable piece of advice as I developed my manuscript for his publishing house: "Write to *teach*, not 'talk about'; exemplars ('what') are good; instructions ('how to') are better." This harkened back to the classic theatre adage I learned about compensating for dialogue-heavy scripts with visual support through actor movement and scenography such as stage properties and lighting: "Show it, don't tell it." And as a classroom teaching methods instructor, I was highly attuned to the best instructional practices for maximizing student learning. During my entire professional life, I've been teaching students how to act, how to direct, how to design, how to write, how to research and, most important, how to teach. "How to" is my modus operandi. In theatre production and in the classroom, things must get done. And it's my job, my responsibility, to teach others "how to." That same work ethic drives my research methods writing.

I write about research methods as if I'm teaching them aloud in a classroom. I assume that the knowledge will be new (and sometimes intimidating) to my students, so the material is presented in a highly organized format with succinct clarity:

1 Introduce the method with the most essential theoretical and methodological foundations;
2 Define and explain any unique terms and concepts;
3 Provide a concrete example of the method from the literature;
4 Apply the method through a practical guided activity with new data;
5 Discuss and reflect on the method and its applications to qualitative inquiry.

Some may view this systematic teaching approach as too streamlined or even pedagogically oppressive. But my own experience has informed me that students appreciate a well-organized classroom and clear instructional delivery from a teacher with a nurturing ethos. I don't "dumb down" the learning; I "smarten up" the teaching.

I write like I teach. I teach "how to" and I write "how to." I use the simplest vocabulary needed in order to teach complex principles. I also value utility (because things must get done), so theoretically-laden and philosophically-driven content is reserved for other courses in a student's program of study. Theory and philosophy are things to "talk about." In my classroom and in my writing, I tell *and* show "how to."

The first selection in this chapter, "Goodall's Verbal Exchange Coding: An Overview and Example," was an article commissioned by *Qualitative Inquiry*'s guest journal editor Amira De la Garza. She assembled a group of scholars to develop pieces for a special tribute issue dedicated to the work of the late H. L. "Bud" Goodall, a beloved and respected writer in the field of communication. I was familiar with his qualitative research methods books and his Verbal Exchange Coding approach to conversation analysis, which I had profiled in three editions of *The Coding Manual for Qualitative Researchers*. Each article submission for the special tribute issue was limited in the number of manuscript pages, so the "talk about" sections had to be brief in order to focus more on the "how to." Strict parameters such as page, word, and time limits force the writer to make hard yet often good decisions about what and what not to include in a report.

The second selection is an excerpt from my textbook, *Thinking Qualitatively: Methods of Mind*. The chapter included, "Thinking Narratively," focuses on writing methods and seemed an appropriate choice for this volume. *Thinking Qualitatively* was developed out of an instructional frustration I heard from a fellow professor who complained, "I can't teach my students how to think." What she meant, of course, is that she felt her students couldn't independently transcend toward richer analytic insights with their data and write-ups: finding interrelationships between categories, synthesizing initial analyses, finding new and fresher perspectives on the phenomenon, formulating theory, or extending beyond a case to higher levels of interpretation and meaning.

To me, teaching how to analyze data is quite easy. Analyzing data on your own is hard. Thus, I assembled an array of thinking strategies and approaches to inquiry to first bring an *awareness* to readers of the methods available to them. The text focuses on how to think about and reflect on social life, and to examine textual, visual, and mediated data beyond standard data analytic techniques. If the researcher herself is considered the primary instrument of an investigation, then the mind – not the data gathered – is the central process of and for rich inquiry. As case study methodologist Robert E. Stake (1995) wisely observed, "Good research is not about good methods as much as it is about good thinking" (p. 19).

Each chapter of *Thinking Qualitatively* begins with a set of major learning objectives, but rather than phrasing them in conventional educational language ("The student will . . ."), the objectives hone in on the desired mental applications ("Your mind will . . ."). The primary theme of the chapter is discussed first (e.g., Thinking Symbolically), followed by the topic's related modules (Thinking Conceptually, Thinking Abstractly, Thinking Capsulely, Thinking Metaphorically, and Thinking Phenomenologically). Each module includes a clear description, a discussion of its purpose and importance for qualitative inquiry, an example from a discipline (e.g., education, health care, sociology), references to the related literature, and occasional personal experiences and reflections from the writer.

The book was written in such a way to include not just information about brain-based learning, but to utilize its principles for maximizing reader impact. Information is provided in organized, thematically unified "chunks" rather than lengthy narratives to better insure conceptual retention. The vocabulary is geared toward an undergraduate reading level for easier comprehension, and the text is written in a first-person perspective to better connect with its readers.

A mixture of both vivid research-related and personal stories is woven throughout the book to embed the knowledge as narrative structures in the memory. Summaries are presented after each module to reinforce key concepts and to stimulate action "for your mental Rolodex." Illustrations such as photographs and diagrams appear strategically throughout the text to maintain visual engagement. (Unfortunately, none are included in the sample chapter below due to copyright restrictions for republication.) Recommended end-of-chapter activities are designed to cognitively and kinesthetically synthesize key learnings for retention and transfer. *Thinking Qualitatively* attempts to practice what it preaches through its reflexive tone and metacognitive structure. It discusses both how the mind thinks and how to think about thinking for social inquiry.

Reference

Stake, R. E. (1995). *The art of case study research*. Thousand Oaks, CA: Sage.

GOODALL'S VERBAL EXCHANGE CODING: AN OVERVIEW AND EXAMPLE

Abstract

This article provides a descriptive overview and brief example of Bud Goodall's Verbal Exchange Coding, a method profiled in his book, *Writing the New Ethnography*. Verbal Exchange Coding categorizes conversation into five forms of verbal exchange, then into five practices or cultural performances of everyday life. Written reflection stimulates the analyst to create storied accounts that weave the researcher's personal experiences into meaning in ways that serve as an analysis of culture. The example is a poignant verbal exchange between the author and a stranger at an airport boarding area.

Keywords

Bud Goodall, Verbal Exchange Coding, conversation analysis, qualitative data analysis, interpretation, culture

Bud Goodall's (2000) Verbal Exchange Coding, a method outlined in his book *Writing the New Ethnography*, is perhaps one of the least utilized methods cited and profiled in the author's *The Coding Manual for Qualitative Researchers* (Saldaña, 2013). Verbal Exchange Coding consists of verbatim transcript analysis and interpretation of the types of conversation and personal meanings of key moments in the exchanges. Goodall (2000), however, opted not to prescribe mechanistic approaches to the method, preferring instead and encouraging researchers to create an "*evocative representation* of the fieldwork experience," the "writing of a *story of culture*" (p. 121, emphasis in original).

Goodall's introductory approach to the analysis of talk and text is just one of many extensive and systematic approaches to conversation and discourse analysis (e.g., Agar, 1994; Drew, 2008; Gee, 2011; Gilligan, Spencer, Weinberg, & Bertsch, 2006; Jones, Gallois, Callan, & Barker, 1999; Lindlof & Taylor, 2011; Rapley, 2007; Silverman, 2006). However, unlike several of these methods, which include detailed notation systems for microanalyses, Goodall advocates a more holistic and truly interpretive approach to the data by novices. The outlined description and analyzed example below should not suggest that users must adhere to a formulaic framework for Verbal Exchange Coding. I simply provide a streamlined summary of Goodall's recommendations for reader guidance. His methods are applicable to both transcribed dialogic exchanges and preexisting fictional and non-fictional texts.

Verbal Exchange Coding Method

Goodall describes a "coding" method that first determines the generic type of conversation, followed by analytic memoing or reflection to examine

[Originally published in *Qualitative Inquiry*, vol. 22, no. 1, 2016, pp. 36–39; doi 10.1177/1077800415603395; edited slightly for this publication.]

the meaning of the conversation. This memoing and reflection often make it directly into the text. It begins with a precise transcription or recollection of conversation, ideally including all pauses and non-verbal cues. The analyst then draws from a typology/continuum of five forms of verbal exchange Goodall suggested for identification of the units. Those familiar with the field of human communication studies might recognize the established emphases areas from the study of discourse and interpersonal communication:

1. *Phatic Communion* or *Ritual Interaction*, a "class of routine social interactions that are themselves the basic verbal form of politeness rituals used to express social recognition and mutuality of address." Simple exchanges can communicate cultural patterns such as status, gender, race, class differences, and so on;
2. *Ordinary Conversation*, "patterns of questions and responses that provide the interactants with data about personal, relational, and informational issues and concerns, as well as perform the routine 'business' of . . . everyday life";
3. *Skilled Conversation*, which represents "a 'higher' or 'deeper' level of information exchange/discussion" between individuals, and can include exchanges such as debates, conflict management, professional negotiations, and so on;
4. *Personal Narratives*, consisting of "individual or mutual self-disclosure" of "pivotal events in a personal or organizational life"; and
5. *Dialogue*, in which conversation "transcends" information exchange and the "boundaries of self," and moves to higher levels of spontaneous, ecstatic mutuality.

(Goodall, 2000, pp. 103–104)

This first stage of Verbal Exchange Coding also explores the personal meanings of key moments by examining facets such as speech mannerisms, non-verbal communication habits, and rich points of cultural knowledge (slang, jargon, etc.). The categorization then proceeds to examine the *practices* or the "*cultural performances* of everyday life" (p. 116). Notice that these five also suggest a continuum ranging from everyday matters to the epiphanic episode:

1. *Routines and Rituals* of structured, symbolically meaningful actions during our day;
2. *Surprise-and-Sense-Making Episodes* of the unanticipated or unexpected;
3. *Risk-Taking Episodes* and *Face-Saving Episodes* of conflict-laden exchanges;
4. *Crises* in a verbal exchange or as an overarching pattern of lived experience;
5. *Rites of Passage*, or what is done that significantly "alters or changes our personal sense of self or our social or professional status or identity."

(pp. 116–119)

Selected questions assist the analyst in coding, interpreting, and reflecting on the content and meaning of the verbal exchange: What is the nature of the relationship? What are the influences of fixed positionings (gender, race/ethnicity, social class, etc.)? What are the rhythms, vocal tones, and silences contributing to the overall meaning? (pp. 106–107).

The overview described above should not suggest an overly systematic approach to analyzing verbal exchanges. For Goodall, these could be quick reflective analytic moves. His suggested heuristics are basic categorization of overheard conversation followed by reflective narrative, rather than coding's traditional unitizing of data and symbolic notation of them through words or short phrases (Saldaña, 2013). His approach evocatively explores "the new ethnography" – storied accounts grounded in the data that weave "the personal experience of the researcher into meaning in ways that serve as analyses of cultures" (Goodall, 2000, p. 127). Following is an example of how I employed my interpretation of Goodall's suggested method.

Example

(I stand waiting for my flight to New York-LaGuardia at a Delta Airlines gate at the Raleigh-Durham airport on Friday, July 26, 2013, approximately 5:30 p.m. I am separated from the other seated passengers' waiting area, occasionally puffing on my electronic (e-)cigarette. The gate agent makes an announcement over the speaker system. An average-build White man in his late 50s with salt-and-pepper hair and a neatly trimmed goatee, dressed in a light gray suit but with no tie, approaches me; I call him the SWEDE because we never exchanged our actual names, and it was only later in our conversation that he revealed his nationality.)

SWEDE: What did she say? *(I detect a slight European accent in his voice, but am not sure which country he's from. His voice is medium pitched, moderate volume, and gentle in tone.)*

JOHNNY: She said that boarding was going to be delayed until the captain calls New York to find out if we can land OK and on time.

SWEDE: Oh. *(referring to my e-cigarette)* Are those things any good?

JOHNNY: *(making a grimace)* They're satisfactory but not satisfying.

SWEDE: I used to smoke, too.

JOHNNY: I smoked for 40 years before I quit.

SWEDE: I *had* to quit.

JOHNNY: Me, too. A friend of mine smoked the same amount of time as me, probably the same amount each day, and he ended up with lung cancer, he's on chemo, so bad. Me, I stopped, got my lungs x-rayed and, thank God, I'm clean as a whistle.

SWEDE: I had cancer, too, spent a year in the hospital.

JOHNNY: Wow.

SWEDE: *(smiling)* They cut me from here to here *(pointing and moving from one side of his jaw to the other)* and took it out.

JOHNNY: *(almost apologetic)* Oh, I'm so sorry.

SWEDE: (*laughing*) No, that's OK, it's not your fault.
JOHNNY: I mean that I'm sorry for what happened to you.
SWEDE: It was hard. My wife had to take care of me for nine months in the hospital.
JOHNNY: Wow. (*in an affirming tone*) But you're here, and that's good!
SWEDE: (*smiling*) Yes.
JOHNNY: Do you live in New York?
SWEDE: I'm originally from Sweden and moved there to work.
JOHNNY: I'm going to New York to see some shows for a day, then going right back home. I'm from Arizona.
SWEDE: I was here for just the day, and flying back. I've been here since eight o'clock this morning.
JOHNNY: Wow.
SWEDE: And you?
JOHNNY: I was teaching at one of the universities here for a week.
SWEDE: Lots of universities here.
JOHNNY: Yes.
SWEDE: What did you teach?
JOHNNY: Research methods for an institute. What do you do for a living?
SWEDE: I'm an investment planner.
JOHNNY: Are you with a bank or an investment firm?
SWEDE: Investment firm.
JOHNNY: Yeah, I've been thinking a lot about investments and savings lately. I'm going to retire from my job in May 2014.
SWEDE: What kind of plan are you on?
JOHNNY: I'm on a pension plan with my state.
SWEDE: (*rolling his eyes slightly*) Good luck with that.
JOHNNY: It's a pretty good plan but it's not going to be the same as what I'm making now. It's both scary and exciting. . . .
(*We continue chatting about our jobs for a while, and the conversation veers back to smoking.*)
SWEDE: I still like to be around smokers and smell it.
JOHNNY: Me, too. The smell of it comforts me even if I can't smoke.
SWEDE: My wife doesn't like the smell of it at all. She goes away from it, makes a face, "Ah, that smells terrible!" She hated it when the smell of smoke was in my clothes, in my coat.
JOHNNY: I know, I got so self-conscious of the way I smelled, but now that's not a problem.
SWEDE: I look at people smoking and I miss it.
JOHNNY: I like to hang around smokers and just smell it. I don't need to smoke, I just want to be around them. I know that if I had just one more cigarette, I'd probably get hooked again. I have a very addictive personality.
SWEDE: I quit once for two weeks long ago. But a friend of mine said, "Ah, just have a cigarette with me," we were in a bar. So I smoked one from him, and when I was on my way home, I thought, "Ah, I'll just buy a pack," and I started up again.

JOHNNY: I couldn't do that. I know that all it'll take is just one cigarette and I'll be hooked again.

SWEDE: Yes, well.

JOHNNY: I have nicotine tablets, too, because you can't smoke these (*referring to and holding my e-cigarette*) on the plane.

(*The gate agent makes an announcement for first-class and priority passengers to line up. The SWEDE smiles at me and says, "Here we go. See you." Later, when my section of seats is called to board, I enter the plane and pass the SWEDE sitting in first class on my way to the coach section. We make eye contact; he grins and reaches out to grasp my arm and pats it strongly; I quickly grin back and pat his arm with the same strength.*)

CODING: Our initial exchange bypassed introductory *Phatic Communion* and began with *Ordinary Conversation* through information exchange about flights. Our discussion of work and retirement matters were brief interludes of *Skilled Conversation*, but it was our smoking and smoking related illness stories that dominated and took us rather quickly and easily into assorted *Personal Narratives* throughout our exchanges. I would classify our final moment of arm patting on the plane as a significant moment of non-verbal *Dialogue*, explained below.

REFLECTION [excerpts]: Ex-smokers readily share with each other their *Ritual* stories of addiction, the trials of quitting, and their nostalgia for a former bad habit. Strangers quickly bond when they share the habit/culture of smoking, and non-smoking exes gravitate to each other to discuss with a person who truly understands an experience they genuinely miss. Smoking, quitting, and its constituent elements (length of habit, non-smokers' annoyances, withdrawal strategies, etc.) are frequent and easily generated topics for conversation. The *Surprise-and-Sense-Making Episode* of the Swede's bout with cancer was followed by my apologetic *Face-Saving Episode*, but the Swede graciously laughed it off. The stigma of carrying a bad "smell" (uttered frequently in one conversation section) and, sometimes, recovery from severe illness brought on by smoking are shared not as chaos narratives (Frank, 2012, p. 47) but as badges of honor and points of mutual connection.

The Swede might never have spoken to me had he not seen me with my nicotine substitute prop: an electronic cigarette. He was an investment planner, dressed in a suit, well groomed, and had a first-class seat on the plane. I was dressed in very casual clothing and destined for coach, but he had no problem striking up a conversation with me, of a different ethnicity and social class – yet each of us within the same age range and with graying facial hair. We both shared a former bad habit, and this transcended all other demographic attributes. His line, "I look at people smoking and I miss it," is *exactly* what I myself feel. If we can no longer smoke together and share the bonding that comes with mutual engagement in the habit, then former smokers can at least find comfort and empathetic understanding with someone who shares the memory of what it used to be like.

Our shared stories of addiction and withdrawal are our emotional nicotine substitutes. A patch, lozenge, and electronic cigarette satisfy our ongoing psychological and physical needs for a mild high. However, the human affirmation of someone who's been there gives us a sense of community, of cultural belonging. Virtually nothing connects recovering addicts more than sharing a (former) bad habit. Me and the Swede never told each other our names, but that didn't matter. Our identities were rooted in and revealed through a similar past experience.

The *Rite of Passage* moment of patting each other's arm strongly while grinning on the plane was a "dialogic" moment that capped two strangers' fleeting conversation, cemented our temporary yet quickly formed relationship, and reinforced a sense of kinship, brotherhood, and an affirmation of triumph: "We're here, and that's good!" Two men in their late 50s, occasionally reflecting on our mortality as we grow older, were still being "bad boys" by symbolically high-fiving our shared pasts, shared accomplishments, and shared ex-smoker's culture.

Conclusion

Goodall recommends Verbal Exchange Coding as a preliminary analytic step toward a more evocative write-up, perhaps drafted as vignettes or profiles (Erickson, 1986; Seidman, 2013). Research genres such as action and practitioner research (e.g., Fox, Martin, & Green, 2007; Stringer, 2014), narrative inquiry (e.g., Holstein & Gubrium, 2012; Riessman, 2008), phenomenology (e.g., Smith, Flowers, & Larkin, 2009; Wertz et al., 2011), and arts-based research (e.g., Knowles & Cole, 2008; Leavy, 2009) lend themselves well to representing and presenting an analyst's inquiry and discoveries through Verbal Exchange Coding. Although Goodall did not mention it, his approach also serves as an excellent way for performance ethnographers/ethnodramatists to delve deeply into the texts they construct to exhibit the nuanced actions, reactions, and interactions between their participant-characters (Saldaña, 2011).

Goodall's legacy of Verbal Exchange Coding is perhaps an overlooked method from his prolific writings that instructors of qualitative research methods may wish to reexamine for their coursework readings and student exercises. The approach provides both structured and open-ended guidance for internal reflection and analysis of conversation. It is recommended as an introductory way to holistically explore the subtleties of dialogue and culture before venturing into more systematic methods for analyzing talk and text.

References

Agar, M. (1994). *Language shock: Understanding the culture of conversation*. New York, NY: Quill-William Morrow.

Drew, P. (2008). Conversation analysis. In J. A. Smith (Ed.), *Qualitative psychology: A practical guide to research methods* (2nd ed.) (pp. 133–159). London, England: Sage.

Erickson, F. (1986). Qualitative methods in research on teaching. In M. C. Wittrock (Ed.), *Handbook of research on teaching* (3rd ed.) (pp. 119–161). New York, NY: Palgrave Macmillan.

Fox, M., Martin, P., & Green, G. (2007). *Doing practitioner research*. London, England: Sage.
Frank, A. W. (2012). Practicing dialogical narrative analysis. In J. A. Holstein & J. F. Gubrium (Eds.), *Varieties of narrative analysis* (pp. 33–52). Thousand Oaks, CA: Sage.
Gee, J. P. (2011). *How to do discourse analysis: A toolkit*. New York, NY: Routledge.
Gilligan, C., Spencer, R., Weinberg, M. K., & Bertsch, T. (2006). On the listening guide: A voice-centered relational method. In S. N. Hesse-Biber & P. Leavy (Eds.), *Emergent methods in social research* (pp. 253–271). Thousand Oaks, CA: Sage.
Goodall, H. L., Jr. (2000). *Writing the new ethnography*. Walnut Creek, CA: AltaMira Press.
Holstein, J. A., & Gubrium, J. F. (Eds.). (2012). *Varieties of narrative analysis*. Thousand Oaks, CA: Sage.
Jones, E., Gallois, C., Callan, V., & Barker, M. (1999). Strategies of accommodation: Development of a coding system for conversational interaction. *Journal of Language and Social Psychology, 18*, 123–152.
Knowles, J. G., & Cole, A. L. (2008). *Handbook of the arts in qualitative research: Perspectives, methodologies, examples, and issues*. Thousand Oaks, CA: Sage.
Leavy, P. (2009). *Method meets art: Arts-based research practice*. New York, NY: Guilford Press.
Lindlof, T. R., & Taylor, B. C. (2011). *Qualitative communication research methods* (3rd ed.). Thousand Oaks, CA: Sage.
Rapley, T. (2007). *Doing conversation, discourse and document analysis*. London, England: Sage.
Riessman, C. K. (2008). *Narrative methods for the human sciences*. Thousand Oaks, CA: Sage.
Saldaña, J. (2011). *Ethnotheatre: Research from page to stage*. Walnut Creek, CA: Left Coast Press.
Saldaña, J. (2013). *The coding manual for qualitative researchers* (2nd ed.). London, England: Sage.
Seidman, I. (2013). *Interviewing as qualitative research: A guide for researchers in education and the social sciences* (4th ed.). New York, NY: Teachers College Press.
Silverman, D. (2006). *Interpreting qualitative data: Methods for analyzing talk, text and interaction* (3rd ed.). London, England: Sage.
Smith, J. A., Flowers, P., & Larkin, M. (2009). *Interpretative phenomenological analysis: Theory, method and research*. London, England: Sage.
Stringer, E. T. (2014). *Action research* (4th ed.). Thousand Oaks, CA: Sage.
Wertz, F. J., Charmaz, K., McMullen, L. M., Josselson, R., Anderson, R., & McSpadden, E. (2011). *Five ways of doing qualitative analysis: Phenomenological psychology, grounded theory, discourse analysis, narrative research, and intuitive inquiry*. New York, NY: Guilford Press.

CHAPTER 10 – "THINKING NARRATIVELY": FROM *THINKING QUALITATIVELY: METHODS OF MIND*

Learning Objectives and Summary

- Your mind will reflect on different narrative approaches to qualitative research presentation.
- Your mind will explore a variety of literary representations for social inquiry.

This chapter explores how the writing of qualitative research studies can be enhanced through different ways of thinking about presentations aside from traditional scholarly article prose and formats. These methods of mind consist of

- Thinking narratively
- Thinking monologically
- Thinking dialogically
- Thinking poetically
- Thinking proverbially

The purpose of this chapter is to acquaint you with various prosaic and poetic forms of thinking and writing for evocative qualitative research representation and presentation. (Dramatic writing is another literary genre, but that modality is addressed in Chapter 7's "Thinking theatrically" and in several of this chapter's sections).

Thinking Narratively

A narrative is a storied account of events, a symbolic representation of knowledge and experiences. It documents, in written, visual, or oral form, participant actions and emotions, yet does so in such a way as to grab the reader's or listener's attention and engagement with the tale. A *literary* narrative adds stylistic dimensions to the telling, providing a potentially evocative and aesthetic experience. Read this descriptive field note passage:

> At the outdoor social, a man sits on a brick ledge looking at other people standing in front of him and talking to each other.

The composition of this note jotted in the field serves its purpose in documenting the action the researcher observed. But notice how, with a few carefully selected words and different syntax, yet remaining firmly rooted in the original observation, a different picture of life is created:

> Howard sat by himself on the hard brick ledge as sunset approached, feeling so alone as he gazed at the crowd drinking and noisily socializing around him.

[Originally published in *Thinking Qualitatively: Methods of Mind* by Johnny Saldaña, Thousand Oaks, CA: Sage Publications, 2015, pp. 169–183; edited slightly for this publication.]

If my intended effects as a writer have been successful, I have accomplished several things. First, I have assigned a pseudonym to the participant ("Howard"), but in doing so I have transformed him from an anonymous person into a central character. I have portrayed a sense of time and place ("sunset," "hard brick ledge") and established a problem, conflict, or tension, interwoven with an emotion ("feeling so alone"). Lastly, I have chosen the omniscient observer as a point of view that can reveal the internal thoughts and feelings of people. Much has been accomplished in just one sentence, and the next steps are to set these initial prompts into motion in my narrative describing the phenomenon of *social isolation*. I could just as easily have begun my account with a more objective and general assertion, such as:

> Individuals experiencing social isolation often initiate their own physical separation from other people.

But by reporting a mere fact, I have potentially distanced my reader from the essential *feeling* of the phenomenon – a key facet of understanding the nature of social isolation. What if the research story were to begin like this:

> Alone and lonely. No one but you, even in a crowd. Afraid to make contact. Fear of rejection. Keep to yourself. Safer that way.

Thinking narratively considers the stylistic writing choices available for conveying to readers the journey and destination of the research. It is heightened attunement to various storied forms of social experience – the construction of vignettes, short tales, chronicles, poems, life lessons, life trajectories, and especially the characterization of our participants as we document their lives. Our minds retain information longer when a narrative string connects the memories. And if that narrative possesses an aesthetic dimension that carries emotional impact, we can cement the memory more firmly in our readers' brains.

Fictional and nonfictional literature tends to get classified according to its *genres*, *elements*, and *styles*. Genres or forms are literary types, such as short story, biography, poetry, and drama. Elements refer primarily to literary devices incorporated throughout a work, such as protagonist, antagonist, symbolism, foreshadowing, and alliteration. A style suggests the overall tone of the work: for example, tragedy, comedy, satire, romance, or fantasy.

Qualitative research also has genres, elements, and styles (Saldaña, 2011). The genres or forms range from methodologies such as grounded theory to phenomenology to ethnography. The elements of inquiry are not just literary but functional: participant observation field notes, interview transcripts, literature review, and so on. The styles of qualitative research refer to its write-ups and the various approaches to tale-telling: realistically, confessionally, critically, analytically, interpretively, and so on (Van Maanen, 2011; Wolcott, 1994). It is these styles of writing that primarily determine a study's narrative texture.

A classic design saying goes, "For every choice, there is a sacrifice," meaning that if you choose to summarize in your own words what a participant said, rather than quoting her or him verbatim in your report, that choice sacrifices direct evidence for researcher interpretation. If you choose to present your study's write-up in the straightforward, descriptive manner typical of most traditional reports, you sacrifice the possibilities of critical, poetic, dramatic, and other representational and presentational genres and styles. And if you choose to document your ethnographic fieldwork and findings as a scripted, performed work for the stage, some readers may find the choice bold and innovative while others may find the play artistically self-indulgent and lacking in rigor and credibility. The precision of quantitative research rests in its statistical accuracy. In qualitative research, precision rests in your word choices.

If someone were to ask you, "So, what's your research about?" your answer would generally be the plot (or, overall structure) of your research story. When you develop the purpose statement of your study, you are formally composing its plot. A statement for a project might read:

> The purpose of this study is to explore how doctoral candidates perceive their college/university coursework as preparation for their independent research projects.

The characters of a qualitative study are its participants. Their actions, recalled through interviews or observed in the field, generate various storylines within the plot. Monologues may emerge from individual interviews with the participants, while dialogues may be documented as you observe participants in seminars with a professor and peers. As for the life lessons learned by the participant-characters as their action storylines progress through the research plot, those might consist of a key assertion, a core category, a set of themes, or a theory you construct from your data analysis.

The parallels between a research study and literature can extend further when you consider how diverse literary styles such as romances, mysteries, and tragedies can inspire more creative nonfictional writing for your reports (Gibbs, 2007). An interesting question I once heard at a qualitative research conference presentation by Daryl Ward was, "What classical or contemporary piece of literature does your research remind you of?" A project exploring stigma or shame might evoke recollections of Nathaniel Hawthorne's novel *The Scarlet Letter*; participants feeling trapped in unfulfilled lives are reminiscent of multiple characters from the plays of Anton Chekhov. A return to literary masterworks can provide a researcher additional insights on the human phenomena under investigation. Just because a work is considered fiction doesn't mean it isn't truthful in some ways.

Creative nonfiction employs the devices and conventions of exemplary literary writing for the reportage of rigorous, systematic investigation. The work is not "based on a true story," as is often claimed when media producers take creative license in their dramatization of the facts. Creative nonfiction simply tells the

114   *Writing About Method and Methodology*

research story in an engaging way for its readership. Social scientist Brené Brown muses, "Maybe stories are just data with a soul." Narrative inquiry has made great strides in this field, and this methodology has much to offer more traditional qualitative researchers in terms of the representation and presentation of their work (see Clandinin & Connelly, 2000; Coulter & Smith, 2009; Gutkind, 2008; Holstein & Gubrium, 2012; Murray, 2008; Riessman, 2008). For an amusing and intricately designed online reference to narrative elements, see The Periodic Table of Storytelling (http://designthroughstorytelling.net/periodic/index.html).

Thinking narratively is a necessary method of mind that serves several purposes:

- It stimulates the search for stories in the data and thus the character and processes of participants.
- It encourages you to document your own and your participants' perceptions in written forms and formats that best represent their intended meanings.
- It offers a variety of choices for literary genres, elements, and styles to consider as you compose the account.
- It stimulates creative ways of rendering the qualitative report through more progressive forms of writing for enhanced reader engagement.
- It forces meticulous attention to language as a powerful medium for communicating human insights.

The following methods of mind profile other modalities of narrative representation and presentation for qualitative inquiry: *thinking monologically, dialogically, poetically*, and *proverbially*.

FOR YOUR MENTAL ROLODEX: As you conduct fieldwork, stay attuned to the storylines of action within the social settings you observe. In interviews, actively prompt and solicit self-standing stories from participants. Consider how your own written account of the study might take on literary dimensions for the representation and presentation of fieldwork experiences.

Thinking Monologically

A monologue is an extended, one-person account told in the first person. It most often appears as a performance convention of plays, teleplays, screenplays, and stand-up comedy, but monologic accounts can also be found in standard research articles as longer, indented passages of an interviewee's transcribed text. Monologues are also solo narratives of varying length, such as individual blogs, vlogs, Facebook postings, and even the occasional tweet on Twitter. In fact, the single-authored narrative about the study itself functions as a monologic account.

When we think to ourselves, our minds experience stream-of-consciousness monologues. These internal, solo narratives are rapid and complex thoughts to and for ourselves that reason, reflect, panic, problem-solve, and carry out other processes that we enact most often when we speak aloud to others in everyday life. Psychology's thinking-aloud protocol (Ericsson & Simon, 1993) attempts to record what a person is thinking and feeling as she or he voices uncensored the thoughts going through her or his mind while working on a task like solving a math problem, reading, or watching a film. One of its purposes is to construct a cognitive map of mental processes through a detailed microanalysis of thought sequences and patterns. Writing monologically for qualitative inquiry more coherently documents one person as she or he thinks out loud, preferably with the same uncensored complexity one would use when thinking to oneself.

Some perceive the monologue as a one-sided, even oppressive concept because the opportunity for dialogic exchange and meaning-sharing is missing. But monologues should be treasured as opportunities to read or listen to a person's valued perspective, uninterrupted. Monologues provide not just forums for one's voice; they are participant portraits in miniature. These solo works offer windows into the person's private mind – her or his values, attitudes, beliefs, emotions, and experiences. Monologues give our participants an "open mike" to address an audience with vulnerability and honesty.

Thinking monologically finds passages in your database where participants say things that you cannot possibly "top" through your own words. These are moments when gripping stories are told, when poignant moments are expressed, when the little things seem important, when strong emotions prevail, and when profound insights are made. But they must also add value to the monologic account by revealing something about a participant's personality and character.

Alan Peshkin's (1986) *God's Choice: The Total World of a Fundamentalist Christian School* includes several monologic passages from key teachers and students in the setting. Chapter 1 consists primarily of an extended monologic narrative from Pastor William Muller, headmaster of the school, expressing his personal religious beliefs, the philosophy and approach of the school, and the way he perceives the world today. An excerpt from that monologue reads:

> There is no way of getting in to heaven except through Jesus Christ. Fewer and fewer people believe in the fact that Jesus was God. You're extreme if you do, and I point out in this speech that we are extreme in our belief of the Virgin Birth. We are extreme in believing that Jesus is coming again, we are extreme in believing in salvation by faith, and we are extreme in witnessing to others.
>
> What I'm saying is that Christians are extremist in the eyes of the world. I don't look at myself as a conservative. I can see kooky people to the right of me, but if somebody else looks at me from their perspective, and if they're outside the fold of Christ, they'd look at me as a conservative. I see myself as obeying the Bible. Our belief has got to affect our behavior; if we're Christians, our behavior is going to be conservative politically.
>
> We look around us and see Satan. He's prince and power of this age and he has stronger involvement with this world than Christians do.
>
> (p. 6)

Seidman (2013) advocates three separate interviews with the same participant for qualitative case study research. One of the analytic approaches he prescribes is the creation of a "profile," a monologic assemblage of the richest passages from transcripts – approximately one-third of the total corpus. The researcher cuts and pastes transcript excerpts on a monitor screen to create a more organized narrative in terms of chronology, storyline, climactic build, and so on. In the resulting self-standing account, the participant tells her or his own story for the researcher to analyze further, or for a reader to learn about from a first-person perspective. Remember that there are times when the participant herself or himself can take center stage in the study without researcher intervention.

I myself prefer to document for my readers verbatim accounts by participants, including all original grammatical constructions, erratic flows of speech, and extraneous utterances like "um" and "uh." Some label this verbal debris, but I consider it part of an authentic *voiceprint*, as it's called in theatre parlance. I do not attempt to spell out phonetically any cultural dialects, nor do I include "sic" whenever an error (as I perceive it) appears in the transcribed text. The monologue must showcase and honor the participant's unique voice.

But don't forget that you, too, have a researcher's voice. Your thoughts and feelings, especially when they venture toward the confessional and impressionist or the critical and advocacy tales of writing (Van Maanen, 2011), can engage your readers with their up-front starkness. I once wrote a conference presentation about one of the most frustrating students with whom I've ever worked, a young man whose intellectual stubbornness brought out the anger in me, and labeled it not a case study but a "case rant." My 15-minute diatribe was an experiment in autoethnographic storytelling that set aside the conventions of academic decorum and focused on the "messy truth" of what sometimes runs through a teacher's mind. Autoethnography (Chang, 2008; Jones, Adams, & Ellis, 2013; Poulos, 2009; Spry, 2011), a methodology of qualitative inquiry, situates the researcher's personal lived experiences front and center in the writing. In fact, I recommend that all researchers do some soul-searching and undergo the examination of themselves in a report. Doing so will heighten your awareness of what you're asking your participants to do for you. As I advocate in my workshops, "You can't learn how to tell someone else's story until you first learn how to tell your own."

FOR YOUR MENTAL ROLODEX: As you investigate social life, construct monologic work from your participants or yourself that offers insight about human experiences.

Thinking Dialogically

A form not seen too often in academic writing is dialogic exchange. Most qualitative research projects collect data through one-on-one interviews, so documentation of interaction between participants is sparse. There is abundant methods literature on conversation analysis, but studies from that genre tend to parse the narratives extensively through their analytic detail, interrupting the flow of dialogue on the page.

Thinking dialogically finds passages of text from your data that reveal participants engaged in dialogue – that is, significant conversational action, reaction, and interaction. It reflects carefully on how the power and nuances of language don't just communicate but influence and affect things into motion. Thinking dialogically examines how the conversationalists themselves perceive the verbal exchange, and how you as the researcher retrospectively interpret what was spoken between them. Some interviews contain dialogic exchanges between the researcher and participant, but most of these tend to consist of question/answer turn-taking. Focus group transcripts however, particularly during tension-laden passages, contain rich sources for dialogic encounters. Chapter 6's "Thinking communicatively" offered several considerations for conversation analysis, such as Goodall's (2000) Verbal Exchange Coding and the microanalysis of dialogic "moments." This section focuses on the documentation and writing up of those conversations for your readership.

The formatting of conversation generates different effects on readers. When dialogue is woven into a prosaic rendering, the narrator has the opportunity to add supplemental description and commentary. Below is an excerpt from Finley and Finley's (1999) narrative inquiry account of homeless youth in pre-Katrina New Orleans. Two young men, nicknamed Tigger and Roach, plan their strategies to "sp'ange" (ask passersby for spare change):

> Tigger has several years of practice and a high school diploma to separate himself from the rank and file gutter-punk. He was even in the military, for a short while, but couldn't get through the boot camp thing. Often times, he's the voice that gets things moving along.
>
> "We better make quick work of the schwillies, man," Tigger says in a quick aside to Roach, then addresses the entire group. "We gotta sp'ange enough for all weekend today; it's gonna rain tomorrow."
>
> "How do you know that?" Roach feels comfortable challenging Tigger. It's always done in a friendly tone, and his challenges often let Tigger explain his rationale, swaying the whole group to his point of view. Roach takes a long swig of whiskey in his turn. "Are you a weather man now?"
>
> Tigger rolls his eyes. "I read it in the paper. Town is gonna be packed and we can make bank. The Clover has a sign welcoming some conference, so there's plenty of green around. We just gotta get it while the weather holds."
>
> (p. 327)

Now examine the same dialogic exchange, adapted and formatted as an ethnodramatic script:

TIGGER: We better make quick work of the schwillies, man. We gotta sp'ange enough for all weekend today; it's gonna rain tomorrow.

ROACH: How do you know that? Are you a weather man now? (*he takes a long swig of whiskey*)

TIGGER: I read it in the paper. Town is gonna be packed and we can make bank. The Clover has a sign welcoming some conference, so there's plenty of green around. We just gotta get it while the weather holds.

(adapted from Saldaña, 2005a, p. 147)

Both formats are available to qualitative researchers, and each offers its unique advantages as a rendering of social life. Prosaic formats permit more nuanced descriptions reminiscent of field notes and an omniscient point of view. Dramatic formats provide an economic sense of action happening "here and now" and ask the reader to make more inferences and interpretations of the dialogic exchanges. Your format choice for a written report should be strategically selected to render the account in its most powerful manner.

One of the more fascinating methodological genres of qualitative inquiry to evolve recently is duoethnography (Norris, Sawyer, & Lund, 2012; Sawyer & Norris, 2013). Duoethnography is a collaborative research methodology in which two (or more) researchers juxtapose their life histories to provide multiple understandings of a social phenomenon. Duoethnography compensates for the potentially limited vision of a one-person autoethnography, and the potentially diffuse findings from large-team research, by establishing a two-person project.

Each writer provides both individual contributions and commentary on the other researcher's reflections, usually but not exclusively through e-mail exchanges. Individual positions can be supplemented, enhanced, supported, challenged, and revised through dialogic response. Awareness becomes further heightened when two individuals from different backgrounds collaborate as duoethnographers (e.g., when gender issues are discussed between a man and a woman or sexual orientation and identity politics are discussed between a straight man and a gay man). The premise of the genre is based on the simple adage, "Stories beget stories," meaning that one person's shared personal experiences stimulate and generate additional narratives from another. Both researchers play the roles of storyteller *and* listener in this new methodology. Perhaps the most refreshing quality of duoethnography is its honesty. The methodology, and thus the writing, permits collegial and unpretentious exchanges of thoughts and insights. However, contributors do not sacrifice rigor for their straightforwardness. They cite the professional literature when necessary and propose new theories as ideas accumulate – not as intellectual "talking heads" but as collegial interactants reflecting on the issue. Duoethnography is scholarly conversation at its best. Topics vary from the small details of everyday living to the grand and important meanings of life. Feelings are just as valid as facts, and insights deepen from the opportunity to exchange and build upon another's perspectives.

Even a researcher and a key participant can dialogue (in real time or electronically) as duoethnographers, so long as the time and effort do not tax the respondent. I have conducted many interviews with participants who contributed profound insights on the topics I investigated, but I have not had many opportunities to "talk shop" with them about the nature of the study itself and its data analysis. When those exchanges did occur, a few of them offered me intriguing factors to consider and even some "Aha!" revelations. As time permits, dialogue with your participants about the research process itself – not just as a means of conducting member checks to confirm accurate data documentation and reportage, but to gain their perspectives on how to go about understanding the very phenomenon you're attempting to study.

FOR YOUR MENTAL ROLODEX: As you investigate social life, listen for and extract significant conversational moments between your participants. Understand that dialogue is not just communication but inquiry in its broadest sense.

Thinking Poetically

Poetic inquiry (Prendergast, Leggo, & Sameshima, 2009) is a methodological approach to qualitative research that utilizes the conventions of poetry as representational and presentational modalities. The poetry can originate from the researcher's own reflections about her or his experiences, or it can be adapted from the qualitative data collected (most often from interview transcripts) and constructed as "found poetry." As an example, the following poem (Miles, Huberman, & Saldaña, 2014, p. 187) represents an elementary fine arts magnet school's philosophy and curriculum goals according to its principal. The words were extracted from a portion of a one-hour interview and arranged by the researcher to capture essential content and, hopefully, to stimulate an aesthetic experience for its readers. The mission of this arts-centered school is to

Teach attitudes
    create whole people
    lifetime learners
Learn attitudes
    a love of problem solving
    elegance of expression
Teach and learn
    respectfully
    supportively
    joyfully

Performance artist Anna Deavere Smith (2000) asserts that people speak in "organic poetry" through their everyday discourse. She takes the most intriguing portions of their verbatim interview transcript texts and arranges them in free poetic verse formats for monologic presentation. An example of this technique is taken from an interview with a second-year doctoral student regarding his university program of study:

> I'm 27 years old and I've got over $50,000 in student loans that I have to pay off and that scares the hell out of me. I've got to finish my dissertation next year because I can't afford to keep going to school. I've got to get a job and start working.
>
> (Saldaña, 2013, p. 18)

If this excerpt were arranged into poetic form, it might read thus:

I'm 27 years old
and I've got
    over $50,000 in student loans   that I have to pay off
and that scares
the hell
    out of me.

I've got to finish my dissertation next year because
    I can't afford to   keep going to school.
I've got to get a job
    and start
        working. . . .

The parsing (i.e., each phrase on one line) and selected indents are strategies for emphasizing the constituent thoughts and erratic emotional journey of the doctoral student, which may get lost in an unbroken prosaic quotation. All the words in the poem are exactly the same as in the original quote, but the reformatting highlights each specific struggle and heightens the tension of the participant's dilemmas. Such exercises attune the analyst to each and every word of the text and force the careful search for nuances of meaning. See Mears (2009) for powerful examples of how organic poetic transcription and found poetry assist analysis.

Another approach to poetic inquiry is the researcher as self-reflective poet, composing original work synthesized from field experiences, methodological or analytic musings, or autoethnographic memories. As I composed this paragraph, I thought poetically about how to best express an example. What emerged (after five drafts) was the following poem about my ways of working as a qualitative researcher:

Method is my life partner.

I smile when I think of him
and his intricate complexity,
    grasping my hand firmly as I
    search for meaning.

He almost never leaves my mind.

Thinking poetically is analyzing and condensing large amounts of data into as few words as possible for the capture and evocation of core meanings – goals comparable to those of the methodologies of phenomenology and grounded theory. But this is not just about the quantity of words; it's also about the careful selection and arrangement of them to stimulate from readers and listeners powerful "wow" moments, or what is known among artists as aesthetic arrest. As you review text-based data from your study, find key words and phrases in your field notes, interview transcripts, documents, and so on that will serve the purposes of poetic composition. *In vivo* coding (using words or short phrases spoken by the participant) is one method to help get you there, but also rely on your intuitive capacity for determining what feels right artistically.

This thinking modality is not for everyone. I profiled poetic inquiry as a descriptive research method in one of my research methodology textbooks (Miles et al., 2014). A reviewer of the book's early manuscript questioned the inclusion of this approach with the critical comment, "Poetic inquiry – I just don't get it." I smiled and thought to myself, "Of course you don't." Researchers accustomed to more traditional conventions of quantitative and systematic qualitative data analysis (e.g., codes, categories, themes, theories) may find poetry a questionable approach to social investigation. Perhaps it is sometimes assumed that such inquiry is "fluff" or "less than" more rigorous analytic methods. You may be able to find receptive audiences among the poetically inclined, but, depending on your discipline, you may encounter strong resistance against and critical judgment of your work. Thus, poetic inquiry may serve as a viable method for the researcher's eyes only – a private data display for personal reflection that can stimulate later conventional forms of writing for public audiences.

FOR YOUR MENTAL ROLODEX: As you listen to participants in the field and review interview transcripts, remain vigilant for the organic poetry inherent in the data. Reformat some of your texts into poetic structures to explore how new meanings and understandings might be generated.

Thinking Proverbially

Aesop's fables have morals. Our research stories have theories. The classic tale of Aesop's "The Tortoise and the Hare" teaches readers that "Slow and steady wins the race." But a modern theory about achievement, developed from a case study of a university's unit reorganization, might propose that *Significant and sustained institutional change should occur by mandate from executive levels of power for initiation and transformation within limited time parameters.*

Our everyday lives are sometimes guided by folk wisdom in the form of proverbs – theories for productive living. When considering whether to indulge ourselves with a frivolous purchase, we might remember that "All that glitters is not gold." So we decide not to spend our hard-earned money carelessly because our reckless, "penny-wise and pound-foolish" buying experiences have taught us that "A fool and his money are soon parted." Having made a bad decision like this in our past makes us "Once bitten, twice shy." Instead, we refrain from making the purchase and take pride in our self-discipline, confident that "A penny saved is a penny earned." After all, "You never know what the future holds," so we should always "Set aside something for a rainy day" because "It's better to be safe than sorry."

Proverbs are theories about life and living. Recall from previous chapters that a theory (as it is traditionally conceived of in research) is a generalizable statement with an accompanying explanatory narrative that

- predicts and controls action through an if/then logic,
- accounts for variation in the empirical observations,
- explains how and/or why something happens by stating its cause(s), and
- provides insights and guidance for improving social life.

A proverb such as "If you lie down with dogs, you'll wake up with fleas" meets the criteria for a theory because it possesses an if/then logic, accounts for variation in behavior (good vs. bad), states the consequences of an action, and gives us insight into how we should conduct ourselves (i.e., we need to choose our companions and social settings cautiously to keep us out of trouble).

Different professions pass down insider knowledge or ways of working through aphorisms. Those in building construction teach their apprentices, "Measure twice, cut once." Veteran teachers share with novices, "Teachers don't always see what grows from seeds they've planted." A university professor of multicultural issues continually cautions his students, "This classroom will be safe, but it may not be comfortable." And a marriage counselor may regretfully advise clients, "Sometimes the best way to heal a relationship is to end it." Those who belong to Facebook might read friends' posts that share short quotes by famous people or nuggets of folk wisdom and motivational passages with accompanying pictures: "Do not judge by appearances: A rich heart may be under a poor coat" or "How others see you is not important; how you see yourself means everything."

Thinking proverbially succinctly phrases the life lessons heard during or suggested by your study. It works as a heuristic for collecting and analyzing the folk wisdom purported by your participants to discern the values, attitudes, and beliefs that may guide their actions. Your observations may also remind you of proverbs, pithy sayings, famous quotes, and the like from your own prior knowledge that are applicable to your study. One veteran teacher I observed reminded me that "All you need is love" for your students to get through difficult circumstances in the classroom. A bipolar, suicidal adolescent I interviewed said of himself (as his parents were recovering from drug and alcohol abuse), "What doesn't kill you makes you stronger."

If these pieces of folk wisdom are laypeople's informally phrased theories, then "Measure twice, cut once" might be expanded to read: *Significantly fewer errors will occur if the builder double-checks the measurements before cutting into construction materials*. But the simplicity and rhythm of "Measure twice, cut once" has more impact on one's memory. Kahneman (2011) advises that these proverbs or sayings have more staying power in our memories if they're elegant and especially if they rhyme ("An apple a day keeps the doctor away"). Hahn (2011, pp. 32–33) also suggests that we examine a proverb's opposing perspective to ensure that the first life lesson proposal for our study is not undercut by disconfirming evidence. We might posit that our participants confirm the adage, "You're never too old to learn." But is there anyone among the sample who supports, "You can't teach an old dog new tricks"? And don't forget to explore the canon of folk wisdom from other cultures, which offers unique insights on life. For example, we have these proverbs from Latin America: "The devil lurks even behind the cross," "Virtues all agree, but vices fight one another," and "He who speaks sows, and he who listens harvests" (Zona, 1996).

Many stage plays, teleplays, and screenplays are well known for their one-liners – memorable passages or quotable quotes that make an impact with their insight, irony, or poignancy (Trimble, 2006). Shakespeare's King Henry IV observed, "Uneasy lies the head that wears the crown." An adolescent character from the TV series *Boy Meets World* advises, "Life's tough; get a helmet." Dorothy from *The Wizard of Oz* film learns, "There's no place like home." These one-liners are comparable to proverbs, and in daily social life we should stay alert to such passages spoken by our participants that strike us as noteworthy nuggets of wisdom, for they have the potential to be built into a theory about our case. "Uneasy lies the head that wears the crown" begins a theoretical treatise on the emotional toll of responsibilities and hazards for those in leadership positions. In the everyday, real-life workplace, a disgruntled employee may observe about others, "Some people want all of the authority but none of the responsibility." This one-liner sets into motion an investigation of the validity of his assertion to further a study on power dynamics and relationships among an infighting staff.

The participants we interview or observe may occasionally say something offhandedly that strikes us as a profound insight. In my action research project with elementary school children to reduce bullying (Saldaña, 2005b), I was puzzled about why my efforts to teach peacekeeping and positive negotiation strategies were thwarted by young people's preferences for combative solutions. It all became clear when a fourth-grade girl told me, "Sometimes, you can't be nice to deal with oppression." That single quote became the throughline for the study's key assertion on power dynamics among youth. As another example, a university colleague and I once discussed how to achieve success in the entertainment industry, and I offered the legendary, "Well, it's not what you know but who you know." He countered with, "Wrong. It's not 'who you know'; it's *who knows you*." And as I reflect on the invitations offered to me by others in influential positions, I realize he was right. I now offer his advice instead of my tired cliché – affirmation that not all proverbs should be accepted unquestioningly.

If you feel unable to develop a formal theory about your research, first listen for what types of proverbs, folk sayings, and folk wisdom might be used by participants in their everyday interactions or during interviews, and reflect on what classic proverbs might seem relevant to your particular case. Though it may seem pedantic, reflect on what moral, life lesson, or cautionary advice might be suggested by your study. Think about not what you learned, but what your participants learned. And always keep your ears open for those significant participant one-liners that seem to summarize what the study is all about.

FOR YOUR MENTAL ROLODEX: As you investigate social life, attend to proverbs, folk wisdom, and significant quotes offered by participants. Use these as the basis for theory development from your study.

Closure

Sometimes what separates a great piece of research from a mediocre one is its writing finesse. New ideas certainly make an impact on readers, but the literary accessibility of a journal article, chapter, or book comes from the author's ability to communicate ideas in an engaging manner. "The essence of persuasion, communication, and self-understanding has become the ability also to fashion a compelling narrative" (Pink, 2006, p. 66). Writing is all about choices; the genres, elements, and styles you select to represent and present your study embody the totality of your inquiry.

Writing is also thinking. Therefore, writing poetically necessitates thinking poetically. Writing theoretically means thinking theoretically. And writing well requires thinking well. What you type on a keyboard, what appears on a monitor screen documents the thoughts formulated in your mind. What you create is a product of your thinking. The past ten chapters have offered various lenses, filters, and angles for your vision, in its broadest sense. It is now time to apply them on an as-needed, as-remembered, and as-inspired basis for your qualitative research studies.

Exercises for Thinking Narratively

1   Compose a one-page narrative monologue – a rant – about a social issue that easily angers you (e.g., economic disparity, ineffective government, gender inequality). Write your thoughts in everyday language and with uncensored honesty. Then privately voice out loud, nonstop, what you've written. Reflect on the experience of how verbalizing rather than just writing your thoughts may have impacted you.

2   Visit a field site where conversational exchanges are frequent (e.g., a restaurant, mall, social gathering). Listen to dialogic exchanges between people and focus not just on the content of the conversation but on the action, reaction, and interaction patterns they employ (e.g., turn-taking, question/answer, support, negation, disagreement, confirmation, laughter, verbal fluency).

3   Generate a two- to three-page selection from an interview transcript and apply *in vivo* coding to the text. (*In vivo* codes are words or short phrases

spoken by the participant that the researcher interprets as significant; see Saldaña, 2013, pp. 91–96.) Use the *in vivo* codes as resources to create a found poem about the participant's experiences.

4   Brainstorm a list of folk sayings, folk wisdom, or proverbs from your particular discipline – for example, in education, "To teach is to learn twice"; in counseling, "You can't see the frame when you're in the picture"; in design, "Less is more." Write about or discuss with a peer the possible origins and bases of experience of one or more of these proverbs from your field. Critique the proverbs' legitimacy, credibility, and applicability to contemporary thought and practice in your discipline.

References

Chang, H. (2008). *Autoethnography as method*. Walnut Creek, CA: Left Coast Press.
Clandinin, D. J., & Connelly, F. M. (2000). *Narrative inquiry: Experience and story in qualitative research*. San Francisco, CA: Jossey-Bass.
Coulter, C. A., & Smith, M. L. (2009). The construction zone: Literary elements in narrative research. *Educational Researcher, 38*(8), 577–590.
Ericsson, K. A., & Simon, H. A. (1993). *Protocol analysis: Verbal reports as data* (Rev. ed.). Cambridge, MA: Massachusetts Institute of Technology.
Finley, S., & Finley, M. (1999). Sp'ange: A research story. *Qualitative Inquiry, 5*(3), 313–337.
Gibbs, G. R. (2007). *Analysing qualitative data*. London: Sage.
Goodall, H. L., Jr. (2000). *Writing the new ethnography*. Walnut Creek, CA: AltaMira Press.
Gutkind, L. (Ed.). (2008). *Keep it real: Everything you need to know about researching and writing creative nonfiction*. New York: W. W. Norton.
Hahn, D. (2011). *Brainstorm: Unleashing your creative self*. New York: Disney Editions.
Holstein, J. A., & Gubrium, J. F. (Eds.). (2012). *Varieties of narrative analysis*. Thousand Oaks, CA: Sage.
Jones, S. H., Adams, T. E., & Ellis, C. (Eds.). (2013). *Handbook of autoethnography*. Walnut Creek, CA: Left Coast Press.
Kahneman, D. (2011). *Thinking, fast and slow*. New York: Farrar, Straus and Giroux.
Mears, C. L. (2009). *Interviewing for education and social science research: The gateway approach*. New York: Palgrave Macmillan.
Miles, M. B., Huberman, A. M., & Saldaña, J. (2014). *Qualitative data analysis: A methods sourcebook* (3rd ed.). Thousand Oaks, CA: Sage.
Murray, M. (2008). Narrative psychology. In J. A. Smith (Ed.), *Qualitative psychology: A practical guide to research methods* (2nd ed.) (pp. 111–132). London: Sage.
Norris, J., Sawyer, R. D., & Lund, D. E. (2012). *Duoethnography: Dialogic methods for social, health, and educational research*. Walnut Creek, CA: Left Coast Press.
Peshkin, A. (1986). *God's choice: The total world of a fundamentalist Christian school*. Chicago: University of Chicago Press.
Pink, D. H. (2006). *A whole new mind: Why right-brainers will rule the future*. New York: Riverhead Books.
Poulos, C. N. (2009). *Accidental ethnography: An inquiry into family secrecy*. Walnut Creek, CA: Left Coast Press.
Prendergast, M., Leggo, C., & Sameshima, P. (Eds.). (2009). *Poetic inquiry: Vibrant voices in the social sciences*. Rotterdam: Sense Publishers.
Riessman, C. K. (2008). *Narrative methods for the human sciences*. Thousand Oaks, CA: Sage.

Saldaña, J. (Ed.). (2005a). *Ethnodrama: An anthology of reality theatre*. Walnut Creek, CA: AltaMira Press.

Saldaña, J. (2005b). Theatre of the oppressed with children: A field experiment. *Youth Theatre Journal, 19*, 117–133.

Saldaña, J. (2011). *Fundamentals of qualitative research*. New York: Oxford.

Saldaña, J. (2013). *The coding manual for qualitative researchers* (2nd ed.). London: Sage.

Sawyer, R. D., & Norris, J. (2013). *Duoethnography*. New York: Oxford.

Seidman, I. (2013). *Interviewing as qualitative research: A guide for researchers in education and the social sciences* (4th ed.). New York: Teachers College Press.

Smith, A. D. (2000). *Talk to me: Listening between the lines*. New York: Random House.

Spry, T. (2011). *Body, paper, stage: Writing and performing autoethnography*. Walnut Creek, CA: Left Coast Press.

Trimble, E. (2006). *Quote unquote volume 4: Movie quotes for unscripted moments*. Sherman Oaks, CA: Autumn Leaves.

Van Maanen, J. (2011). *Tales of the field: On writing ethnography* (2nd ed.). Chicago: University of Chicago Press.

Wolcott, H. F. (1994). *Transforming qualitative data: Description, analysis, and interpretation*. Thousand Oaks, CA: Sage.

Zona, G. A. (1996). *Eyes that see do not grow old: The proverbs of Mexico, Central and South America*. New York: Touchstone.

7 Writing for the Research Studio

The Art of Teaching Research Methods

I always refer to my qualitative methods classroom or workshop space as a *research studio*, meaning a place to experiment mentally, physically, and creatively with inquiry processes. My other course teaching assignments in educational drama – acting, puppetry, improvisation, and so on – are active, participatory studio courses, and my research methods classes and workshops are no exception. I cannot teach any other way except through on-your-feet experiential pedagogy. Lecture time in my theatrical studio classes is kept to a minimum. Bodies are guided in motion to develop essential skills for presentation and performance. Student voices offer personal expression with emotional layers and nuances of character. But what happens in my qualitative research methods courses, whose topics are normally instructed in and relegated to the seminar or colloquium format?

Just as performance courses begin with physical and vocal warm-ups to prepare the actor's instrument, every research methods class begins with a five-minute mental warm-up. Students, in pairs, play the card game *Three for All!* (http://bit.ly/1fQVijS; also see www.remote-associates-test.com/) the first half of the semester to develop their coding and categorization skills, plus to exercise their cognitive capacities for inductive, abductive, and deductive reasoning. The second half of the semester we play *Set* (www.setgame.com/), an advanced card game that strengthens students' classification and data analytic capacities further. My research methods workshop warm-ups with in-service professionals utilize the card game *Pickles to Penguins!* (www.outsetmedia.com/games/pickles-to-penguins/party-game), which initiates them to the analytic concepts of pattern construction, data interrelationships, story-line, unity, and influences and affects (the qualitative parallel of the quantitative paradigm's "cause and effect"). All these exercises are intended to develop students' data analytic skills from the very beginning of and throughout the semester, rather than saving them for application during the latter portion of the course where qualitative data analysis is traditionally relegated. To me, data analysis is one of the most difficult subtopics of inquiry for novices to grasp, so the earlier I can introduce and cultivate these essential skill sets, the better (Saldaña & Omasta, 2018).

Drama educators create simulated social worlds in the classroom where students can improvise in imaginary circumstances as appropriate characters. My research methods classroom simulates fieldwork with exercises in students interviewing each other, and visiting an on-campus site to practice participant observation and field note writing before venturing into authentic research projects off-campus. Analytic exercises utilize index cards and sticky notes with data, codes, categories, themes, and assertions laid out, arranged, and rearranged on large tables. Sometimes we embody the data and move through the studio space to kinesthetically explore analytic concepts such as taxonomies, hierarchies, processes, trajectories, synthesis, causation, and influences and affects.

Film is the digital cousin of live theatre, and selected titles in cinema are viewed in the research methods classroom and workshop to both engage students through pedagogical novelty, and to illustrate principles of inquiry through artistic metaphor (Saldaña, 2009). The opening scene of *Kinsey* is only 90 seconds in length, but packed into that clip are virtually all the principles of an effective interview protocol with participants. We watch the excerpt and discuss its relevance and application to qualitative research practice. The opening scene from the documentary *Super Size Me* serendipitously parallels the qualitative research design process. Other film excerpts from titles such as *A Beautiful Mind*, *The Final Cut*, and *Arrival* illustrate and simulate the researcher's analytic processes. Films are metaphors for human experience. Strategically selected excerpts from them serve as metaphors for the research enterprise.

Classroom questions, discussion, and oral reflection are certainly important components for a course in human inquiry, but talk alone does not maximize learning. A classic teaching proverb goes, "I hear and I forget; I see and I remember; I do and I understand." If the greatest learning comes from doing (and educational research supports this), then the research methods classroom should be as physically active as possible. We cannot assume that all upper-division and graduate students are intrinsically motivated to give their full, focused attention during a sit-down seminar that demands higher-order thinking skills. The instructor is responsible for making learning participatory and, if possible, even joyous for learners of all ages.

This chapter includes the individual, small group, and whole class exercises and activities designed to accompany *The Coding Manual for Qualitative Researchers* (Saldaña, 2016). They represent the types of active learning approaches used in my research methods classroom and professional development workshops. These activities cannot be completed sitting still at a table or in a desk. Participants must be on their feet, moving their whole bodies, hands, and manipulatives to explore the research principles and concepts inherent in these activities. I abandoned long ago the stifling term "lesson plan" to refer to my written class preparation. I instead use the term *session design* to suggest a more artful composition for a dynamic classroom experience, regardless of subject or topic.

Professors and workshop facilitators are encouraged to integrate these ideas into their own courses. They have been written to facilitate easily by the first-time instructor. Published materials on research methods pedagogy are scant, so these selections are included in this volume to share a set of field-tested resources with fellow educators. It's what teachers do for one another.

References

Saldaña, J. (2009). Popular film as an instructional strategy in qualitative research methods courses. *Qualitative Inquiry, 15*(1), 247–261.
Saldaña, J. (2016). *The coding manual for qualitative researchers* (3rd ed.). London: Sage.
Saldaña, J., & Omasta, M. (2018). *Qualitative research: Analyzing life*. Thousand Oaks, CA: Sage.

EXERCISES AND ACTIVITIES FOR CODING AND QUALITATIVE DATA ANALYTIC SKILL DEVELOPMENT: FROM *THE CODING MANUAL FOR QUALITATIVE RESEARCHERS*

These activities can be conducted alone or with classmates and are intended to attune the researcher to basic principles of coding, pattern development, categorization, and qualitative data analysis. See this book's companion website [text below] for small and large group exercises.

Know Thyself

This exercise is prompted by the question, "Who are you?" Empty your purse, wallet, backpack, or briefcase and place all items on a table. Arrange, organize, and cluster those items that share similar characteristics (e.g., all writing instruments in one pile, all credit cards in one pile, all makeup in one pile). Give each pile its own label or category name, but avoid descriptive nouns such as MAKEUP; use more evocative labels such as GLAMOUR or MASKING MYSELF. Write an analytic memo on yourself that explores the assertion, "our identities are supported and altered by various forms of identification" (Prior, 2004, p. 88). Also address the higher-order analytic question: What do all the piles (categories) have in common? What is the Pattern Code?

Ten Books

This exercise can be done by one person. The purpose is to explore how many different ways you can categorize, classify, and order a data set.

Choose ten books (paper, not digital) at random from your personal library. Lay them on a table and explore as many different ways possible to organize them into patterns, clusters, and hierarchies. For example:

- one pile or group of hardback books, and one pile or group of paperback books
- one pile of fiction, and one pile of non-fiction
- laid out in order, from the smallest number of pages to the largest number of pages
- in order from the lightest in weight to the heaviest
- in order of copyright date
- from the most worn out to the most pristine
- in clusters of single and multiple (two, three, etc.) authors
- in order of probable resale price at a used bookstore
- from what you'd like to read over and over to what you'd most likely never read again

[Originally published in *The Coding Manual for Qualitative Researchers* (3rd ed.) by Johnny Saldaña, London: Sage Publications, 2016, pp. 311–313; edited slightly for this publication.]

- in clusters of illustrations included (non-illustrated, photographs, line drawings, color plates, mixed, etc.)

Exhaust a variety of additional ways to organize the ten books. Then write an analytic memo reflecting on the exercise and how this simulates the way researchers might explore and analyze a set of qualitative data.

Color Cards

This exercise can be done by one person. The purpose is to explore how to label and thus code a spectrum of data and categorize it.

Visit a paint retailer and pick up several different color card samples with three or four tints, hues, and shades of color on each card. Notice how the manufacturer often creates evocative names for each color. For example, a color palette of oranges I found on one Behr Paint card includes the names "Trick or Treat" (a light tan), "Roasted Seeds" (a pastel orange), "Pumpkin Puree" (a dark tan), and "Jack O Lantern" (a light brown). As an analytic and categorization exercise, name what these four color "codes" in the palette have in common – their theme. One possible (if not obvious) category label is "Halloween." But the goal is to make the category as creative as the related paint color codes. Thus, more evocative category names like "Fall Festival" or "October Night" to represent the four colors might better serve. Conduct this exercise with a few other color cards.

To further exercise your synthesizing abilities and creativity, put two different colors from separate color cards next to each other. For example, one combination might be "Moonlight Sonata" (a dark shade of blue) placed next to "Pancake" (a very light beige). If these two colors were literally or metaphorically mixed or swirled, what would be the name of the new combination? One label might be "Pancake Supper"; another could be "Blueberry Muffin." The analogy is that the two colors could be subcodes, and their combination is their parent code; or the two colors are separate categories that join together to form some type of relationship. Explore this exercise with a few varied two-color combinations.

Next, transfer this exercise to actual excerpts of qualitative data. . . . Collect three or four related interview or document excerpts and code them creatively, as done with paint colors. Then develop an evocative category label or thematic statement that unifies the codes.

Reference

Prior, L. (2004). Doing things with documents. In D. Silverman (Ed.), *Qualitative research: Theory, method and practice* (2nd ed.) (pp. 76–94). London: Sage.

GROUP EXERCISES: FROM *THE CODING MANUAL FOR QUALITATIVE RESEARCHERS*

These activities can be conducted with small or large groups and are intended to attune the researcher to basic principles of coding, pattern development, categorization, and qualitative data analysis.

The Pattern of Patterns

Patterns are ubiquitous in social and natural environments. Humans have a need and propensity to create patterns for order, function, or ornamentation, and those needs and thus skills transfer into our analysis of qualitative data. In a classroom or other average-size indoor environment (such as an office, small restaurant, or bedroom), look for and list all patterns observed. These can range from patterns in the architecture or décor (e.g., rows of fluorescent lighting tubes, slats in air conditioning vents) to patterns in furnishings and their arrangements (e.g., desks lined up in rows, vertically arranged cabinet drawers). Next, organize the individual items in your master list into categories – a "pattern of patterns." For example:

- *Decorative patterns* – those patterns that are purely ornamental or aesthetic, such as stripes on upholstery fabric, painted marbling on a wall
- *Organizational patterns* – those patterns that bring order to the environment or its artifacts, such as books of similar topics shelved together, various office supplies in appropriate bins
- *Other types of patterns you construct.*

Conduct the same exercise above in an outdoor/natural environment. However, create a different classification system for the individual patterns you observe (e.g., petals on a flower, leaves on a tree, clusters of cacti).

Next, list the patterns of actions in your own life you've experienced thus far today (e.g., not just what happened more than once today, but what series of actions happened today that were repeated from previous days). Formulate categories or themes to appropriately cluster and label these patterns (Saldaña, 2015, p. 45). Compare the patterns of your life with someone else's.

T-shirt Codes

This is a group exercise. Visit a clothing store, or have all members of a class wear a favorite t-shirt to a session. Address the following:

[Originally published on the Companion Website for *The Coding Manual for Qualitative Researchers* (3rd ed.) by Johnny Saldaña, London: Sage Publications, 2016; https://study.sagepub.com/node/31740/student-resources/chapter-6; edited slightly for this publication.]

What is the t-shirt made of? Look at the label (if any) sewn into the garment. That label, with information on the fabric composition and country of manufacture, is like an *Attribute Code* for the clothing item's contents. The label – the code – summarizes the entire t-shirt's basic contents.

What size is the t-shirt? Again, look at the label (or better still, try it on). The symbols S, M, L, XL, XXL, XXXL are *Magnitude Codes*. The experience of trying it on yourself gives you a better understanding of what that size code actually means. These days, what passes for "medium" in one brand of clothing may be labeled "large" by another manufacturer's line. If there is no label that specifies the t-shirt's size, use observation and comparison with other t-shirts to assess its probable size.

What words and/or images (if any) are on the front or back of the t-shirt? Those words and images are both textual and non-verbal *In Vivo Codes* for the garment. Cluster together with others wearing similarly coded shirts (a form of *Focused Coding*) and discuss not only what the messages have in common but also what the people wearing them have in common. What you identify for each cluster or category of people might be called a *Pattern Code*, based on the collective values, attitudes, and beliefs of the wearers – a form of *Values Code*.

Come, My Neighbor, If . . .

This popular theatre game is intended to build community, but it also serves as an exercise that demonstrates inclusion and exclusion criteria – in other words, categorization.

All participants stand in an open area that permits simple walking movement. One person at a time moves to an unoccupied area of the room calls out, "Come, my neighbor, if," followed by a prompt intended to learn who shares a similar quality. For example, if the prompt is, "Come, my neighbor, if you've ever taken a statistics course," all those who meet that criterion walk to and join the person, while those who have not move away from the person. Prompts can be descriptive or values-laden but should not be too personal. Examples include:

- "Come, my neighbor, if you've attended a college in a different state or country."
- "Come, my neighbor, if you love science fiction."
- "Come, my neighbor, if you're scared of the dark."
- "Come, my neighbor, if you've ever stayed overnight in a hospital."
- "Come, my neighbor, if you believe in the death penalty."
- "Come, my neighbor, if you feel you trust others too much."

After playing 15–20 prompts, group members discuss what they learned about each other through the exercise, and how binary or dichotomous categorization can sometimes be problematic.

Properties and Dimensions

The purpose of this exercise is to explore grounded theory's components of properties and dimensions. With peers, collect at least ten different fabric samples, swatches, or articles of clothing that are all the same general color (for example, all green) but vary in texture, saturation, pattern, and other design elements (for example, one article with green sequins, a swatch of green felt, a calico fabric with green motifs, and so on).

Lay the ten articles on a table and, with a small group, negotiate the arrangement of the items along several continua – for example, from the brightest tint to the darkest shade, from the roughest texture to the smoothest texture, from the most seemingly luxurious to the most seemingly homespun. Also explore the possible categorizations of the ten items – for example, a cluster of six that appear natural and a cluster of four that appear synthetic; or a cluster of three that suggest childhood, five that suggest maturity, and two that suggest elder status. Discuss the decision processes among the group that led to the results, and how the property of green has various dimensions.

Infer and interpret how each green fabric piece might symbolize different human personalities – for example, a dark green velvet as an upper class socialite, and a light green felt as a warm, nurturing parent. Discuss how their assigned attributes are comparable to the dynamics or range of human qualities, and how the variances play a role in grounded theory's search for the properties and dimensions of data.

The Spectrum of Difference

The Spectrum of Difference is a popular theatre game which demonstrates how people's attributes, preferences, opinions, and values, attitudes, and beliefs can be represented in three-dimensional space. The game serves as a way of simulating, diagnosing, and understanding how our research participants hold multiple perspectives on an issue. It also demonstrates how grounded theory's properties and dimensions of categories operate.

Players imagine that a line the length of a typical room is drawn on the floor. A prompt is called out and participants walk to and stand on a place on the imaginary line that represents their position about a descriptive or values-laden issue. The imaginary line is a continuum and each endpoint represents opposite sides of the prompt. For example, the leader calls out, "Are you a cat person (*pointing to one end of the imaginary line*) or a dog person (*pointing to the other end of the line*), or do you like both equally or have no opinion (*pointing to the center*)? Or maybe you align yourself more toward the cat side or dog side but not completely at the far ends (*pointing toward the one-third and two-thirds areas*). Go." Participants then move to and stand on the part of the line that they feel best represents their individual preferences for cats and/or dogs. They do not have to stand in single file; clusters around a point on the line are acceptable. The group diagnoses and discusses the results.

This same technique is repeated with a series of prompts prepared by the leader or offered by the participants. Prompts for the continuum can be realistic or metaphoric, and can focus on intrinsic, social, or thematic issues. For example:

- Are you a morning person or a night person?
- Are you a risk taker or do you play it safe?
- Are you the wind or the wings?
- What's more important to you: questions or answers?
- "I'm pro-life" or "I'm pro-choice."
- "Protect our borders" or "Tear down the wall."

Prompts such as the latter two are examples of "hot button" issues that can generate fruitful discussion and reflection by the group if facilitated with care.

The Landscape of Difference

Aside from The Spectrum of Difference, there is The Landscape of Difference which places participants in two- and three-dimensional positions according to multiple criteria. For example, the leader can prompt, "What do you prefer: pie or cake?" Players place themselves on the imaginary line in a continuum as they each see fit. But then the line becomes a landscape by prompting: "From the general area where you're standing, cake people: move to this side of the line if you're into white cake, this side of the line if you're into chocolate cake, and stay on the line if you're into specialty cakes like marble, yellow, or red velvet. Pie people: from the general area where you're standing, move to this side of the line if you're into fruit pies, this side of the line if you're into cream pies, and stay on the line if you're into other pies like mincemeat or pecan." The landscape can become even more dimensional if you ask: "From where you're standing, raise your hand high if you'd like a cold beverage with that dessert, or just a thumbs up if you'd prefer a hot beverage."

The Landscape of Difference positioning techniques can now be applied to more complex or nuanced prompts for participants to explore. Explore only topics you and the group feel comfortable with. Discuss the individual and collective process and results after each set of prompts:

- First Dimension (on the line): "I know who I am" or "I'm still searching for my identity." Second dimension (on either side of the line): "Other people have had more influence on who I am" or "I myself create who I am." Third dimension (hands up or thumbs up): "I've got a lot of work to do" or "I'm OK for now."
- First Dimension: "Public parking" or "No trespassing." Second Dimension: "On the ground" or "In the air." Third Dimension: "Maybe," or "Maybe not."

Advanced or willing groups can even explore a fourth dimension: movement in time. From the third dimension position, players can create a self-sculpted image, repeated gesture, or whole body movement that synthesizes and embodies the three dimensions' prompts. For a fifth dimension, players add repeated, evocative sounds or keywords to accompany their movement.

The Spectrum and Landscape of Difference are gaming diagnostics to assess the varying perspectives of the group, but they are also exercises to explore how qualitative data analysts can map out the properties and dimensions of data. After several rounds of play, the discussion can focus on how we interpret and write about these diverse positions and clusters of meaning in our reports. Discussion can also focus on how these three-dimensional displays can transfer into drawn displays on paper or as graphics with computing software.

Grounded Theory Carnival

This is a group exercise. "Carnival in Rio" (also known as "Homogenous Rhythms"), a game developed by theatre artist Augusto Boal, is a movement and sound exercise that, serendipitously, parallels the processes for developing grounded theory (GT). I facilitate the game in my research methods workshops to demonstrate how GT "works."

A large group of people first divides into smaller groups of three. Each of the individual small-group members creates a simple gesture (such as a hand wave or head tilt) that can be replicated and repeated easily by the other two in the small group, accompanied with a nonsensical sound (such as "beep" or "woop") that others can imitate. Then the other two small-group members each offer their own unique gesture – sound combinations to their partners for replication and repetition.

(ANALOGY: *Think of each person in the small group as a datum; their unique gestures are Process Codes, and their unique sounds In Vivo Codes. The preliminary sharing is a form of Open or Initial Coding.*)

After each small-group member shares a gesture and sound, they then *simultaneously* enact their unique sounds and gestures *repeatedly*. Through the processes of individual negotiation and non-verbal communication, the small group of three "morphs" or synthesizes their individual gestures and sounds so that all three evolve toward making the exact same gesture and sound repeatedly. The final small-group sequence might consist of one person's gesture combined with another person's sound, or a new composite movement that integrates two gestures with one person's sound, and so on.

(ANALOGY: *Think of the process above as Focused Coding to develop an initial category. Whatever thoughts run through an individual's mind are an analytic memo.*)

Each small group of three, now enacting its newly collective gesture and sound, joins another group of three doing its own unique gesture and sound. The process of morphing/synthesizing continues so that ever-increasing groups of 6, 9, 12 and so on evolve into more and more people gesturing and sounding the exact same way. Sometimes one gesture will dominate because it is easy to replicate; perhaps a sound will dominate because it is the loudest; perhaps a particular gesture/sound combination will dominate simply because most group members are doing it and the minority acquiesces to the majority; or a whimsical gesture/sound combination will prevail because its qualities appeal to the group.

(ANALOGY: *Think of the processes above as GT's Axial and Selective Coding.*)

The whole group eventually assembles standing in a circle as all participants continue to evolve their gestures and sounds. The goal or culminating product (ideally) is everyone making the exact same gesture and sound.

(ANALOGY: *The process above represents Theoretical Coding, resulting in the core category.*)

The group stops and reflects on the process. I clarify how each stage of game playing simulates the analytic stages of GT. We share our thought processes (the analytic memos) as we played to discover how we arrived at our "core category" and what the final gesture/sound combination might mean – our grounded theory (Birks & Mills, 2015, pp. 122–3).

Board Games

Several commercial board/DVD/electronic/app games actually provide valuable experience with exercising necessary analytic skills for the qualitative researcher, such as pattern recognition, coding and categorizing, and inductive, abductive, and deductive reasoning. A few of these games can be played by one person, but most work best with two or more players. Selected Internet sites about the games are listed; try Googling for additional sites:

- *Pickles to Penguins!* (www.outsetmedia.com/games/pickles-to-penguins/party-game)
- *Three for All!* (http://bit.ly/1fQVijS)
- *The $100,000 Pyramid* (http://pyramidanswers.blogspot.com/)
- *Scattergories* (www.hasbro.com/games/swf/scattergories_demo3.swf)
- *Simon* (www.kidsmathgamesonline.com/memory/simon.html)
- *Set* (www.setgame.com/)
- *Tribond* (http://tribond3.blogspot.com/)
- *Remote Associates Test* (www.remote-associates-test.com/)
- *Word Warp* (www.universaluclick.com/puzzles/wordwarp)

See also Waite (2011) for a clever classroom exercise in sorting a deck of playing cards to stimulate student discussion about categories and discrepant cases.

Popular Film Viewing

Selected popular films include scenes that illustrate the characters in analytic life dilemmas (Saldaña, 2009). These conflicts are artistic metaphors, comparable to what the qualitative researcher encounters when coding and analyzing data. View and reflect on relevant scenes from the titles below with peers to discuss how certain principles of qualitative inquiry are depicted and can transfer to your own work.

Research Genres

- Case studies: *The Final Cut, The Truman Show, 49 Up* (and the entire *Up* series)
- Survey research: *Kinsey*
- Quantitative (and qualitative) research: π [*Pi*], *A Beautiful Mind*
- Longitudinal research/change: *The Truman Show, 56 Up, Half Nelson, Boyhood*
- Action research: *Dangerous Minds, Kindergarten Cop*
- Life course research: *The Final Cut, 56 Up*
- Phenomenology: *Silence of the Lambs*
- Field experiments: *Super Size Me*
- Critical ethnography: *Bowling for Columbine*
- Performance ethnography/ethnodrama: *Twilight: Los Angeles, The Laramie Project, The Exonerated, United 93, Howl, The Stanford Prison Experiment*

Research Methodology and Methods

- Epistemology and ontology: *The Matrix, Inception, Source Code, Interstellar*
- Research design: *Super Size Me, Experimenter: The Stanley Milgram Story*
- Research ethics: *The Truman Show, Krippendorf's Tribe, Miss Evers' Boys, Experimenter: The Stanley Milgram Story, The Stanford Prison Experiment*
- Participant observation/fieldwork: *The Truman Show, Gorillas in the Mist, Looking for Comedy in the Muslim World, Kitchen Stories, WALL-E, Avatar, Arrival, Following* (1998), *Dark Mysterious Austria* [available on YouTube]
- Interview techniques: *Kinsey, 49 Up, The Laramie Project, The Guys, Looking for Comedy in the Muslim World, The Help*
- Inductive, abductive, deductive, and retroductive reasoning: *Memento, Fargo,* π [*Pi*], *Silence of the Lambs, A Beautiful Mind, Sherlock Holmes* (2009), *Sherlock Homes: A Game of Shadows*
- Codes and categories: *The Final Cut*
- Triangulation: *Minority Report*
- Cause and effect, influences and affects: *The Butterfly Effect, World War Z*
- Correlation/interrelationship: *An Inconvenient Truth, The Number 23*
- Data analysis: *A Beautiful Mind, Contact, The Final Cut, Silence of the Lambs, The Imitation Game*
- Mixed methods: *Super Size Me*

References

Birks, M., & Mills, J. (2015). *Grounded theory: A practical guide* (2nd ed.). London: Sage.

Saldaña, J. (2009). Popular film as an instructional strategy in qualitative research methods courses. *Qualitative Inquiry, 15*(1), 247–261.

Saldaña, J. (2015). *Thinking qualitatively: Methods of mind*. Thousand Oaks, CA: Sage.

Waite, D. (2011). A simple card trick: Teaching qualitative data analysis using a deck of playing cards. *Qualitative Inquiry, 17*(10), 982–985.

8 Writing Research as Reader's Theatre

Presenting Performatively

I become easily frustrated when I see and hear poor presenters at conferences. Their monotone voices, lack of eye contact, nervous body language, and robotic delivery style disengage me from their reportage. We teach scholars how to write well, but not many know how to speak effectively in front of a small audience of peers. I remember virtually nothing of what these boring presenters said.

My own academic conference presentations are frequently scripted. I feel more secure with a prepared text in front of me, permitting my mental energies to focus on my oral delivery. But what I do that perhaps others don't are three things: (1) rehearse, (2) rehearse, and (3) rehearse. I practice my presentations out loud and non-stop a minimum of three times before the actual event. I practice in the vocal volume I might actually need for the presentation, and I deliberately practice eye contact with an imaginary audience in front of me. After each rehearsal reading I reflect on the text and how it might be revised to make me more comfortable as a speaker and more accessible to a listener.

This is also a flaw of poor conference presenters. Sometimes their prepared texts are written in discourse appropriate for a peer reviewed journal article but inappropriate for a live audience *hearing* their presentations for the first time. A research paper laden with technical terms, dense vocabulary, and overly long sentences is somewhat difficult to take in and comprehend, especially if the presenter speaks rapidly in order to meet a required time limit.

Conference presentations should be written to be audience-friendly: in everyday language as much as possible, with results presented toward the beginning of the paper rather than the end, and scripted elegantly to permit speaking at a relaxed rate. Too often when we prepare research material for oral presentation, we tend to write as if its destination is a print medium. Instead, consider how the paper might be written to *sound* effectively to a listener.

One of my assertions about researchers is that we try to prove to others how smart we are. That drive might motivate the need to compose our oral texts in formal structures with complex sentences and an advanced vocabulary. The smartest presenters, to me, are those who recognize that I'm hearing about their work for the very first time. The smartest presenters are those who look me in the eye and talk *to* me, not at me. The smartest presenters are those who know how to tell a good story with both simple language and rich voices. The smartest presenters are those who have thought carefully about every word they're going to say, and who have rehearsed delivering those words for maximum impact. You needn't be a trained actor or public speaker to present well; you just need to be honest, genuine, and sincerely believe what you're saying to your fellow researchers.

Reader's theatre has been called "theatre of the mind" because it relies primarily on the reader's voice to conjure evocative imagery in the listener's head. Traditional reader's theatre uses a minimal amount of stage production elements such as large scenery and lighting effects, but small-scale hand properties, connotative dress, projections, and music/sound effects are sometimes utilized. The text – whether fiction or nonfiction, prosaic, poetic, or dramatic – is central to this presentation genre, but it also relies on readers with the ability to engage an audience through dynamic vocalization, and thoughtful interpretation of the writer's ideas. The minimalist production demands of reader's theatre make it an accessible presentation method for a variety of venues including research conferences.

The selection in this chapter represents a collaborative effort between a four-member research team. Our first published report, written as a conventional research journal article, can be accessed from McCammon, Saldaña, Hines, and Omasta (2012). Below, we present the scripted reader's theatre presentation delivered at one research conference and at a research awards presentation sponsored by our professional association, The American Alliance for Theatre & Education.

Our mixed methods study, "Lifelong Impact: Adult Perceptions of Their High School Speech and/or Theatre Participation," collected online quantitative and qualitative survey responses from 234 participants. All respondents, ranging in age from 18 to 70+, participated in high school speech and/or theatre classes and related extracurricular programming (e.g., speech tournaments, play productions). The primary purpose of the study was to determine in what ways participation in these high school subjects may have positively influenced and affected adults after graduation. The second purpose was to identify, describe, and advocate the potentially beneficial and lifelong impacts speech/theatre participation during adolescence can contribute to adulthood.

All four research team members are theatre artists, so the presentation of our findings would be performative in some way through our practiced oral delivery skills. But the format of our presentation took an interesting shape as we discussed how it would be done and who would say what. Since the study examined speech and theatre, it seemed only natural that we use those field's devices to represent and present our research. Reader's theatre, described in the article below, served as the modality for our conference report.

A handful of scholars before us had already employed reader's theatre for their research publications and presentations, so our approach was not novel or unique. But what *did* emerge during rehearsals and performances was a shared phenomenon among the four team members: Voicing out loud the participants' testimony gave us new and heightened awareness of the data. As actors, we instinctively embodied the inferred personalities of the survey respondents when we spoke aloud what they wrote to us. Our performative immersion when telling their stories in front of an audience led to a state of consciousness we labeled *reinteracting* (explained later). Perhaps that is why I advocate that qualitative researchers should physicalize their analyses through abstract movement or even dance – to think not just with the mind but with the body. Performing the "character" of our participants, in their own words, brings us closer to understanding their worldview.

"The Reader's Theatre Script for 'Lifelong Impact: Adult Perceptions of Their High School Speech and/or Theatre Participation'" from *Youth Theatre Journal* will describe the development of the piece, and offer commentary on how dramatizing our research *and performing it* may lead to powerful insights about whom and what we study.

Reference

McCammon, L. A., Saldaña, J., Hines, A., & Omasta, M. (2012). Lifelong impact: Adult perceptions of their high school speech and/or theatre participation. *Youth Theatre Journal*, *26*(1), 2–25.

THE READER'S THEATRE SCRIPT FOR "LIFELONG IMPACT: ADULT PERCEPTIONS OF THEIR HIGH SCHOOL SPEECH AND/OR THEATRE PARTICIPATION"

Laura A. McCammon, Johnny Saldaña, Angela Hines, and Matt Omasta

Abstract

This article includes a reader's theatre script adapted from a full-length qualitative study, "Lifelong Impact: Adult Perceptions of Their High School Speech and/or Theatre Participation." The report first reviews reader's theatre as an arts-based form of research representation and presentation, then surveys key figures from qualitative inquiry and theatre education involved with interdisciplinary collaborations. The coauthors then discuss one of their key learnings from their experiences with performing the research, labeled "reinteracting the data" – a triple compound word of acting, reacting, and interacting with the dramatized text and our audiences.

Reader's Theatre and Performance as Research Modalities

Reader's theatre as a form of qualitative research representation and presentation has been employed for several decades in such diverse fields as education, sociology, and nursing (e.g., Bloom et al., 2009; Donmoyer & Yennie-Donmoyer, 1995, 2008; Lewis, 2011; McIntyre, 2009; Pardue, 2004; Walker, Pick, & Mac-Donald, 1991; cf. Downey, 2008). A few distinguished scholars from educational research, such as Robert Donmoyer, also have theatre training and experiences in their backgrounds. Donmoyer's reader's theatre (and general) presentations at national conferences of the American Educational Research Association (AERA) demonstrate a performative finesse through a confident presence, rich voice, and purposeful movement comparable to stage blocking.

Other noted researchers and methodologists in the field of qualitative inquiry, such as Valerie Janesick, Patricia Leavy, and Yvonna S. Lincoln, do not focus on theatre as their current fields of study, yet they do have experience with high school theatre as either students or teachers and draw on those experiences to inform their rich writings and conference presentations. Others in the field of educational research, such as Tara Goldstein (2001, 2002, 2004, 2006, 2008), have experimented with adapting their participant observation field notes and interview transcripts into ethnodramatic play formats yet have done so without a theatre background. Goldstein became so invested in the process of performance ethnography that she enrolled in a playwriting program as a postdoctoral student for her professional development as an artist. And one of the most

[Originally published in *Youth Theatre Journal*, vol. 26, no. 1, 2012, pp. 26–37; doi 10.1080/08929092.2012.678218; edited slightly for this publication.]

internationally recognized qualitative research methodologists, Norman K. Denzin (1997, 2003), learned midcareer about the power of performance and now champions it within the research community as one of the most powerful ways to interrogate and represent human experience.

During the two past decades, there seems to have been an accelerated interest among selected social scientists for performance ethnography and other dramatic forms of research representation, initiated by a slew of influential, multidisciplinary writings by Dwight Conquergood, Jim Mienczakowski, and Richard Schechner (and, of course, the seminal work of sociologist Erving Goffman and anthropologist Victor Turner before them). Noted performance studies scholars within the discipline of human communication, such as Bryant Keith Alexander, Ronald J. Pelias, and Tami Spry, have been particularly present and influential at the International Congress of Qualitative Inquiry (ICQI) with their readings and productions.

Selected scholars within the American Alliance for Theatre & Education's membership and our sister organizations worldwide also attend and network within AERA and ICQI. Veteran educational theatre researchers, such as George Belliveau, Diane Conrad, Kathleen Gallagher, Laura A. McCammon, Robin Mello, David Montgomery, Joe Norris, Monica Prendergast, Johnny Saldaña, Kent Seidel, Philip J. Taylor, Prue Wales, and several others, regularly attend these events and keep theatre actively present within conference programming. ICQI regularly sponsors preconference workshops in performative research for its nontheatre participants. And Joe Norris's (2010) work, *Playbuilding as Qualitative Research*, received the prestigious 2011 Outstanding Book Award from AERA's Qualitative Research Special Interest Group, followed by Johnny Saldaña's (2011) *Ethnotheatre: Research from Page to Stage* as the 2012 winner.

In sum, nontheatre scholars within the field of qualitative inquiry have discovered and generated "the performative turn" (e.g., Denzin, 2003; Janesick, 2011; Knowles & Cole, 2008; Leavy, 2009) for social science research in education, sociology, anthropology, psychology, and even in disciplines such as sports, nursing, and health care, providing a welcome opening and opportunities for theatre educators in higher education to collaborate with and influence receptive colleagues. The arts – theatre in particular – may be relegated to second-class status in many kindergarten through twelfth-grade public education programs but now hold legitimate representational and presentational capital among major qualitative researchers worldwide. It is imperative that researchers and practitioners in educational theatre network with high-profile methodologists in large organizations such as AERA (www.aera.net) and ICQI (www.icqi.org), plus at allied gatherings of such organizations as the American Anthropological Association (particularly its Society for Humanistic Anthropology, www.aaanet.org), the National Communication Association (www.natcom.org), the National Council of Teachers of English Assembly for Research (nctear.org), and *The Qualitative Report* annual conference (http://nsuworks.nova.edu/tqrc/).

The Performance of Our Research

The January 2011 Narrative, Arts-Based, and "Post" Approaches to Social Research (NAPAR) conference in Tempe, AZ, was the first event at which the coresearchers of the "Lifelong Impact" study presented their work. McCammon and Saldaña, as the primary coauthors of the full technical report, instinctively felt that the nature of the conference demanded not a conventional lecture presentation but an arts-based approach to harmonize with conference goals. Because the study itself focused on educational theatre and speech, it seemed almost a "given" that a reader's theatre adaptation and performance of the report would be presented.

The thirty-minute time limit for the conference session forced us to dramatize only a portion of the full study, so we focused on participant responses to the survey question, "In what ways do you think your participation in speech and/or theatre as a high school student has affected the adult you have become?" because the participants' answers to this question were the richest in the database. Omasta reviewed more than two hundred responses and selected the most salient and representative, which were then further streamlined into drafts by Saldaña and reviewed by McCammon and Hines.

We opted not to venture into standalone respondent testimony for the reader's theatre script because we felt the outcomes of the research study were just as important to share with our audience of educators. The conventions of traditional text-based reader's theatre scripts, rather than those of more commercial, field research-based play productions such as *The Laramie Project* and *The Exonerated*, seem to permit more scholarly language woven throughout the script. And the contexts of a reader's theatre presentation at research-oriented conference sessions of professional associations permit a more academic tone in its writing. The following reader's theatre script is not what most theatre practitioners might label as high dramatic "art," but we do not suggest that it is. We provide an example, not an exemplar, of dramatized research – a genre that serves a double agenda: (1) to present the major findings of a study, and (2) to present authentic participant testimony that supports the findings.

There is little utility in describing the detailed script development process of the "Lifelong Impact" report for a theatre education readership. Most practitioners familiar with reader's theatre are already acquainted with common adaptation techniques, such as editing, condensing, and summarizing, and the decision-making processes of what seems necessary to include and exclude from the final text. We will, however, focus on one aspect that seems to have made an impact on the coresearchers: the postperformance effects of voicing aloud the data.

Only on rare occasions will a qualitative researcher actually voice out loud what he or she has collected in the field and transcribed or documented. For example, those who use voice recognition software calibrated to one's own voice may listen to the audio recording of an interview, then repeat and speak aloud the participant's words into a microphone that the computer software realizes through automatically generated written text. But most often in qualitative inquiry, the lone researcher works silently with data stored in electronic files or on paper and reflects on the text's meanings in his or her mind.

Saldaña, as an ethnodramatic playwright and journal peer reviewer of nontheatre researchers' scripts, encourages in reviews and revision recommendations that the writer voice aloud, nonstop, the entire script that he or she has written. This technique encourages the researcher to take ownership of each and every single word written on paper. The primary goal is to heighten the researcher/playwright's awareness of language choices, yet the covert purpose is to make the writer realize how fatiguing it may be to read aloud a pedantic, "talking heads" play script in severe need of editing and rewriting. A balance must be found between the rigorous expectations of conventional qualitative research discourse and the more aesthetic properties of effective playwriting. The key advice shared with these nontheatre novice playwrights is, "Stop thinking like a social scientist and start thinking like an artist" (Saldaña, 2011).

When the coresearchers performed our "Lifelong Impact" reader's theatre script at the NAPAR, AERA, and AATE conferences, we noticed ourselves as theatre artists naturally bringing our acting and oral interpretation of literature training into our voicing of the participants' honest and heartfelt stories. But the actual *voicing out loud* of the data, even after months of rigorous and detailed qualitative data analysis on a computer monitor and on paper, brought new cognitive insights to and emotional reverberation with our study. It stimulated nuanced awareness among the coresearchers, sometimes in aesthetic arrest over the power of a team member's interpretation during the performance. Hines noted that the voicing out loud of our data also motivated several audience members to retell their own stories of how theatre and speech participation in high school impacted their lives.

We propose that the oral interpretation of qualitative data – specifically, the participant's own words from an interview transcript or written document such as a journal or open-ended survey response – takes the researcher to a new level or position of understanding the phenomenon that cannot be accomplished through traditional inner monologic reflection and conventionally silent data analytic methods. Some would call voicing aloud one's data as "embodiment" of the experience, but the term has been overused (if not abused) in certain research circles. Others have coined such terms as taking "cognitive ownership" of the empirical materials, or employing "performative ontologies" to suggest what we mean here.

The coresearchers propose that we were *reinteracting the data*. "Reinteracting" is a triple compound word that suggests we were simultaneously acting, reacting, and interacting during performance. We *acted* the lines we were each assigned to speak aloud – sometimes technical and formal text and sometimes participant testimony that we ourselves had experienced and emotionally connected with. We *reacted* to the prompts for our next line and to the meanings our cue lines suggested for our interpretation, as well as to spontaneous reactions to and from our audiences. And we *interacted* as coperformers in a sometimes rapidly cascading series of short texts that demanded our focused attention lest we missed a cue, and we interacted intimately with our relatively small but collegial audiences during the readings. Reinteracting the data is a researcher's arts-based aesthetic that suggests inquiring and performative immersion in an event – a holistic interconnection between the researcher, coperformers, participants, and audience members that hopefully leads to new and deeper understandings about an experience or phenomenon.

Saldaña (2008) asserts that there are "drama" and "poetry" to qualitative method, if the analyst is attuned to the artist within. Some may see thousands of words in a data corpus as a confusing mess to grudgingly wade through, rather than as a beautiful and exciting mystery story waiting to be solved. The latter perspective keeps the researcher better motivated for intense qualitative work and employs what theatre artists already do for a living: analyzing texts carefully to realize them in creative, performative ways.

The four coresearchers and coperformers hope that the reader's theatre version and presentation of our work was novel, informative, and artistically satisfying for those in attendance at the August 2011 AATE Research Awards session, yet still met our colleagues' expectations for a credible and trustworthy research report.

The Reader's Theatre Script: "Lifelong Impact"[1]

(*The four coresearchers are seated facing the audience; they each hold a black notebook containing the script and read aloud from it. All passages in quotation marks consist of participants' written survey responses. LAURA and ANGIE voice female participant responses; JOHNNY and MATT voice the male participant responses.*)

SCENE 1

JOHNNY: "Working in theatre in high school actually helped me become alive as a human being as well as a student."

LAURA: "Theatre gave me confidence that continues with me through today."

ANGIE: "Theatre helped me see life from all sorts of angles more than I did before."

MATT: "Without my theatre program, I have no clue where I would be today."

LAURA: The purpose of the Lifelong Impact study was to determine in what ways participation in high school theatre or speech classes and related extracurricular activities, such as play productions and speech tournaments, may have positively influenced and affected adults after graduation.

JOHNNY: Several published studies exist that describe high schoolers' perceptions of their experiences *as* they're enrolled in secondary school, but virtually no systematic research exists that explores how adults from ages eighteen to seventy-plus [years old] remember and reflect on those same events.

LAURA: Coresearchers Laura A. McCammon of the University of Arizona,
JOHNNY: and Johnny Saldaña of Arizona State University
LAURA: initiated the project in fall 2009 and collected data through e-mail surveys sent directly to potential participants and forwarded to contacts such as speech and theatre teachers for purposive and referral sampling.
ANGIE: Angie Hines served as a research assistant.
MATT: Matt Omasta served as a research consultant.
JOHNNY: Two hundred and thirty-four respondents returned completed surveys;
LAURA AND ANGIE: approximately two-thirds of the participants are female;
JOHNNY AND MATT: one-third are male.
JOHNNY: Participants were asked to provide basic demographic information such as their location:
(*ALL simultaneously*)
LAURA: "Alabama, Arizona, British Colombia, California, Colorado."
ANGIE: "Hawaii, Illinois, Indiana, Kansas, Louisiana, Michigan."
JOHNNY: "New Hampshire, New Jersey, New York, Ohio."
MATT: "Ontario, Oregon, Tennessee, Texas, Utah, Wisconsin."
MATT: "No Response."
JOHNNY: their years of high school attendance,
(*ALL simultaneously*)
LAURA: "1953, 2009, 2007, 2006."
ANGIE: "1957, 1968, 1999, 1996."
JOHNNY: "1958, 1989, 1988, 1986."
MATT: "1960, 1961, 1965, 1979."
MATT: "No Response."
JOHNNY: the types of drama/theatre classes they took during high school, the types of subject-related activities they participated in, and their current occupation:
(*ALL simultaneously*)
LAURA: "Administrative assistant, history major, nurse, unemployed, acting major, high school theatre teacher, stay-at-home mom."
ANGIE: "Active-duty Air Force, mayor pro-tem, piano teacher, dairy farm owner, pharmacist, textbook editor."
JOHNNY: "High school English teacher, retired, actor/model, law student, volunteer firefighter, CEO of a technology company."
MATT: "Restaurant manager, lawyer, optometrist, military officer, medical software technician, wine marketing consultant, Internet consultant."
MATT: "No Response."
JOHNNY: Participants represented graduation years as early as 1953 to as recent as 2009,
ANGIE: and attended high schools representing thirty-six American states and two Canadian provinces.
LAURA: Approximately 52 percent are currently in theatre-related occupations or studying theatre in higher education,

MATT: while the other 48 percent range in occupation from administrative assistants to biology teachers to attorneys.
LAURA: Participants also responded to survey prompts that asked them to quantitatively rate and qualitatively reflect on:
JOHNNY: their high school theatre and speech teachers,
ANGIE: their theatre and speech participation,
MATT: challenges they faced,
LAURA: favorite memories,
ANGIE: major learnings and outcomes,
MATT: and speculation on how participation in high school speech and theatre may have influenced and affected the adults they became.

SCENE 2

JOHNNY: The key assertion of this study is: Quality high school theatre and speech experiences can not only significantly influence but even accelerate adolescent development and provide residual, positive, lifelong impacts throughout adulthood.
LAURA: Speech and theatre teachers who maintained high standards for and expectations of quality work, and who nurtured their students personally and artistically with an ethic of care and encouragement in safe environments, were regarded by survey respondents as those who made a lifelong impact on their adulthoods.
JOHNNY: Survey question: In what ways do you think your participation in speech and/or theatre as a high school student has affected the adult you have become?
ANGIE: High school English teacher, Class of 2006: "Although I don't feel like being involved in theatre has changed my life, it definitely changed my high school experience. It was something I worked hard at, enjoyed, and looked forward to."
LAURA: Global leader for a major corporation, Class of 1984: "Any career success I've experienced is largely due to the combination of process thinking developed in engineering school and, more significantly, my theatre, speech, and debate experience in high school. I learned to communicate effectively, write well, speak clearly and distinctly, engage and hold an audience with pacing, inflection, movement."
JOHNNY: Quality manager for a manufacturing company, Class of 1982: "It really has not changed my adult life at all."
MATT: Hollywood sound effects and dialogue editor, Class of 1999: "Theatre and speech saved mine and my brother's lives."
JOHNNY: Four categories of outcome were constructed from survey data:
LAURA: Lifelong Self-Confidence,
MATT: Lifelong Thinking and Working,
ANGIE: Lifelong Living and Loving,
JOHNNY: and Lifelong Legacy.

SCENE 3

ALL: Lifelong Self-Confidence.

JOHNNY: CEO of a technology company, Class of 1988: "Theatre gave me confidence, experience in public speaking, the ability to react quickly with a 'show must go on' attitude when things go wrong."

LAURA: Survey respondents overwhelmingly testified that a sense of *self-confidence* was a significant outcome of their high school theatre and/or speech programming. Students physically and vocally transcended their "comfort zones" and made themselves open to performance and presentation experiences that, across time, developed expressive, outgoing, and independent personas:

ANGIE: Part-time work and part-time college student, Class of 1997: "I have a great deal of self-confidence and self-esteem now. If I can get up in front of an audience and act as part of a cast, I can do anything."

JOHNNY: Though the interrelationship will be discussed later, self-confidence comments were linked to public speaking/communication, self-esteem, leadership, and cognitive/thinking affects:

MATT: Youth program and worship arts coordinator, Class of 2002: "I think theatre has helped me to be OK with being nervous on stage. It helped me be more willing to try 'scary' things. Turns out that many 'scary' things are worth participating in! Theatre has also helped me be more relaxed in pressure situations – after all, only the end of the world is the end of the world. It helped me realize that I can be at least OK at just about whatever I want to be involved in as long as I give it a good attempt."

SCENE 4

ALL: Lifelong Thinking and Working.

ANGIE: Assistant education director for a nonprofit theatre for youth, Class of 2001: "Developmentally, I became the person I am today because of the experiences in the arts I had in high school. I learned about responsibility, teamwork, dedication, commitment, self-expression, communication, and much more through the arts."

MATT: Participants felt they gained public speaking and communication skills that enabled them to speak articulately and persuasively with heightened "presentations of self" and "a sense of performance," most notably in nontheatrical contexts such as classes and employee seminars:

JOHNNY: Military officer, Class of 2001: "I'm now involved in a field that emphasizes my ability to speak in front of a crowd, think on my feet, and present information succinctly to others. Even though I originally signed up in the military as an engineer, I'm now involved in public affairs, and this career wouldn't have been open to me were it not for a certain amount of dramatic skill. I learned in high school that even if the bulk of my talent lies in the math and science realm, I would always enjoy the artistic side more."

ANGIE: Various cognitive processing skills were other subcategories of outcome. The term refers to the capacity for thinking quickly, intellectually, critically, and creatively, particularly in "high pressure" and risk-taking situations:

LAURA: Executive director of a pedestrian coalition, Class of 1994: "As a teacher, a fundraiser, and a director of an advocacy nonprofit, drama has come in very handy. Every time I start to think of a task as too daunting to complete, I think of things in theatre I have done before that dwarf the obstacles. Speaking at a press conference? How can that possibly be more difficult that executing 120 light cues on a manual board in a two-hour show? I mean, seriously. Doing a new lesson plan for an ESL (English as a second language) class? What's that compared to memorizing two hours of lines for a packed house within a week?"

MATT: Hollywood sound effects and dialogue editor, Class of 1999: "In my business, you can't hesitate for a second on a solution; you have to know your options and come through with something or else people lose money and you lose your job. I can trace nearly every ounce of my ability to thrive in the film business back to my high school speech and debate team. With only thirty seconds to come up with an impromptu speech on some esoteric topic, you feel like you can accomplish anything because, no matter what, you have the tools to improvise quickly and the fearlessness to try new solutions."

ANGIE: Respondents testified their work habits and work ethics were cultivated through high school theatre and speech participation. Teamwork or working collaboratively with others was nurtured, as were time management, organization, and goal setting for meeting deadlines and task completion, plus ethics of self-motivation, perseverance, and responsibility to oneself and to others:

LAURA: Bank employee, Class of 1987: "It certainly gave me the confidence to speak up and taught me that sometimes pretending to be something can make that something be true. It was also my first lesson in understanding that you have to work with people you don't like and you have to do it well."

ANGIE: Theatre major, Class of 2009: "During my time in the theatre, I became the person I always wanted to be. Throughout my life I was struggling to find my niche, as well as finding who I truly was. Theatre, and all the people involved, helped me find these two things. Theatre made me."

SCENE 5

ALL: Lifelong Living and Loving.

LAURA: Social worker, Class of 1998: "For me, it gave me fond memories of high school and a sense of belonging when I didn't fit in or wanted to be a part of the athletes or other cliques. This absolutely supports one's sense of self during the difficult stage of adolescence."

ANGIE: The category of Lifelong Living and Loving is composed of the affective, intrapersonal, and interpersonal domains of learning. Like earlier survey findings, some respondents noted the lifelong friendships that were initiated during their high school years. But most prominent here was the formation of one's personal identity. Theatre and speech were opportunities to discover one's talents and strengths, and thus to find one's focus or purpose:

JOHNNY: Hollywood sound effects and dialogue editor, Class of 1999: "You meet so many amazing and interesting people in theatre, all with their own personal life stories and worldviews. It's one of the most diverse tribes in any school. You really get a sense of just how big the world is and how worthy of respect each person is. We change each other for the better in that environment."

MATT: Selected respondents testified they experienced emotional growth though such conceptual processes as self-esteem, self-worth, values clarification, maturity, and personal character development. For some, speech and theatre were conduits for discovering "what mattered," particularly in domains of human awareness and social interaction:

LAURA: University theatre major, Class of 2008: "I learned to handle responsibilities. I also learned that one person cannot do everything. A show is created by a team. I learned to let myself be vulnerable as well. I used to be very shy and very closed off to people. Now I know that even if I might get hurt later, it is better to open up and learn to be close to people."

JOHNNY: University audio technology and English major, Class of 2006: "Theatre has helped me pursue my dream of becoming a writer. Working in that environment taught me that if I'm going to be successful and fulfilled in life, I must do what makes me happy. I'm not saying theatre prevents wrong turns in life and it's perfect and it's the answer to all! No! But it does have a perfect fit to your unique situation at your own unique time. You can always tell the difference between a theatre student and nontheatre student. You don't think so? Take another look."

SCENE 6

ALL: Lifelong Legacy.

MATT: Artistic director at a nonprofit musical theatre company, Class of 1985: "Theatre and speech have driven my adult career as an actor, director, producer, educator, and consultant. My creative capacity is one of my greatest assets."

JOHNNY: For the 52 percent of respondents who chose and pursued theatre as a vocation or college/university major field of study, continued participation after high school was a "given." For some, theatre has become a living, and for others, a way of life:

LAURA: Unemployed, Class of 1968: "Theatre is all I've ever wanted to do. That won't be true for everyone, though. All of the other kids in my high school drama group went in other directions than theatre. I am the only one who hung on and hung in."

JOHNNY: A prominent theme from both theatre *and* nontheatre adults was a sense of "paying it forward" and leaving a "legacy" as an arts patron and advocate, particularly by those who chose to teach theatre to children and adolescents:

ANGIE: Graduate theatre major, Class of 2003: "Because I had such a negative experience in high school theatre, I now find myself committed to ensuring that younger students do not have the same experience. My thesis on the exploration of democratic and collaborative play development is a very obvious result of feeling so disempowered when I was younger."

MATT: Graduate student in educational theatre, Class of 2000: "I have always wanted to be as free and myself as I was onstage in that high school class. I am pursuing this educational theatre degree, in part, because I want to regain that freedom and let others feel it, too."

SCENE 7

ALL: Closure.

MATT: Call center manager, Class of 2004: "I can sum up theatre's impact on my life as making me a leader, refining my work ethic, and creating lifelong friendships. So many of the friends I still talk to, including my best friend, I met through high school theatre. The bonds of friendship built in theatre – through the hard work and emotional discoveries – cannot be found in other activities."

ANGIE: History and business management major, Class of 2003: "I appreciated the limitless possibilities I had with theatre, and although I never pursued it further with my education, I loved doing the work and being a part of an ensemble, it's unforgettable."

LAURA: Data analysis suggests that quality high school speech and theatre programming develops in most young people during adolescence and through adulthood, regardless of future occupation:

MATT: (*stands*) increased self-confidence;

ANGIE: (*stands*) collaborative teamwork, problem-solving, and leadership skills;

JOHNNY: (*stands*) public speaking, communication skills, and presentations of self;

LAURA: (*stands*) pragmatic work ethics such as goal setting, time management, and meeting deadlines;

MATT: heightened historic, cultural, and social awareness;

ANGIE: empathy and emotional intelligence;

JOHNNY: identity, values systems, and a sense of personal significance;

LAURA: lifelong friendships;

MATT: and artistic living and patronage.

JOHNNY: Overall, theatre and speech experiences, according to survey respondent testimony:

LAURA: empower one to *think and function improvisationally* in dynamic and everchanging contexts;

MATT: deepen and accelerate development of an individual's *emotional and social intelligences*;

ANGIE: and expand one's verbal and nonverbal *communicative dexterity* in various presentational modes.

JOHNNY: Internet strategy consultant, Class of 1999: "I have a measure of confidence and composure that would not exist if it wasn't for speech. I wouldn't have the same set of job skills and abilities. I wouldn't have had the same influences that created my political ideologies and many of my individual beliefs. I believe that my participation in speech and theatre in high school has influenced who I am as an adult more than any other single influence in my entire life."

Acknowledgments

The coresearchers thank the 2011 American Alliance for Theatre & Education [AATE] Research Awards Committee and jurors for their support of this work. We also extend our thanks to the 234 "Lifelong Impact" survey respondents who shared their personal testimonies with us. This article includes the scripted adaptation of the full-length "Lifelong Impact" study. . . . It is included in *Youth Theatre Journal* as an example of arts-based educational research representation and presentation through the genre of reader's theatre. The script was performed by the four coauthors at the August 2011 AATE Research Awards session in Chicago.

Note

1 Portions of this script will appear in a forthcoming chapter for *Performing Scholartistry*, a volume of the Arts-Informed Inquiry Series published by Backalong Books (www.backalongbooks.com). Earlier versions of this script were developed for and performed at the NAPAR and AERA conferences. Saldaña and McCammon's university institutional review boards approved the "Lifelong Impact" study in the fall of 2009.

References

Bloom, L. R., Reynolds, A., Amore, R., Beaman, A., Chantem, G. K., Chapman, E., Fitzpatrick, J., et al. (2009). Identify this . . . A reader's theatre of women's voices. *International Review of Qualitative Research, 2*(2), 209–228.

Denzin, N. (1997). *Interpretive ethnography: Ethnographic practices for the 21st century.* Thousand Oaks, CA: Sage.

Denzin, N. (2003). *Performance ethnography: Critical pedagogy and the politics of culture.* Thousand Oaks, CA: Sage.

Donmoyer, R., & Yennie-Donmoyer, J. (1995). Data as drama: Reflections on the use of reader's theater as a mode of qualitative data display. *Qualitative Inquiry, 1*(4), 402–428.

Donmoyer, R., & Yennie-Donmoyer, J. (2008). Readers' theater as a data display strategy. In J. G. Knowles & A. L. Cole (Eds.), *Handbook of the arts in qualitative research: Perspectives, methodologies, examples, and issues* (pp. 209–224). Thousand Oaks, CA: Sage.

Downey, A. L. (2008). No child left untested: Docudrama in six scenes. *Youth Theatre Journal*, 22, 47–66.

Goldstein, T. (2001). Hong Kong, Canada: Playwriting as critical ethnography. *Qualitative Inquiry*, 7(3), 279–303.

Goldstein, T. (2002). Performed ethnography for representing other people's children in critical educational research. *Applied Theatre Researcher*, 3. Retrieved from www.griffith.edu/au_data/assets/pdf_file/0003/54975/performed-ethnography.pdf

Goldstein, T. (2004). Performed ethnography for antihomophobia teacher education: Linking research to teaching. *The Canadian On-Line Journal of Queer Studies in Education*, 1(1). Retrieved from http://jqstudies. oise.utoronto.ca/journal/viewissue.php?id=3

Goldstein, T. (2006). Toward a future of equitable pedagogy and schooling. *Pedagogies: An International Journal*, 1(3), 151–169.

Goldstein, T. (2008). Multiple commitments and ethical dilemmas in performed ethnography. *Educational Insights*, 12(2). Retrieved from www.ccfi.educ.ubc.ca/publication/insights/v12n02/pdfs/goldstein.pdf

Janesick, V. J. (2011). *'Stretching' exercises for qualitative researchers* (3rd ed.). Thousand Oaks, CA: Sage.

Knowles, J. G., & Cole, A. L. (Eds.). (2008). *Handbook of the arts in qualitative research: Perspectives, methodologies, examples, and issues*. Thousand Oaks, CA: Sage.

Leavy, P. (Ed.). (2009). *Method meets art: Arts-based research practice*. New York: Guilford.

Lewis, P. J. (2011). Collage journaling with preservice teachers: A reader's theatre in one collage. *International Review of Qualitative Research*, 4(1), 51–58.

McIntyre, M. (2009). Home is where the heart is: A reader's theatre. *The Canadian creative arts in health, training and education journal*. Retrieved from www.ijcaip.com/archives/CCAHTE-Journal-7-McIntyre.html

Norris, J. (2010). *Playbuilding as qualitative research: A participatory arts-based approach*. Walnut Creek, CA: Left Coast Press.

Pardue, K. T. (2004). Introducing reader's theater! A strategy to foster aesthetic knowing in nursing. *Nurse Educator*, 29(2), 58–62.

Saldaña, J. (2008). The drama and poetry of qualitative method. In M. Cahnmann-Taylor & R. Siegesmund (Eds.), *Arts-based research in education: Foundations for practice* (pp. 220–227). New York: Routledge.

Saldaña, J. (2011). *Ethnotheatre: Research from page to stage*. Walnut Creek, CA: Left Coast Press.

Walker, R., Pick, C., & MacDonald, B. (1991). 'Other rooms: Other voices': A dramatized report. In C. Pick & B. MacDonald (Eds.), *Biography, identity and schooling: Episodes in educational research* (pp. 80–93). Washington, DC: Falmer Press.

9   Writing Autoethnography

Telling Your Own Story

Autoethnography is a recently developed methodology in qualitative inquiry in which the researcher herself is the primary subject of study. Adams, Jones, and Ellis (2015) explain that the genre is an "artistic and analytic demonstration of how we come to know, name, and interpret personal and cultural experience" (p. 1). Autoethnography is the introspective examination of one's life, identity, and meaning through a culture-of-one's experiences. At its best, the genre blends case study intimacy with ethnographic revelation. A few of the most outstanding autoethnographies I've read can be accessed from Sonny Nordmarken (2014) reflecting on his transgender "in-betweenness," Alejandra Martínez (2015) coping with her father's mental illness, and Tony E. Adams's (2011) masterwork blending ethnographic and autoethnographic research on same-sex attraction.

A folk proverb teaches, "You can't learn how to tell someone else's story until you first learn how to tell your own." As wise as that sounded when I first heard it, I now realize it must be taken with a grain of salt. I have been fortunate to witness many autoethnographic presentations at conferences. Some presenters offer compelling stories about their lives which extend beyond the autobiographical and who relate their tales to the social world at large. But a few presenters seem to employ autoethnography as a self-indulgent forum for wrestling with personal demons in front of an audience when they would be better served in the privacy of a one-on-one counseling session. Also, a few scholars seem to focus exclusively on the genre, devoting their careers to studying one's personal life without venturing beyond their own spheres to study in-depth the lives of their fellow human beings.

Rather than flatly accepting the adage, "You can't learn how to tell someone else's story until you first learn how to tell your own," I offer the following as autoethnographic writing qualifications:

- Study other people first; learn about *their* lives.
- Concurrently, examine how you yourself relate to the lives of those you're studying.

- When you've conducted at least two studies about other people, study yourself and write about it autoethnographically.
- Go back to studying other people, better informed of what it takes to examine a life.
- Write other autoethnographies occasionally, but don't make a career out of it. You're not the only one in the world.

I believe that all qualitative researchers should write at least one autoethnography in their professional lifetimes. It truly does heighten one's awareness of what it takes to understand social life. But I published fifteen research articles related to nine different qualitative studies before I wrote my first autoethnographic piece. I feel that track record provided me a solid foundation (if not permission) to write about myself. As a twist on the folk proverb, I now offer that "You can't learn how to tell your own story until you first learn how to tell someone else's."

Both selections in this chapter were presented at academic research conferences. The first, "Gay-Tex-Mex: Autoethnographic Vignettes," was included as part of a plenary session coordinated by Bryant Keith Alexander for the May 2017 International Congress of Qualitative Inquiry assembly. The charge for each of the twelve presenters was to deliver an autoethnographic rendering in under ten minutes on the theme of the cowboy. Since I was born, raised, and educated in Texas, the topic was quite easy to address.

When I was first invited and later accepted to participate in the plenary, Alexander asked each participant for a title and abstract of their paper. I reflected on the cowboy myth and how my personal experiences related to it. What first crystallized in my mind was the stark contrast between the hypermasculine, heteronormative, White cowboy archetype and my gay Hispanic identity. A cascade of memories about my parents, teachers, students, and friends sprang to mind, but the title for the presentation emerged quickly since it embodied three of my cultural worlds: "Gay-Tex-Mex." The title provided a strong focus for the abstract and content to be written – an assemblage of memories about language differences, culture clash, ethnic discrimination, and homophobia. The structure I chose was a string of brief vignettes alternatingly related to one of my three cultural identity markers, which totaled to a poignant conclusion and thematic lesson I learned growing up gay and Hispanic in Texas. Accompanying PowerPoint slides presented key quotes and vivid images suggested by the narrative.

The second selection, "Thank You, Mrs. Whitehouse: The Memory Work of One Student About His High School English Teacher, Forty Years Later," also employs the vignette format. This keynote address was presented at the National Council of Teachers of English Assembly for Research conference in February 2011. The theme of the event (and the title of its published proceedings) was *Time and Space in Literacy Research* (Compton-Lilly & Halverson, 2014). The invitation as a keynote speaker was extended to me based on my previous methodological work in longitudinal qualitative research (Saldaña, 2003).

Since this was an English teachers' gathering, I immediately honed in on the general topic – memories about the most influential teacher in my lifetime: my high school junior-level language arts teacher, Mrs. Ann Whitehouse. And since time was a thematic emphasis for the conference, the keynote address jumps playfully from past to present throughout with each vignette identified with one of three headings: **Flashback** (past actions or memories), **Flashforward** (present states or advancing in time from the previous vignette), and *Flashsideway* (an aside, commentary, or reference to the academic literature). During the presentation, I embodied each time frame by taking a step backward for a flashback, walking forward for a flashforward, and moving sideways for a flashsideway.

I did not originally label this piece autoethnographic but instead used the term *memory work* – a therapeutic, action research methodology tangentially related to longitudinal qualitative research, and which seemed to have evolved concurrently with autoethnography. "Thank You, Mrs. Whitehouse" discloses personal, stream-of-consciousness thoughts triggered by yet related to vivid memories of one of the most exciting classes I've ever taken as a student. The work pays homage to a gifted master teacher who significantly influenced my love of American literature and my own teaching practice throughout my career.

References

Adams, T. E. (2011). *Narrating the closet: An autoethnography of same-sex attraction.* Walnut Creek, CA: Left Coast Press.

Adams, T. E., Jones, S. H., & Ellis, C. (2015). *Autoethnography.* New York: Oxford.

Compton-Lilly, C., & Halverson, E. (Eds.). (2014). *Time and space in literacy research.* New York: Routledge.

Martínez, A. (2015). The first death of my father: Reflecting on masculinity, illness, and work. *International Review of Qualitative Research, 8*(4), 408–418.

Nordmarken, S. (2014). Becoming ever more monstrous: Feeling transgender in-betweenness. *Qualitative Inquiry, 20*(1), 37–50.

Saldaña, J. (2003). *Longitudinal qualitative research: Analyzing change through time.* Walnut Creek, CA: AltaMira Press.

GAY-TEX-MEX: AUTOETHNOGRAPHIC VIGNETTES

Texans Are Taught

Texans are taught – literally – taught in school to be proud of living in the Lone Star State. In the 1960s, Mrs. von Rosenberg told us second graders that Texas was the biggest state in the union, until one of the boys in class asked her, "But, isn't Alaska bigger than Texas?" You could see the shock on Mrs. von Rosenberg's face as she realized she was wrong.

Texas Cowboy Culture

Texas has a unique outline shape as a state. It looks bold, vast, rugged. The state's famous anti-littering campaign slogan, "Don't Mess With Texas," was embraced by its arrogant citizenry. In many parts of the state it *was* pure cowboy culture – kick-ass, hell-raising, shit-kicking, tight Wranglers, rodeo, country-western line dancing, barbeque, potato salad, chicken fried steak, Lone Star Beer, Austin City Limits, football games every goddamn weekend, and Baptist brimstone, hellfire, and damnation on Sunday mornings followed by family dinner at Luby's Cafeteria.

Texas Hispanic Culture

But on my side of town – 98% Hispanic – it *was* fiestas, quinceañeras, Mariachi music, with tortillas, fideo, arroz con pollo, borrachos y pachucos y puro chiflada, piñatas on your birthday, La llorona crying by the river at midnight, hiding when a stranger knocked on your front door, cleaning other people's houses and doing other people's laundry, women wearing veils to Catholic mass on Sunday mornings, reciting the rosary every day, and lighting candles or burying raw eggs in the back yard and saying a prayer over them when someone was sick.

Mí Amá

I was proud of our family's surname – Saldaña – because I was the only one in my elementary class who had a mark over one of the letters in his name. My mother, mí amá, told me it came from Spain and that I should always put it over the n in Saldaña. The tilde was different – and it made *me* feel different, special, unique.

[Previously unpublished material, first presented at the International Congress of Qualitative Inquiry conference May 19, 2017 in the session, "Autoethnography: Plenary: 'Mommas Don't Let Your Babies Grow Up to Be . . .': Revisiting Western Imagery and Grown-Up Cowboys".]

In the 1960s, there was hushed talk in my neighborhood about a very strange man who liked to dress up in women's clothes. I walked in on my mother and aunt talking about it in shocked and disapproving tones. My mother looked at me, realized I had overheard the adult conversation, pointed her finger at me and said, "Johnny, don' you ebber turn out like that!"

I loved my mother's thick Spanish accent. She was born in Spain, yet raised in Mexican American culture. My parents didn't teach me Spanish as I grew up because they had become more fluent in English by that time. But mom would still have problems pronouncing certain words like "frerijerater" or "compooter," and when she got mad at another driver for taking a parking space in a lot she'd yell from her car, "You son of a beesh!"

Mí Apá

My father, mí apá, was quite the do-it-yourself man, hardened from picking fruit and cotton in the fields and manual labor as a carpenter and a cook most of his life. When I was nine or ten years old I was helping my father fix the car – or rather, standing next to him holding a wrench he would later need as he tinkered under the hood. He chatted to me about this and that as he worked, which most likely bored me to no end, but then stopped with a brief pause, looked at me and said, "Johnny, don't ever trust the white man."

"Saldaney"

My seventh-grade P.E. teacher was as Texas redneck as they came – a man who reeked of cigar smoke and sweat. Probably ex-military and probably never going to be anything more than he was at the time. He called all of us "lads" by our last names, but he called mine, "Saldaney." I told him it was pronounced "Saldaña." But for the rest of the school year, it was said with outright defiant redneck mockery and a shit-eating grin on his face: "Saldaney."

Wetback

A "wetback" is a demeaning ethnic slur, referring to a Mexican who swims across the Rio Grande River to enter the United States "illegally." After a long morning of high school marching band rehearsal outdoors in the hot Texas sun, we would all come back to the band hall to put our instruments away. The perspiration that was always on the back of my shirt was a running joke among my white friends. They would smirk and pat me gently on the back over and over saying, "Hey Johnny, your back's wet, your *back's wet!*"

Theatre

The University of Texas at Austin's Department of Drama was one of the biggest – of course – in the nation. And there, for the first time, my closeted self was surrounded by openly gay people – theatre queens with bitchy attitude imitating Bette Midler and singing songs from *Cabaret*. Like we said in Texas at the time, "You can't swing a dead cat in here without hittin' a queer!" We called it "theatre" while the lesser educated of rural east and west Texas called it "thee-AY-ter." There was a wild Texas boldness among my classmates – a post-1968 college radicalism that was avant-garde and protest theatre and fuck-you-in-your-face experimental art. Being gay there was not a sin, as Catholic church had taught me. Being gay was a status symbol. Being gay was a badge of honor. But still, it was something never to be spoken of in the presence of my oh-so Hispanic Texas family.

Student Teaching

During my senior year of teacher certification, I student taught one semester at Stephen F. Austin High School, where the old money families sent their children. I asked one of the young white teens if he was going to audition for my play production, and he told me to my face, "No. I don't want to work with a Mexican."

My next student teaching assignment was at David Crocket High School, where the young cowboys from surrounding farms and ranches attended. I walked cautiously down the school's hallways, noticing how these tall, lean young men in straw cowboy hats, rattlesnake skin boots, and brown leather belts with huge gold buckles would stare at me with a look that suggested, "You ain't from around here, are you, boy?" I'd try to butch it up by walking with my legs spread wide and talking in a deeper than normal voice to fit in.

In the Closet

It was the mid-1970s, right after Cesar Chavez and Luis Valdez had made names for themselves with their Chicano social activism. It was right after the Stonewall riots and the birth of the gay pride movement. But there was a good ol' boy Republican state senator – his name escapes me – during my college years, who honestly believed and publicly stated that there was no way there could be gay people living in Texas.

I never told my parents I was gay. There had been too many messages and enculturation growing up from the 1950s to the 1970s that it was not acceptable – not acceptable in Texas, not acceptable among Hispanic families. My father eventually passed, then my mother, eight years later. Yet never a word to them about my identity and beginnings of a long-term relationship with a man in another southwestern state.

In the early 2000s, I had a long-distance phone call with my niece who had grown up in my Texas hometown and who chatted frequently with my mother at the kitchen table before she passed. My street-wise niece figured out that I was gay, for she has an open and loving spirit. And over the phone one night, I confessed to her that I always regretted never telling my mom about being gay. Then she confessed to me, "Uncle Johnny, she knew – she just never told you."

The Cowboy's Ethos

A running joke among Texans is that there are only two states in the U.S. – Texas, and the rest of the country. Texas can be a hard place to live in. There are people with gritty outlooks, toughened up and emboldened from the pride that comes naturally from living in the Great Lone Star State. Not everyone is a cowboy, but you adopt the cowboy's ethos – his leathered spirit, his sunburnt soul. I guess – or rather, I reckon – that living and growing up there has toughened me up, too. I've made it this far in life, and that's good. I'm not a cowboy by any means, but *ah know hauw t' drop a Texas drawwwl as good as eny of 'em – y'all.*

Don't mess with Texas. And, don't mess with me.

THANK YOU, MRS. WHITEHOUSE: THE MEMORY WORK OF ONE STUDENT ABOUT HIS HIGH SCHOOL ENGLISH TEACHER, FORTY YEARS LATER

Flashback, fall 1960, Austin, Texas: I'm in first grade. The teacher is not in the classroom but a few of us students are. I see on top of my teacher's desk – a sacred temple to a six year old – a copy of our math textbook. But hers was different from ours. It was almost twice as large and had in big letters printed on the front cover, "Teacher's Edition." What is this? I thought. I picked up the book and flipped through its pages. It had the same content as our books but the answers to all the math problems were included – in red ink. This was so cool! One of my art projects was to take a sheet of lined notebook paper, fold it in half and fold it again as if to make a small book. I drew a copy of the cover of our math book on the front page with pencil and proudly wrote along the side: "Teacher's Edition." Inside the booklet I included some simple addition problems, but I also included the answers – in red ink. Back in 1960, red ink pens were not so common to children – they were the province of teachers and other professionals. But because my father did his own business accounting, he had red ink pens at home for me to play with. I proudly showed my creation – not to my teacher but to my first grade friends. They were so impressed with what I made that they asked me to make them a Teacher's Edition, too.

Flashsideway: I didn't know it at the time but, fifty years ago, that was my earliest memory of fascination with being a teacher.

Flashforward, the 1980s, Tempe, Arizona: I can't remember the specific year but it was most likely within that decade. I'm a university professor in theatre education at Arizona State University ordering textbooks for my Methods of Teaching Theatre class. One of the standard titles on my recommended list was a well-known textbook for high school students. I wanted future educators to know what most high school theatre programs adopted as a core textbook for adolescents. But one year, I thought, instead of just the textbook, maybe I should order the Teacher's Edition of it for my university students. So, that's what I ordered. The university bookstore contacted me a few months later stating that the publisher was reluctant to ship those books because the Teacher's Edition was only authorized for full-time secondary school teachers, not pre-service education majors. Why? I asked them. Security reasons, they said. The Teacher's Edition of the textbook has the answers to standardized tests they composed for classroom use.

Flashsideway: "Memory work" originated in Europe in the 1980s as a form of feminist participatory action research. One's personal past is individually and then collectively examined with others to recall moments of oppression that formed gender socialization. The agenda of memory work is therapeutic

[Originally published as Chapter 1 in *Time and Space in Literacy Research*, edited by Catherine Compton-Lilly and Erica Halverson, New York: Routledge, 2014, pp. 19–32.]

and emancipatory. One's memories of actions, motives, and emotions are key experiences that form the construction of one's present identity. Ultimately the purpose of memory work is not the exploration of "Who am I?" but rather, "How did I get to be this way and, if necessary, how can I change?" (Liamputtong, 2009, pp. 130–131).

Flashback, fall 1960: I was taught by and grew up on Dick and Jane readers:

Oh, oh, oh.
See Spot run.
Oh, Puff. Funny, funny Puff.

Flashforward, the 2000s: In my fifties, I am on avid searches for Dick and Jane books in antique stores and online sites. I find a few titles from my childhood that evoke memories of "Yes, this is one I actually read!" Scott, Foresman and Company: I even remembered the publisher. The books had a distinctive look; they had *style*. It was a world of children. They were all the perfect white nuclear family, but race or ethnicity didn't matter to me back then. The words were big, the pictures were colorful, the workbooks were fun. I was learning how to read. And in my adult searches for these collectable items, about $15 to $125 each depending on the condition, I bought old cover-worn copies of *We Look and See* and *Guess Who* and, yes, the Teacher's Edition of *Fun With Dick and Jane*.

Flashsideway: Memory work is the rewriting of memories of past oppression in order to find liberation. As we go through life, we experience "important events and their memories and the reconstructions of these form a critical part of the construction of self" (Grbich, 2007, p. 100). We trace back to find out how our selves became who we are – how we've been socialized. We transform ourselves as a result of this. The individual attempts to find significant themes. We look not only for what is present, but also what is missing.

Flashback, fall 1967, 8th grade English: Our teacher was crazy. We were scared to death of her. I did my best to please her just to keep her from yelling at me as she often did to others. One day I sat down in class before the bell rang and opened my three-ring notebook, getting solidly prepared for class. The teacher walked up to me with a frown on her face, literally yanked my notebook away from my desk, took it up to hers, and slammed it down. I was stunned and she offered me no explanation for why she did it. She was crazy. Everyone at school said so.

Flashsideway: Don't worry. This keynote address is not some trauma-filled purging or exorcising of personal demons. On the contrary, it's an upbeat success story yet tinted with just enough genre variety and occasional tension, humor, and revelation of juicy stuff to keep you engaged.

Flashforward, fall 1969, high school sophomore English: The teacher was a pleasant enough woman, beautiful penmanship on the chalkboard, but not a very good instructor. She would frequently venture off into tangents with stories about her husband and family. The content was weak and classes were generally boring. I remember very, very little about them, except for reading *Julius Caesar* – yawn – and John Steinbeck's *The Pearl*. Latin American characters – oh yeah, I could relate. Simple, beautiful language, like poetry. And the literary *elements*: symbolism, irony, foreshadowing. Now this was literature! I would read it over and over again throughout the next decade. I even constructed English tests for myself about the novel to show how well I knew it. And I put the answers in red ink.

Flashsideway: For memory work, once a theme has been chosen for exploration, memories are recalled and written down by the individual. The originators of the method advise writing one's memories in the third person to provide a sense of detachment and bird's-eye perspective. But I choose to employ writing in the first person since I'm working on my own rather than with a collective. I write in the first person to take deep ownership of my memories.

Flashforward, spring 1978: I took a graduate-level anthropology course in folklore because the subject sounded really interesting. I had taken a course in children's literature the semester before and immersed myself in reading folk tales from around the world. But I was way over my head in that seminar with the anthropology majors and I only lasted about five weeks before I withdrew. But I learned a lot. We were coding African stories' motifs. And it was there that I learned the concept of what a motif was. I got up to speed by reading Stith Thomson's books on the subject, and found it to be a very intriguing literary element.

Flashsideway: Filmmaker Jean-Luc Godard is credited with saying, "Every story should have a beginning, a middle, and an end. But not necessarily in that order."

Flashback, spring 1972, high school senior English: We were studying dramatic literature of the late 19th and early 20th century Great Britain, and our teacher was trying to discretely explain the notoriety of Oscar Wilde. After some skirting around the issue, one of the school thugs blurted out, "You mean he was a *homo*?"

Flashforward, the late 1970s: I've moved away from home, and I'm coming to terms with my own sexual identity. I bought a paperback copy of Walt Whitman's *Leaves of Grass*. Read it cover to cover, looking for "those" passages. Found them, savored them – and underlined them in red ink.

Flashsideway: We study the personal to get to the historical, social, political, and cultural. I present a hybrid form of time study in this address – a qualitative mixed methods genre of memory work, autoethnography, and longitudinal qualitative research (Saldaña, 2003). As anthropologist Clifford Geertz (1983) mused, "Life is just a bowl of strategies" (p. 25). Life is adaptation and I am a notorious adaptor. I take what is necessary for me and reshape and blend it to suit my own purposes.

Flashback, summer 1971: I took the first semester of high school senior English during summer school, just to get ahead of my program of study. We had an import teacher from another high school that term – admittedly and frankly an old, bitter queen of a man. We read *Hamlet*, as most seniors will in that course.

A hard play, especially for a high schooler, to digest. But this teacher asked us to read the entire play on our own rather than guiding us through it one act at a time for whole class discussion. On the first day we discussed the Shakespearean work the teacher asked me, "Johnny, what's the theme of *Hamlet*?" I remember being taken aback and feeling the need to say something – anything – lest I appear that I didn't read the play. I cannot remember what I said to him in front of the class but I knew I said something – a desperate fledgling answer. But the teacher's sarcastic reply, almost forty years later, will never be forgotten. He said, "Well, that's very interesting, Johnny. What a shame it doesn't have a damn thing to do with the play."

Flashforward, the 1980s through 2000s, Methods of Teaching Theatre class: When we study the teaching of dramatic literature. I tell my students that story, and I encourage them to never ask someone what's *the* theme of a play. Instead, I encourage them to ask their students to look for those lines in the play that strike you as the most interesting, and why.

Flashsideway: Holstein and Gubrium (2000), in *Constructing the Life Course*, conceptualize that

> The life course and its constituent parts or stages are not the objective features of experience that they are conventionally taken to be. Instead, the constructionist approach helps us view the life course as a social form that is constructed and used to make sense of experience. . . . The life course doesn't simply unfold before and around us; rather, we actively organize the flow, pattern, and direction of experience in developmental terms as we navigate the social terrain of our everyday lives.
>
> (p. 182)

Flashback, fall 1970: When you're a beginning high school teacher and presumably on a low or modest salary, Mrs. Ann Whitehouse, my junior year English teacher, would wear the same outfits frequently throughout the year. There were two in particular that I remember: a bright orange and cream white polyester pants suit (well, that *was* the fashion at the time), and a dark blue knee-length dress flecked with gold motifs. The dark blue dress in particular was remembered because it was a bit low cut at the top – somewhat scandalous for a female high school teacher in 1970. But Mrs. Whitehouse looked *stunning* in those outfits. Add her long brunette hair, sparkling eyes, pleasant smile, and bright red lipstick, and she was *pretty*.

Flashforward, the 1980s: I dress in my beiges, tans, and browns phase.

Flashforward, the 1990s: In mid-life crisis I dress in my tight jeans, Harley T's, and leather phase.

Flashforward, the 2000s: I dress in my blacks and whites and grays phase. A graduate student once asked me, "Johnny, why do you always dress in blacks and whites and grays?" I sincerely replied, "I guess it's like a uniform, a sense of professionalism." But I learned later, on my own, that that was not the real reason.

Flashsideway: There are five categories of memories for memory work. The first is *accretion* – how memories accumulate meaning over time; the second is *condensation* – how meanings intensify and become simpler over time; the third is *secondary revision* – how we create retrospective narratives to fit with present needs; the fourth is *repression* – material that is forgotten or pushed to the unconscious; and the fifth is *melancholia* – an inability to let go of what is lost – a form of hyper-remembering (McLeod & Thomson, 2009, pp. 26–27).

Flashback, summer 1971: Remember senior English, bitter old queen, the theme of *Hamlet*? Before that, we read *Beowulf*. Not just excerpts from it, the whole poem. Couldn't figure out what was going on; hated it.

Flashforward, fall 1973: University sophomore English. We had to read *Beowulf* again. Still couldn't figure out what was going on; hated it.

Flashforward, the mid 1990s: Me in my forties and in mid-life crisis. For some strange reason, felt compelled to re-read *Beowulf* on my own. *Loved* it! Knew *exactly* what was going on!

Flashsideway: I've always been good at recalling memories from childhood through the present day. In theatre, this is actually part of actor training – sense memory and emotional recall, two tools of the trade which help an actor imaginatively reconstruct from his own experiences believable circumstances on stage when portraying a fictional character.

Flashback, fall 1970: Mrs. Whitehouse was giving us instructions and deliberately and gleefully used the word "ain't" as if she had just uttered an obscenity. The class mockingly gasped and "oohed" in wicked delight.

Flashforward, spring 1971: We were reading O. Henry's short story, "The Cop and the Anthem," and Mrs. Whitehouse explained to us what the term "goose egg" in the story meant, and read the line aloud in an Irish dialect.

Flashforward, a summer in the late 1980s: I discover that the teacher's voice, my voice, needs to be performative in order to communicate effectively with students.

Flashsideway: McLeod and Thomson (2009) wisely note that "The language of social science is not always best suited to express the subtleties of temporal processes, and for this reason we employ literary examples along the way" (p. 15). Thus, to study time and change, writing can creatively incorporate genre, metaphors, symbols, and motifs.

Flashback, fall 1970: In the high school hallway, I was walking to my next class, and I saw Mrs. Whitehouse walking briskly toward her classroom. She moved with speed, with confidence, with *style*.

Flashsideway: Life has motifs, those recurring elements that pop up now and then in the serendipitous of times and places. I employ motifs in my original playwriting, and even in my academic writing. I feature Motif Coding in my book, *The Coding Manual for Qualitative Researchers* (Saldaña, 2009). I explain that a *motif* is "the smallest element in a tale" that has something unique about it such as characters, significant objects, and single incidents of action (Thompson, 1977, pp. 415–416).

Flashback, fall 1970: In Mrs. Whitehouse's class, we had to read an American novel on our own time, and since I liked *The Scarlet Letter* I picked another Hawthorne novel, *The House of the Seven Gables*. My, what a lot of exclamation points it had! But what a story! I was telling all my friends, "You have *got* to read this book!" I told Mrs. Whitehouse, "This should be required reading for an English class!"

Flashforward, the 1990s: I am a peer reviewer of article manuscripts for professional journals, and I wrote in my comments that a particular author had used far too many exclamation points in her writing.

Flashsideway: In memory work, McLeod and Thomson (2009) advise, "We're not uncovering the nature of the event but the meaning that the event had for us then and now" (pp. 23–24).

Flashback, fall 1970: Mrs. Whitehouse was smiling, as she often did, as she told us about the works of Herman Melville, such as "Bartleby the Scrivener" and *Moby Dick*, to which the class clown smirked and asked, "Moby's what?" Mrs. Whitehouse kept smiling and, without missing a beat, ignored the remark and moved on with her lecture.

Flashforward, summer 1975: I took a summer school class in early American literature at the University of Texas at Austin for my English Education minor. I can't remember the professor's name; I simply recall that he was an elderly, bearded, gentle soul of a man. Over the course of six weeks we were to read an American literature anthology of approximately one thousand pages plus a few American novels – including *Moby Dick*. And I immersed myself in this country's literary heritage and came to class each day ready to excitedly discuss these works with that kind and amiable man. In *Moby Dick*, though, there's that rather awkward and inference-laden passage about Ishmael's hand in the barrel of whale sperm from the chapter titled "A Squeeze of the Hand," which the professor read aloud:

> Squeeze! squeeze! squeeze! all the morning long; I squeezed that sperm till I myself almost melted into it; I squeezed that sperm till a strange sort of insanity came over me; and I found myself unwittingly squeezing my co-laborers' hands in it, mistaking their hands for the gentle globules. Such an abounding, affectionate, friendly, loving feeling did this avocation beget; that at last I was continually squeezing their hands, and looking up into their eyes sentimentally; as much as to say, – Oh! my dear fellow beings, why should we longer cherish any social acerbities, or know the slightest ill-humor or envy! Come; let us squeeze hands all round; nay, let us all squeeze ourselves into each other; let us squeeze ourselves universally into the very milk and sperm of kindness.

And I so wanted to blurt out to my English professor about Melville: "You mean he was a *homo*?"

Flashsideway: After the memories' social meanings have been constructed, they are thematically organized and theorized.

Flashback, fall 1970: We had mint green-colored vocabulary workbooks, and we had to research the definitions on our own for about fifteen new words each week. On vocabulary days, Mrs. Whitehouse would call on each student randomly to present the definition of a word. And if you didn't have your homework completed, you would get a mark in her grade book. One day, she called on a particular student – not exactly the smartest one in our class – to give the definition for the first word on the list. "I don't have it," he said. Mrs. Whitehouse reached for her grade book and proceeded to put a mark in it as she asked, "You didn't do your homework?" The student raised his vocabulary workbook to show her: "I have the definitions for the other fourteen words, I just don't have the first one." Mrs. Whitehouse looked puzzled and asked, "Why don't you have the first one answered?" The student replied, "Well, I work backwards by starting at the bottom and working my way up to the top, and I ran out of time and didn't get the last one – or, the first one – done." There was a brief pause of silence in the room as we all basked in that rather surrealistic moment. Mrs. Whitehouse stared at him with a confused look, shook her head, laughed, and erased the mark from her grade book.

Flashsideway: What is the accretion of these memories?

Flashback, fall 1970: Mrs. Whitehouse would occasionally read poetry to us, as most every English teacher will do. She read aloud Walt Whitman's "Young Grimes," and told us ahead of time it was one of his early attempts and a fairly shaky poem, not his best, and so she read it with slight tongue-in-cheek glee:

When old Grimes died, he left a son –
   The graft of worthy stock;
In deed and word he shows himself
   A chip of the old block.
In youth, 't is said, he liked not school –
   Of tasks he was no lover;
He wrote sums in a ciphering book,
   Which had a pasteboard cover.

But I will never forget her reading of Whitman's "O Captain! My Captain!" During the first two verses, her eyes were riveted to the book. I could tell she wasn't performing for us; she seemed to be genuinely moved by its power:

O Captain, my Captain! our fearful trip is done;
The ship has weathered every rack, the prize we sought is won;
The port is near, the bells I hear, the people all exulting,
While follow eyes the steady keel, the vessel grim and daring:
   But O heart! heart! heart!
   O the bleeding drops of red,
   Where on the deck my Captain lies,
   Fallen cold and dead.

Flashsideway: I believe that there is pattern and purpose to everything. Like that old bitter queen of an English teacher might have asked me, "Johnny, what's the theme of your existence?" I'm afraid that after I give an answer, he'll reply with, "Well, that's very interesting, Johnny. What a shame it doesn't have a damn thing to do with your life."

Flashback, fall 1970: We were about to read *The Adventures of Huckleberry Finn*, required reading those days in junior English just a year before Austin's mandatory school bussing and integration. But everyone knew the book had the "n" word in it. Only back then, Texans didn't call it "the 'n' word," we said it out loud. Mrs. Whitehouse, in her discrete way, forewarned us that the word would be read throughout the novel and told us, "It's a word you needn't be embarrassed by, it was used frequently during the time the book was written."

Flashforward, the 1990s through 2000s: I model how to teach monologue reading to my Methods of Teaching Theatre class, and I use a selection from Jane Wagner and Lily Tomlin's one-woman show, *The Search for Signs of Intelligent Life in the Universe*. I tell my students, "You're going to read the word 'lesbian' in this monologue and it's a word you needn't be embarrassed by; it's not a derogatory slur, it's a clinical term."

Flashsideway: If there's a direct link between past and present, it's because I've constructed it as such. I'm a weaver, an integrator of disparate threads. I was trained as a costumer, so I sew. I put things together and I repair them. It's a male thing: fix things if they're broken. Find the solution. Find the answer.

Flashback, spring 1971: It was either a Bret Harte or Stephen Crane short story we had been reading, and Mrs. Whitehouse explained to us the symbolism and foreshadowing in the tale: sunrises and the east represented birth, while sunsets and the west represented death.

Flashforward, summer 1975: One day my university American literature professor asked the class why we thought a writer would choose to set death-related action of a story in the west. One student thought it was related to this obscure literary reference about an ancient culture's soldiers marching off toward the west to their defeat, to which the teacher said, "OK." Then I told him what Mrs. Whitehouse taught us about the east and west, and sunrises and sunsets, and birth and death, to which he smiled and said, "That's right." Then it occurred to me: I'd bet anything that Mrs. Whitehouse had this professor as a teacher, too.

Flashsideway: My life has a through-line because I've constructed it as such. There's pattern and purpose to everything because that's what I believe. There's symbolic meaning because I've attributed it. I am the symbol for myself and of myself, representing and hiding who I really am.

Flashback, spring 1971: We had small group reports to make to Mrs. Whitehouse's class, and my contribution was how to read and voice Emily Dickinson's poetry. I read aloud some of her verses to show the class that it was not to be spoken in artificial sing-songy fashion, but as free verse with parsed thoughts, paying careful attention to the punctuation as clues for when to stop and flow.

I showed them the wrong way first and, like Mrs. Whitehouse, spoke it with that Whitmanesque "Young Grimes" attitude:

Be*cause* I *could* not *stop* for *Death* —
He *kindly stopped* for *me* —
The *Carriage held* but *just* Our*selves* —
And *Immortality*.

And then I showed the class the right way to read Dickinson's poetry:

If I can stop one heart from breaking,
I shall not live in vain;
If I can ease one life the aching,
Or cool one pain,
Or help one fainting robin
Unto his nest again,
I shall not live in vain.

Flashforward, the 1990s through 2000s: In my Methods of Teaching Theatre class, I teach the mechanics of voice. All my students have heard of pausing but virtually no one's heard of parsing. I explain it to them, and demonstrate with a reading from *Macbeth*.

Flashsideway: I played the clarinet in high school band and I loved the complexity of the keys, found beauty and intrigue in the codes of its music instruction manual notation. I even made up foreign language written alphabets because the beauty of symbol was so intriguing. It was the code I was after. I was not just in pursuit of meaning, I was in pursuit of symbol — something else, something different, something that captured the essence and essentials of what something was and is. The act of decoding is about mysteries to be solved, but encoding is deep dark secrets to savor and to sometimes strategically keep hidden from others.

Flashback, spring 1971: We were to have read a short story by Ernest Hemingway for the day, and when we walked into Mrs. Whitehouse's classroom the word "juxtaposition" was written in large letters across the chalkboard. This was the literary element we were to learn and notice in a particular passage from Hemingway's story. I can't remember the short story's title, but I will never forget the "juxtaposition" of ideas.

Flashforward, the 1990s through 2000s: When I lecture on methods of teaching dramatic literature, I use scenes from Tennessee Williams' *The Glass Menagerie* as an exemplar. I list on the board the literary elements found most often in his plays such as symbolism, irony, foreshadowing, motif, and juxtaposition.

Flashsideway: Why *do* I always dress in blacks and whites and grays?

Flashback, spring 1971: It was mystery day. Each student in Mrs. Whitehouse's class was given a copy of Edward Arlington Robinson's poem, "How

Annandale Went Out," and we were asked to read it on our own and to answer a series of questions about it:

They called it Annandale – and I was there
To flourish, to find words, and to attend:
Liar, physician, hypocrite, and friend,
I watched him; and the sight was not so fair
As one or two that I have seen elsewhere:
An apparatus not for me to mend –
A wreck, with hell between him and the end,
Remained of Annandale; and I was there.
I knew the ruin as I knew the man;
So put the two together, if you can,
Remembering the worst you know of me.
Now view yourself as I was, on the spot –
With a slight kind of engine. Do you see?
Like this . . . You wouldn't hang me? I thought not.

And after first reading this poem silently to myself I thought, "What the hell?" For thirty minutes as a class we each sat in silence trying to decode and decipher the mystery of this poem. All of us were lost and confused, but after the independent study time Mrs. Whitehouse talked us through the poem one line at a time. And when she told us that the "engine" was a syringe for euthanasia I thought, "What the hell?" I left frustrated that day that I couldn't figure out what the poem meant. *Me*! But, I was Mrs. Whitehouse's best student! I was a junior in high school and I knew *everything*!

Flashsideway: Red ink. The answers. There's a personal need for things to stand out – to bring forward what is important, salient, to capture the essence and essentials. I've been coding all my life – not reducing data but distilling it, condensing it, symbolizing it.

Flashback, spring 1972: I cheated on one of my senior weekly English exams. I was a teaching assistant that semester and had access to the textbook room for some of my responsibilities. I knew that our senior English teacher used the standardized tests from the Teacher's Edition of our textbook, so I peeked at the answer key for our upcoming test. Today, I'm afraid of "getting caught" in so many ways. We all have deep dark secrets – I'm convinced of that. Just as in first grade when I looked at the answers in the Teacher's Edition of the math textbook, here I was in twelfth grade looking at the answers for a standardized quiz. That was the first and only time I ever cheated in school.

Flashsideway: The significance of the Teacher's Editions: I like answers. I want answers. I need answers. I hate unanswered questions. In research, I grow easily frustrated at the string of unanswered questions that sometimes comes at the end of an article. Every time I read this series of questions the researcher is too lazy to answer on his or her own, I think, "Why are you asking *me* this, don't *you* know?" I state that, in your writing, if you don't have an answer, don't ask the question. And I know some of you don't want to hear that. But to me, if you can't come up with answers or, at the very least, educated guesses to the questions you ask, then you have no business calling yourself a researcher. It's not the questions that are interesting, it's the answers that are interesting. It's the answers that are profound.

Flashback, spring 1971: We had a short answer quiz on a piece of literature, and our answers were to be just one to two sentences in length. But I wanted to impress Mrs. Whitehouse with how much I knew and how much I cared. So my short answers were not just one to two, but three to five sentences in length. I gave her what she wanted and more! My test paper was returned the next day – a good grade as I recall – but in red pencil she had crossed out my extended passages and wrote "extra" next to the irrelevant portions. "Extra."

Flashforward, the 1990s through 2000s: I am a promoter of simplicity, elegance, of finding the essence and essentials. Get to the point, already – my time is short. Death will be stopping for me.

Flashsideway: Mrs. Whitehouse embodied, symbolized, all that I loved about *teaching*, not of learning. She symbolized what I wanted to become, though I only vaguely knew it at the time. She unknowingly planted in my soul a seed that would grow, after a few years of my own personal journey, into a rebirth of teaching, a renaissance within myself of discovery; that my voice was not always right but that it was important; that after my own fumbling trial and error in the classroom, realizing that she got it right and that I could, too. I would reflect during my early career, "Gee, I wish I could be as good a teacher as she was." And then one day it hit me – I *could*. I could become who she was by nothing harder than simple replication of her pedagogy – her techniques, her mannerisms, her language, her organization, her patterns, her *style*. And I did, and I am, and I hope I will be until I retire. Even my death will be highly organized – the will's in a safe, the contingency info for my partner's up to date, and my memorial service, according to my last wishes, will have *style*. Yes, Ms. Dickinson, death will stop for me, too, but only at the specific intersection I tell him to pick me up.

Flashback, the 1990s through 2000s: When I read my students' dissertations, I prefer to review them on hard copy, not reading them on a computer monitor with that electronic "comment" function. I use red pen to point out the grammatical errors and to make recommendations for revision. Red pen is better than gray carbon pencil. Red pen will insure that the student sees my notes on the black and white of their document. Red pen says, "Hey, look here. Fix this – it's broken."

Flashsideway: Style. It's one of the most elusive processes in art yet it's something all artists strive to accomplish. It's simple to define but very slippery to achieve. If you want to discover the meaning of your life then closely examine the *style* of it.

Flashback, spring 1971: I was in theatre at the time and had fallen in love with the plays of Anton Chekhov. And Mrs. Whitehouse allowed me to perform a monologue I had memorized from *The Cherry Orchard* as a final class presentation. It was an American literature class, but she allowed me to make a presentation of something from Russia – something I was passionate about.

She even wrote in my report card for that six-weeks reporting period that I had done an "excellent" job with it.

Flashforward, spring 1976. For part of my student teaching practicum in Texas, I am assigned to teach an English class called "Paragraph Writing" at my high school site. Back then, "Paragraph Writing" was code for "the remedial students who really need a lot of help with their composition and writing skills." I remember a breaking-in period in which I had to gain the confidence of the Hispanic gang members and redneck cowboys in the class, but we eventually got along. Yet my personal success story was tutoring and encouraging a young African American woman to write not what she thought I wanted to read, but to write what was truly in her mind and in her heart. Her grades rose that semester from C's to A's. And I told her how proud I was of her *excellent* work.

Flashsideway: Think back, remember deeply, write it down, cut and paste, create the categories, look for patterns. If you're lucky and if you're open, themes will emerge and disparate threads will be woven together. But don't connect the dots; connect the *motifs*.

Flashback, May 2009: A PhD student whose dissertation I supervised was graduating, and we were excitedly waiting for the ceremony to begin. She had been in my research class a few years back and felt she could finally ask me: "Johnny, why *do* you always dress in blacks and whites and grays?" I looked at her, smiled, felt she had earned the real answer; so I told her, "I dress in blacks and whites and grays because sometimes I feel as if there's no color in my life. Except for red ink, of course."

Flashsideway: Never underestimate the power of one teacher. Never forget that what you say and do in the classroom – every single day – has the potential for lifelong impact. Don't you *dare* take teaching for granted. Teaching is meticulous craft. Teaching is an art form. It is *enduring* art.

Flashback, the middle of spring 1971, close to the end of the school year: I loved Mrs. Whitehouse so much for junior English that I wanted her for senior English, too. I told her after class one day, "You know, the junior class is pretty big, and I don't think the senior English teacher can handle all of us by herself next year." "Really?" she said. "Yeah," I replied and stated as a bold hint, "You should teach a section of senior English, too."

Flashforward, the end of spring 1971: Students learn through the grapevine that Mrs. Whitehouse will not be returning to our high school next year.

Flashforward, summer 2010: I keep my high school yearbooks stored in my bedroom's chest of drawers. As I wrote this keynote address, I remembered that I had them and went searching for what I might find. In the 1971 edition on the faculty pages, Mrs. Whitehouse's picture is in it – looking a bit too serious for some reason. But I did ask her to sign my yearbook for me and she wrote me this message:

Johnny,
You don't need my good wishes. I know you'll do well. It has been a pleasure to know you. You'll make a fine teacher.

Ann Whitehouse

Flashback, November 11, 2009: I initiated a Google and Facebook search for "Ann Whitehouse" and came across a listing of an English faculty member at Austin Community College. I e-mailed to the truncated address:

Ms. Whitehouse,
I'm searching for a former high school English teacher of mine. By chance, are you Ann Whitehouse who used to teach junior/11th grade English at Wm. B. Travis High School in Austin, Texas during the early 1970s? Thank you.
Johnny Saldaña, Professor
Arizona State University
School of Theatre and Film

Flashforward, November 12, 2009: An e-mail reply from Ann Whitehouse:

Yes, Johnny, and in my mind's eye I can see your face, looking up at me and smiling. I've been teaching a long, long time, but when I read your name on the subject line, you and our English classroom at Travis High came into focus. Look at you! Fill me in on the journey that took you to ASU teaching in the School of Theatre and Film. Thanks for writing....

Flashforward, today: Thank *you*, Mrs. Whitehouse, for accepting me just as I was; for instilling in me not just an appreciation but a love of American literature; for showing me the power, the grace, the *style* of excellent teaching; and for making me be the best teacher I try to be today. It took me forty years to tell you this, and for that, I am truly sorry. For maybe there was a time earlier in your life when you really needed to hear what I'm saying now. But now you know. Like Emily Dickinson, you have not lived in vain. You have serendipitously and significantly influenced a human life, and the lives of those I've taught, and the lives of those they teach now.

O Captain ... My Captain ...

References

Geertz, C. (1983). *Local knowledge: Further essays in interpretive anthropology.* New York: Basic Books.
Grbich, C. (2007). *Qualitative data analysis: An introduction.* London: Sage.
Holstein, J. A., & Gubrium, J. F. (2000). *Constructing the life course* (2nd ed.). Dix Hills, NY: General Hall.
Liamputtong, P. (2009). *Qualitative research methods* (3rd ed.). South Melbourne: Oxford.
McLeod, J., & Thomson, R. (2009). *Researching social change.* London: Sage.
Saldaña, J. (2003). *Longitudinal qualitative research: Analyzing change through time.* Walnut Creek, CA: AltaMira Press.
Saldaña, J. (2009). *The coding manual for qualitative researchers.* London: Sage.
Thompson, S. (1977). *The folktale.* Berkeley, CA: University of California Press.

10 Writing Poetry

Poetry as Scholarship

Verbatim theatre performer and playwright Anna Deavere Smith attests that everyday people speak in "organic poetry" through their ordinary vocabulary, natural rhythms, and unconscious parsing that evoke prosaic melodies of meaning. David Ian Hanauer's (2015) transformation of interviews with an Iraq War veteran into a stunning poetic suite is an exemplar of the power of organic poetry as scholarship. Unfortunately, many qualitative researchers perceive poetic representation and presentation as niche approaches exclusively for the arts-based research community. What they may not understand is poetry's potential as a rich essence-capturing modality of writing that motivates the researcher to scrutinize every single word choice, and encourages the reader/listener to immerse one's self in evocative literary representations about social life.

The qualitative researcher's poetic condensations and renderings of interview transcripts, field notes, or documents are analytic acts. Poeticizing the data into *found poetry* forces rigorous examination of every single word and the strategic arrangement of language that captures core ideas and evokes vivid mental images. Researchers can also create original poetry about their field experiences that documents their reflexive musings about the participants or themselves. One of my own compositions (Saldaña, 2015, p. 179) speaks to how I feel about my way of life as a qualitative researcher:

Method is my life partner.

I smile when I think of him
and his intricate complexity,
    grasping my hand firmly as I
    search for meaning.

He almost never leaves my mind.

Poetry as scholarship is not accepted by everyone in the research community. A few academic journals even have policies that prohibit poetic submissions. In some cases, poetry can be composed as a for-the-researcher's-eyes-only analytic exercise that can lead to more conventional yet inspired prosaic writing. But some journal editors and professional conferences are quite receptive to this genre, and poets should find those welcoming venues where their voices can be heard.

Monica Prendergast (Prendergast, Leggo & Sameshima, 2009) is one of qualitative inquiry's most dynamic poets and a theatre educator by training. Theatre artists must learn how to read and perform the verse plays of Sophocles, Shakespeare, Molière, and other classic and contemporary playwrights. Poetry is not meant to be read silently – it is meant to be read aloud so that language and voice combine to create intricate harmonies of insight. In my journal peer review comments to anonymous authors of poetry and play scripts, I often read what comes across as stilted verse or awkward dialogue. These submissions are drafted by well-meaning scholars interested in the arts as a qualitative modality of expression, but without a background in literary poetry or drama, the results are often lackluster. One of the most frequent recommendations for revision I offer these writers is,

> Have you yourself voiced out loud, non-stop from beginning to end, everything you've written? Speaking aloud what you've composed will give you a better understanding of your vocabulary choices and the flow of your poetic/dramatic narrative. If you feel comfortable saying what you've written, that's a good sign. But if it feels awkward, unauthentic, or tiresome, then revise the text until it feels "right." If possible, also get someone else to read aloud to you what you've written, listen to it carefully, and ask for their honest responses and comfort with the piece.

The representative selection for this chapter, "This Is Not a Performance Text" from the journal *Qualitative Inquiry*, is a theatre artist's objection to those (usually non-theatre academics) who misuse and abuse the word *performance* in scholarship. When I first attended qualitative research conferences, I was quite surprised and delighted at how several scholars prefaced their presentations by labeling their work a performance. But as I listened to their poor vocal delivery, saw no body movement aside from turning the pages of their paper, and begged for eye contact from the presenter, I became frustrated with the mislabeling of their work. I was also annoyed by good readers of emotionally moving autoethnographic pieces who felt the need to cite the academic literature throughout their presentations, breaking the mood and inhibiting my engagement with their personal stories. As a theatrical director, occasional actor, and ethnodramatic playwright, my conceptualization of performance (albeit rooted in traditional and conventional contexts) was radically different from theirs. And I felt I needed to voice my concern through a publication.

"This Is Not a Performance Text" was inspired by the clever concept and wordplay found in Austrian playwright Peter Handke's *Offending the Audience*, with its mental mind games from actors who tell the audience that they are not watching a play as they are watching the play. This contradiction led me to compose a work that was overtly not a performance, even though some readers may interpret it as such. The confrontational tone of the poem was inspired by the poetry of Mary E. Weems, an African American qualitative scholar whose sometimes angry verse arrests the ear and mind with her word choices and commanding presence in performance readings.

But why poetic form for this piece and not a critical essay or even a stage monologue? Because the terseness of what I needed to say needed a terse format. Prose is too fluid, and dramatic writing would have defeated the purpose of an anti-performance diatribe. Poetry can stutter, repeat, and interrupt itself. It can be harsh when needed, elegant when needed, ironic when needed. Though I did not originally label the work *slam poetry*, "This Is Not a Performance Text" could easily meet the criteria of an emotion-laden, forceful, fast-paced poetic rant. The literary genre we select for our writing should be the one that will best embody our research goals. I do not write poetry often, as some scholars do. I choose it selectively when what I have to say cannot be said in any other form.

References

Hanauer, D. I. (2015). Being in the second Iraq war: A poetic ethnography. *Qualitative Inquiry*, *21*(1), 83–106.

Prendergast, M., Leggo, C., & Sameshima, P. (Eds.). (2009). *Poetic inquiry: Vibrant voices in the social sciences*. Rotterdam, The Netherlands: Sense.

Saldaña, J. (2015). *Thinking qualitatively: Methods of mind*. Thousand Oaks, CA: Sage.

THIS IS NOT A PERFORMANCE TEXT

This is not a performance text.
These are words printed on paper
    (or projected on a monitor
        depending on your subscription format)
in poetic form
published in a journal.

This is a poem.

This is not a performance text.

You are not hearing me
speak these words aloud to you
as I recite them from memory.

You are not seeing me
on a raised platform
with bright lights focused
on my body.

You are not sitting down
in darkness
watching me
read or act or perform.

You are reading a poem –
You are reading a printed artifact.

This is not a performance text.

★ ★ ★

Performance
as a word and concept
has become
overused and abused
within various academic communities.

As a theatre practitioner
in my early fifties
educated during the seventies

[Originally published in *Qualitative Inquiry*, vol. 12, no. 6, 2006, pp. 1091–1098; doi 10.1177/1077800 406293239; edited slightly for this publication.]

at a traditional and
somewhat conservative institution
of higher learning
in the traditional and
conventional forms of theatre,
perhaps my
ingrained
current
and admittedly biased
conception of performance
is too outdated and
not in harmony with
contemporary applications.

But lest you
discount
dismiss
or negate
my perspective
    (all too frequent responses
    I've encountered
    as a gay Hispanic without a PhD)
know that I have read
Goffman
and Turner
and Schechner
and Conquergood
and Madison
and Pelias
and Denzin
and taken from
their glorious work
what resonated within me and,
like a good critical scholar,
questioned what I
believed suspect.

"Digital storytelling"?
I scowl, shrug, and think, "DVDs."
"Embodied methodological praxis"?
I scowl, shrug, and think, "acting."
"Ethnographic performance text"?
I just scowl and shrug.

This is not a performance text.

★ ★ ★

How dare they call it
performance
when it has never been
truly performed?

It annoys me –
like those who put parentheses
around prefixes:
    (re)search
    (re)presentation
    (de)construction
        [and don't get me started on
        power
        and embodiment].

This is not a performance text.

This is a poem.
This is a rant.
This is a poetic rant.

★ ★ ★

You do not determine
whether your work
is or is not performance.
That is my job
my privilege
my right
as an audience member.

At a conference,
when Yvonna sat on a stool
and reminisced about shooting her gun –
that was performance.
    (You should have been there.)

At a conference,
when Charlie

sat behind a table and
told his tales of woe
as a substitute teacher –
that was performance.
    (You should have been there.)

At a conference,
when Mary stood
in front of us and boldly proclaimed
"mothafucka this and mothafucka that" –
that was performance.
    (You should have been there.)

★ ★ ★

I read and hear that
culture is performed
gender is performed
teaching is performance
and that
we live in a performative society.

Yeah, right....

But when Boal[1] declares that
humans are theatre –
that I can understand.
    (and, some of us
      are more theatrical about our lives
      than others.)

Chat room transcripts
are improvised dialogue
documented in play script form.

Home entertainment centers
now rival movie multiplexes –
if not live theatre itself.

When phrases like
"What a drama queen"
and
"What is all this drama?"
entered our everyday speech,
I smiled and thought to myself

"Good.
People are finally catching on –
we are not performative;
we are theatrical."

★ ★ ★

Direct a two-hour play production
that takes hundreds of clock hours to produce –
    three months to prepare
    five weeks to rehearse
    three weekends to perform
and then tell me
what performance is and is not.

Wait backstage in darkness
for your entrance
and feel your
    armpits sweat
    and heart race
    and body shake
and then tell me what
performance is and is not.

Get on a stage
    in costume and make up
    and recall thousands of words
    by memory
    in front of a live audience
    of hundreds of people
    who paid hard-earned money
    to be entertained
and then tell me what
performance is and is not.

★ ★ ★

Go ahead:
use
perform
performance
performing
performative
performativity
and performance studies

as if the words were
intellectual confetti
sprinkled liberally
around the conference
break-out room –
so liberally
and ubiquitous
that they reach
the status of
a, an, and, the.

But know that I
(and perhaps others)
will be sitting
watching
listening
scowling
shrugging
thinking:
This is not a performance text.

Those with
way too much time on their hands
can scrutinize
theorize
and philosophize
all they want
about what
performance is and is not –
for them.

As for me,
I will take back the word
I was taught to hold
special
sacred
and reserved
for the qualified few.

★ ★ ★

This is not a performance text.

This is not a performance.

I am not performing.

There are no
italicized stage directions
prompting me to
sit, stand, cross, scowl, or shrug.

You are reading
what I have already written
in poetic form
long ago.

These are words on a white background.
These are words arranged
in poetic form
on a printed page
     (or on a monitor)
in a journal.

This is a poem.

This is not a performance text.

Note

1 Footnote? Footnote?! I don't need no stinkin' footnote!

11 Writing Ethnodrama

Research as Performance

Chapter 1 describes my projects in research as performance and the terms I've adopted from other writers related to this genre: *ethnodrama* and *ethnotheatre*. Here, I focus on the writing of research-based plays.

There are four primary methods for generating ethnodramatic scripts:

1   Adaptation of interview transcripts
2   Adaptation of nonfiction texts
3   Original autoethnodramatic monologue
4   Devised work through improvisation

(Saldaña, 2011, pp. 16–30)

The adaptation of interview transcripts transforms qualitative data into monologic or dialogic form, though most scripts utilize the former for participant representation. The adaptation can consist of a condensed and rearranged narrative, or verbatim excerpts from a longer interview. Adaptation of nonfiction texts extracts monologic and dialogic passages from different sources and, in some cases, requires the playwright to create plausible oral narratives based on the suggested action.

Original autoethnodramatic monologues are somewhat comparable to the development of autoethnographic texts, but the intent is to stage and perform the work rather than simply write or read aloud one's personal story. Devised work assembles a company of actor-researchers who bring their collected data into the rehearsal studio to improvisationally and collaboratively create a production under a director's helm.

A traditional method of playwriting instruction asks students to compose an original monologue as their first exercise in dramatic writing. The assignment challenges students to think carefully about a single character, his or her possible stories, and the most appropriate language and form for telling one of them. For qualitative researchers, this parallels the one-person case study and provides an opportunity for learning how to adapt an excerpt from a participant's interview transcript into a brief (1–3 minute) self-standing monologic account.

Writing ethnodramatic dialogue exchanged between two or more participant-characters is a more complex endeavor. Naturally occurring conversations documented in field notes or audio recordings can be adapted easily for the stage. Dialogic interactions found in nonfiction texts can also be transformed readily from the page to the stage. But most often ethnodramatists must cull authentic passages from different participants and sources to creatively reassemble them into a coherent dramatic narrative. Another tactic relies on the playwright's imagination to develop plausible stage dialogue inspired by the nonfiction source's prosaic descriptions and summaries of action.

Though it may be stating the obvious, qualitative researchers with a strong theatre background tend to write better ethnodramatic scripts. Several non-theatre scholars experiment with this writing modality, but too often their attempts are little more than a conventional research article – including footnotes, citations, and references to the academic literature – awkwardly adapted into play script format with tedious academic discourse. I try to offer constructive revision recommendations as a peer reviewer of their scholarly work, yet I always include two admonishments: *A play is not a journal article. So, stop thinking like a social scientist and start thinking like an artist.* A playwright is a storyteller in the best sense of the word. And the story an ethnodramatist tells must be told in accessible and authentic language for a lay audience.

The four selections included in this chapter illustrate two of the four methods for generating research-based scripts: writing original autoethnodramatic monologue, and adapting nonfiction texts. (See Chapter 5 for an ethnodramatic example that illustrates the adaptation of interview transcripts and field notes).

The first selection is a brief, self-standing autoethnodramatic monologue about a significant moment from my adolescence. One of my ethnotheatre workshops culminates in each participant developing a personal story from his or her life that can be told aloud in three to five minutes. Participants are given a list of prompts to stimulate memories such as

- a night your parents never found out about
- a time you felt triumphant with an accomplishment
- "the one who got away"
- a time you got into trouble for something you were told not to do
- an encounter with someone of the opposite sex when you had a disagreement rooted in gender issues.

(Saldaña, 2011, pp. 76–77)

Participants select a prompt that triggers a true story that they then workshop into monologic form for informal storytelling presentation to the group. We review the basics of one-character playwriting such as structural arcs and the importance of first and last lines, and performative elements such as gestural motif and physical stance. The example in this chapter is my own autoethnodramatic monologue developed from the prompt: the time you realized you were no longer a child.

The second selection, "*Second Chair*: An Autoethnodrama," is a personal story focused on my high school band experiences. The tale could have been told just as easily – in fact, easier – through a printed, prosaic autoethnographic account. But the commission to develop and present this piece was to demonstrate research as performance for an audience of music researchers and narrative inquirers. *Second Chair* was a monologic keynote performance for the February 2008 Narrative Inquiry in Music Education conference. The complete play script with background information on its development and presentation appeared in the journal *Research Studies in Music Education*. The article provides contextual, backstage information about the ethnodrama and my personal ways of working as a playwright, director, and actor. Four respondents offer their commentary on the play and its performance in volume 30, number 2 (2008) of *Research Studies in Music Education*.

The third selection, "The Drama and Poetry of Qualitative Method," describes the evocative language I found in the writings of educational anthropologist Harry F. Wolcott, which were adapted into the ethnodrama *Finding My Place: The Brad Trilogy*. This chapter was commissioned by co-editors Melisa Cahnmann-Taylor and Richard Siegesmund for *Arts-Based Research in Education: Foundations for Practice*. "The Drama and Poetry of Qualitative Method" includes two scenes from the ethnodramatic adaptation of Wolcott's "Brad Trilogy" articles and explains how I find drama and poetry in the most unlikely of places: academic journal articles and research methods textbooks. The chapter selection proposes how good scholarly writing can be transformed into carefully crafted dramatic narratives. I am particularly pleased with the play's Epilogue, which went through multiple drafts and has even been performed by me at several research methods conferences. The final scene consists of key methodological learnings developed by Wolcott in his various works, woven into a closing monologue that attempts to capture his most insightful words of wisdom for qualitative researchers while reflecting on the meaning of his most difficult case study.

The fourth selection is the complete ethnodramatic script of *Street Rat*, a collaborative project with mother and son researchers Susan Finley and Macklin Finley. I first became acquainted with Macklin at an arts-based research conference where he read aloud his arresting slam poetry on homeless youth (Finley, 2000). I later learned about the ethnographic work he and his mother, Susan Finley, had conducted with unhoused adolescents in pre-Katrina New Orleans (Finley & Finley, 1999). Their narratives and poetry caught my interest since some of my own work in classroom educational drama explored the culture of homelessness.

The Finleys gave me permission to adapt their related unpublished and published works into ethnodramatic form. I integrated Macklin as a character in the play, serving as an omniscient, poetic, Brechtian commentator on the action. The five main characters – Roach, Tigger, Genie, Jewel, and Quiz – are composite creations with dialogue assembled from various sources such as field notes, published pieces, and an unpublished draft of a reader's theatre script. The Finleys' prosaic narratives depicted naturalistic, day-in-the-life experiences of the participants, but the dramatic adaptation utilizes a linear plot centered around Roach's drug use. The script is laced with profanities, yet this is authentic to the young adult participants whose harsh lives are dramatized in the play.

Street Rat is the ethnodrama and ethnotheatrical production I consider one of my best artistic achievements to date. Everything I had studied about theatre and performance ethnography culminated in a work that presented a strong story, staged with authentic artifacts, and co-created with a company of actors and technicians with strong investment in this socially conscious project. Additional information on the play's production development can be accessed from Saldaña's (2005) edited collection, *Ethnodrama: An Anthology of Reality Theatre*.

References

Finley, M. (2000). *Street rat*. Detroit: Greenroom Press, University of Detroit Mercy.
Finley, S., & Finley, M. (1999). Sp'ange: A research story. *Qualitative Inquiry, 5*(3), 313–337.
Saldaña, J. (Ed.). (2005). *Ethnodrama: An anthology of reality theatre*. Walnut Creek, CA: AltaMira Press.
Saldaña, J. (2011). *Ethnotheatre: Research from page to stage*. Walnut Creek, CA: Left Coast Press.

BECOMING A MAN

(*JOHNNY makes a gesture that looks as if he's pushing a drawer shut with two hands*)

JOHNNY: When you grow up named Johnny – not John – you always feel like you're a child. I was quite spoiled as a kid – and as a teenager. Being the youngest, the baby of the family, I was always protected by my parents, always given what I wanted, fed to the extreme and pampered.

In high school, when I was a junior, this guy moved to Texas from New Mexico and came to our school. His name was Jake Simons. And over time, because we both shared an interest in band and drama, we became best friends, but you probably wouldn't think it because we were so, so different. I was a junior, he was a sophomore; I was Hispanic, he was white; I was short, he was tall; I was fat, he was muscular. But we became best friends, nevertheless.

(*makes the drawer pushing gesture, smiles*)

What I admired most about Jake was his confidence. He was a year younger than me, but he seemed so grown up. I didn't have to work as a teenager, but he was working part-time at McDonald's and making spare money – twenty-dollar bills in his wallet, when all I had was one-dollar bills stuffed in my pants pocket. He knew all that manly stuff about sports, machines, and cars. And he had a driver's license – that glorious adolescent symbol of independence – when I hadn't even taken driver's ed. Some girls confessed to me privately that they thought Jake was hot, but were reluctant to tell him so. He was tall and strong and everything I wanted to be.

But he was a year younger than me. So why wasn't I more "mature" than him?

(*makes the drawer pushing gesture, hesitantly*)

It was just an ordinary day, nothing special when I came home after school. But when I walked into my bedroom, I looked around and saw what I had become. At 16 years old, there were still stuffed animals on my dresser and toys on my bookshelves. It looked like a fourth grader lived there.

I thought of Jake and who he was and who he was becoming – then thought of me and realized I wasn't becoming anything.

(*beat*)

That was the time I realized I was no longer a "child."

(*mimes putting things in a drawer*)

So I picked up all the stuffed animals and toys and anything else that was babyish, stored them in the bottom drawer of my dresser,

[Originally published in *Ethnotheatre: Research from Page to Stage* by Johnny Saldaña, Walnut Creek, CA: Left Coast Press, 2011, pp. 79–80.]

(*makes the drawer pushing gesture*)
　　　shut it, and looked around my bedroom.
(*pause, smiles*)
　　　Now, this was the bedroom of an *adult*.
　　　Jake, just by being who he was, just by being my friend, took me out of childhood and helped me grow up. He helped me to, eventually, become what I always wanted to be. He helped me become a man.

192 *Writing Ethnodrama*

SECOND CHAIR: AN AUTOETHNODRAMA

Abstract

Second Chair, an autoethnodramatic one-man play, explores the reminiscences by an older adult of his high school band years and his quest to become first chair clarinetist through an epiphanic challenge. The play is a metaphor for the feelings of lesser status experienced by the marginalized individual in a competitive mainstream society. The full play script is included, accompanied with the author's reflections on the development and performance of the piece, and its implications for narrative inquiry.

Keywords

challenging, culture, clarinetist, high school band, narrative inquiry

Second Chair is a 30-minute, one-man play production, premiered as a plenary session at the second annual Narrative Inquiry in Music Education (NIME2) conference in February 2008 at Arizona State University. As the playwright and actor of my own work, I labeled the script an *autoethnodrama* which, in general terms, is an autobiographical cultural story in play script format intended for performance. Specifically:

> Ethno*theatre* employs the traditional craft and artistic techniques of theatre production to mount for an audience a live performance event of research participants' experiences and/or the researcher's interpretations of data.... The goal is to investigate a particular facet of the human condition for purposes of adapting those observations and insights into a performance medium. Simply put, this is preparatory fieldwork for theatrical production work.
>
> An ethno*drama*, the written script, consists of dramatized, significant selections of narrative collected through interviews, participant observation field notes, journal entries, and/or print and media artifacts such as diaries, television broadcasts, newspaper articles, and court proceedings. Simply put, this is dramatizing the data.
>
> (Saldaña, 2005, pp. 1–2)

*Auto*ethnodrama, as a variant of the form, draws primarily from the writer's personal experiences and memories, which are then documented as a monologue intended for performance by the writer him- or herself. These genres are some of the forms currently explored as a mode of arts-based educational

[Originally published in *Research Studies in Music Education*, vol. 30, no. 2, 2008, pp. 177–191, doi 10.1177/1321103X08097506; edited slightly for this publication.]

research in the field of qualitative inquiry (Cahnmann-Taylor & Siegesmund, 2008; Knowles & Cole, 2008).

Genesis of the Play Script

The NIME2 conference organizers' charge for my plenary session was to acquaint participants with ethnodrama as a literary cousin of narrative inquiry. My original plan was to lecture for one hour and show selected video excerpts of plays from the genre. But as pre-conference planning progressed, I thought it would be preferable to *show* an ethnodramatic performance live, rather than merely talk about the art form with projected media. I had already adapted, directed, and published the scripts of four ethnotheatrical play productions (Saldaña, 1998; 2002; Saldaña, Finley, & Finley, 2005; Vanover & Saldaña, 2005), one of which focused on the classroom turmoil of an inner-city Chicago school teacher who found inner peace by attending the symphony (Vanover & Saldaña, 2005). I considered remounting this production for NIME2, but limited financial resources made that idea impractical. It should also be noted here that, to date, none of my ethnodramatic work had been autobiographical – the scripts were adaptations of other participants' life stories.

Serendipitously, several personal life events occurred months before the conference that collectively led to the development of *Second Chair*. I am a firm believer in pattern and purpose – everything happens for a reason. And the convergence of these isolated yet eventually interrelated matters contributed to and inspired the idea for the script.

First, two former friends from my 1960s-1970s adolescence had recently contacted me via email to reunite. Through our correspondence we reminisced about our wonderful days in high school band. This nostalgia motivated me to search for and purchase CDs of my favorite composer from our concert repertoire – W. Francis McBeth. I listened to four volumes of his music – some selections I myself had played, plus his later work which I found rich and engaging.

Second, I had just completed two chapter submissions about ethnodrama and ethnotheatre for research methods handbooks (Saldaña, 2008a; 2008b), and an unpublished article about the theories inherent in the genre. My focus on the aesthetics of the art form rather than its scholarly methods was now quite prominent and influential in my writing and thinking. By this time I had read almost 200 ethnodramatic play scripts, yet perhaps only 20 of them held high artistic merit in my judgment as both a theatre artist and qualitative researcher.

Third, I was completing the manuscript for my book, *The Coding Manual for Qualitative Researchers* (Saldaña, 2009). One section in the text focuses on coding methods adapted from literary traditions and includes such approaches to qualitative data as Narrative Coding, Motif Coding, and Dramaturgical Coding. Thus, I was increasingly attuned to prosaic, poetic, and dramatic elements in both interview transcripts and documents. (I was also trained as a high school English and theatre teacher, and the instruction of literary elements – symbolism, foreshadowing, juxtaposition, etc. – was emphasized in my curriculum.)

Fourth, during the same semester as the NIME2 conference, I would be teaching my first formal course in ethnotheatre at Arizona State University. One of the options for the course's final project was for students to write a short autoethnodramatic play script and perform it for the class. Though I had already adapted and staged four ethnodramatic works, all of them were other people's stories, not my own. I felt hypocritical asking students to do an assignment I myself had not done before. I asserted on the first day of class: "You can't learn how to tell someone else's story until you first learn how to tell your own." Thus, as an instructor, I needed to "step up to the plate" and develop and perform my own ethnotheatrical piece.

The NIME2 conference was the opportunity and venue for everything described thus far to crystallize. My memory-refreshed music education experiences – which included an epiphanic attempt to compete for first chair clarinetist in my high school band – would serve as the primary topic for the autoethnodrama. The recently purchased McBeth CDs would provide the production's necessary soundtrack – a theatrical element I value highly in my directorial work. My recent writings in the art form had generated within me a heightened consciousness of quality ethnodramatic play script development with attention to such literary elements as complication, motifs, and metaphors. Finally, the need to "walk the talk" for my ethnotheatre class by performing my own story for them, would provide me with the credibility and credentials to assess their final projects.

Rather than describe the actual writing process for *Second Chair* at this point, it would be best to simply present the final version of the play script for readers. My personal commentary and reflections will follow.

The Play Script – *Second Chair*

The following one-man autoethnodrama is a true story; its intended audience is music educators and narrative researchers; the detailed stage directions describe how the production was originally mounted and performed.

(*setting: two metal folding chairs with metal music stands in front of each one; the music stands hold all necessary props for the production; first chair appears shiny and pristine; second chair appears worn, rusty, and beaten*)
(*pre-show music: various selections composed by W. Francis McBeth* (The Feast of Trumpets, Praises, Caccia, Flourishes); *lights rise; JOHNNY enters at the beginning of* Flourishes, *looks longingly at first chair, then sits in second chair and looks occasionally toward the empty first chair; music fades out; he speaks to the audience*)
JOHNNY: In high school band, Tammi Jo thought she was so special. She played an ebony wood Selmer clarinet with a glass mouthpiece, while all I had was this cheap-ass plastic Bundy. Her family was typical middle-class and she

was the only child, thus receiving all of the attention and all of the spoils. My family was transitioning from lower class to middle, but that was kind of hard with so many children to take care of.

In our junior year, I was second chair; and Tammi Jo was first chair.
(*brief pause*)

And I think you know where this story is going.
(*rises*)

I started learning cornet in sixth grade, but became quickly intrigued with the clarinet. All those silver keys looked inviting,
(*picks up a clarinet fingering chart from the music stand and shows it to audience*)
and it fascinated me to see how the fingerings were notated in music instruction manuals. It seemed a lot more exciting to play an instrument with all those keys rather than just pressing the cornet's three valves with its limited configurations.
(*returns the fingering chart to the music stand*)

I was OK at the cornet, but not great. And I hated it when spit and valve oil dribbled all over my pants. Plus, the girls playing woodwinds were a lot nicer than the guys in the brass section. I was two years behind others learning the instrument when I switched, but quickly got up to speed because I was so, so motivated to learn.
(*picks up sheet music from music stand*)

And the sheet music and arrangements for a clarinet were sensational! The trills, with the *tr* and that little squiggly line afterward, and the runs from one note to another with that little squiggly line in-between them. And the grace notes that added a sense of élan to what you were playing.

In high school band, we did it all, from pop tunes to classics, from *Jesus Christ Superstar* to *Carmina Burana*. But my favorite composer
(*returns sheet music; holds up a McBeth CD case*)
was W. Francis McBeth.
(*McBeth's* Lauds and Tropes – Laud II *music up; to an audience member who may be laughing or smirking at that*)

No, really! *Divergents, Masque,*
(*in awe*)

Chant and Jubilo. His music was so different, so . . .
(*at a loss for words. he moves kinesthetically to the music*)

It had a pulse; it had style.
(*music plays for a while as JOHNNY smiles and moves joyously to the music; music fades slowly out; puts CD case away*)

In Austin, Texas in the early 1970s, there were three things that ruled: cowboys, football, and marching band. Competition was drilled into our spirits:
(*fist in the air, chanting loudly, as if at a pep rally*)

We are great! Better than you! We are the class of seventy-two!
(*cheers*)

Texas was the biggest state in the union.
(*aside*)

Actually, Alaska was the biggest state in the union. But to Texans, Alaska didn't really count.

(*picks up a baton, moves a music stand downstage center*)

And with being the biggest came egos to match.

(*he taps the music stand with his baton, raises it sharply and scans an imaginary band in front of him; he swings the baton to the downbeat and conducts; McBeth's* Battaglia *music up*)

Conducting us masterfully with his baton was Mr. Garcia – a great band director who knew his art, taught with passion, demanded nothing less than precision and perfection, and shaped us into the best musicians we could be. And yes, when he got pissed off at our sloppy playing, Mr. Garcia would throw his baton angrily to the floor!

(*he throws baton down; music stops suddenly*)

Then all of us would freeze and stare at him in frightened silence as he scowled.

(*he scowls as Mr. Garcia, glaring at the band in front of him; gestures as if to say, "What the hell's wrong with you?!"; picks up baton*)

Well, there was no time to fool around. Sweepstakes, all-state, first ratings, blue ribbons, gold medals – that's what it was all about. In those days, we weren't told to "do your best," we were told to "*be* the best." And it was not only that way with the entire band, it was that way with me. Young men are taught to strive, to accomplish, to achieve success, to be number one, to be – first chair.

(*returns music stand and baton; sits in second chair*)

But to a young gay man, and second chair, it was not just about competition; it was also about . . .

(*brief pause; looks at first chair*)

jealousy.

(*to audience*)

There are three things gay men are very good at: redecorating a room, preparing brunch,

(*staring at first chair briefly*)

and being petty and vindictive bitches.

Now, Tammi Jo and I were actually quite good friends. We had been sitting next to each other as first and second chair for almost a year already, and we would often joke and laugh, quietly of course, while Mr. Garcia worked with or

(*snickers*)

yelled at the brass and percussion sections. And since I was also involved with high school theatre at the time and quite the closeted drama queen, Tammi Jo and I made a secret pact: as soon as I would win the Academy Award for best actor, she would win the Nobel Prize for medicine.

She was the genius of our school. You know her kind: straight A-pluses on each report card, first on the honor roll, reading Charles Darwin's *The Origin of Species* without being required to, and eventually becoming

valedictorian of our graduating class. She was smart. And skinny – thin as a rail! Me?
(*rises*)
My top weight in high school was 310 pounds.
(*to audience members who may be reacting to that*)
No, really. I was so large that my mom had to custom-sew a new pair of pants for my band uniform because there were none in stock that fit me. Boy, did she jump all over me for that – as she stuffed me with those potato, egg, and flour tortilla tacos.
(*as his mother, in a thick Hispanic dialect*)
"Aye, Johnny, you're too fat!"
(*normal voice*)
And, because it had probably been drilled into her, it was also drilled into me:
(*as his mother*)
"¡Aye, Juanito, mejicanos son pendejos!"
(*pause; normal voice*)
Growing up, I was frequently called "stupid" by my mother.
(*pause*)
Fat *and* stupid. Needless to say, my self-esteem issues were pretty raw back then.
(*returns to second chair; sits, gleefully*)
Oh, but Tammi Jo had *her* baggage. One of the French horn players was this really butch lesbian who was always making the moves on her. And Tammi Jo didn't say no! Rumor spread fast that Tammi Jo was probably, as you said in Texas back then,
(*in a gruff Texas drawl*)
"one of *those* gals."
(*normal voice*)
I don't know if she was or is, but we did wonder. And in high school, once you're labeled, it sticks to you and stinks like cork wax.
(*rises*)
Speaking of labels, there are three things a Hispanic hates being called: lazy, meskin, and wetback. For the uninformed, a "wetback" is a demeaning ethnic slur, referring to a Mexican who swims across the Rio Grande River to enter the United States "illegally."

Swim, river, wet, back. Get it?

After a long morning of marching band rehearsal outdoors in the hot Texas sun, we would all come back to the band hall to put our instruments away. The perspiration that was always on the back of my shirt was a running joke among my White friends. They would smirk and pat me gently on the back over and over saying, "Hey Johnny, your back's wet, your back's wet!"
(*rolling his eyes*)
And I would laugh along, ah-ha-ha-ha-ha-ha . . .
(*pause; scowls*)

Aside from that, they really were good friends.
(looks at then walks to first chair, frustrated)
I was so close to being first chair, so close! Tammi Jo had been first chair for over a year already, even beating out a senior during her sophomore year for the title. And the only reason I progressed from third chair to second chair was that the senior graduated.
(sits in second chair)
So the opportunity was right there in front of me. And one day I seized it, because – I wanted it.
(looks toward first chair)
"Tammi Jo, I think I'd like to challenge you."
(to audience)
That's probably what I told her, the actual memory of what I really said isn't clear in my head. But what I was most likely *thinking* was, "Yeah, Tammi Jo, one day I might win the Academy Award for best actor, and one day you might win the Nobel Prize for medicine, but for right now, at this moment,
(shouting)
it's just between you and me, girlfriend!"
(rises)
The rules of challenging were quite simple. Verbally challenge the player sitting ahead of you, notify the band director, and take one week to prepare a selection of his choice. Mr. Garcia would listen with his back to both of us to keep it anonymous, unbiased, and fair. Then he would immediately announce the results.

On the day of the challenge, my friends – who playfully told me my back was wet – stayed after school to root for me and cheer me on. They could have gone home, but they waited to wish me luck and to find out what would happen. Now that was loyalty – and/or juicy curiosity.

Bad-asses of the school waited in the parking lot to watch two people fight. Band kids waited by the instrument room to hear two people challenge.
(sits in second chair)
Well, this was a major event for everyone in my circle. But to me, this was not just about second chair versus first chair. And this was not just about boys versus girls. And this was not just about Hispanics versus Whites.
(getting angrier and louder)
And this was not just about poor versus middle-class, and this was not just about gays versus lesbians, and this was not just about fat versus skinny, and this was not just about stupid versus smart, and this was not just about *cheap-ass plastic Bundys versus ebony wood Selmers with glass mouthpieces!*
(brief pause; clutches the music stand and seethes in a low voice)
It was all of the above.
(rises, moves music stand to downstage center, music up softly: McBeth's Chant *from* Chant and Jubilo; *JOHNNY mimes holding a clarinet)*

When I played the clarinet, I made it my own. Back then, high school trumpeters were trying to be the next Herb Alpert, while drummers were trying to be the next Keith Moon. But the clarinet was sacred to me. I wasn't trying to be the "next" Benny Goodman; I was trying to be the *first* Johnny Saldaña. I created my own style, my own tone, my own musical signature.

(*conducts with his hands in deep emotion to the music*)

Mr. Garcia conducted with a sense of drama. You could see in his face the emotion of the music we were playing, and he encouraged us to feel it as well. Being in theatre, I understood what he meant; I understood what he was feeling. And that influenced and affected me deeply. I didn't just want to "perform" or "play" my instrument. I tried to *act* with my clarinet.

(*music up; Johnny mimes playing/acting with his clarinet; his emotions take over and his hands move upward as if in glorious flight; music fades out; returns music stand*)

There were strict instructions when you entered the practice room for a challenge while Mr. Garcia had his back to us: Just walk in,

(*sits in second chair*)

sit down, play the selection, and leave. Don't say a word, don't cough, don't even clear your throat – otherwise he would know who it was and the challenge was off.

Maybe I secretly hoped that Mr. Garcia, because he too was Hispanic, would give one of his own kind a break. But I knew he had too much integrity to do something like that. All I could hope for was that the final outcome would not be based solely on the quality of sound made by an ebony wood Selmer with a glass mouthpiece, and a cheap-ass plastic Bundy.

(*McBeth's* Of Sailors and Whales – I. Ishmael *music up softly*)

To be honest, 38 years after the fact, I really can't remember what the selection was that Mr. Garcia had us play for him. Most likely it would have been something we were rehearsing at the time for a concert band performance. Oh, but wouldn't it be delightfully ironic if it had been something composed by W. Francis McBeth?

(*rises*)

So, Tammi Jo and I both played and competed for first chair – she to maintain it, me to achieve it. And then we waited outside the practice room nervously waiting for the results.

Mr. Garcia stepped out of the room, looked at his written notes, and asked which one of us played first and which one of us played second.

One of my friends who had been hanging out by the instrument room heard the news, ran out of the band hall and into the hallway shouting to the others,

(*music rises to its full climax as he extends his hand and shouts*)

"Johnny got first chair!"

(JOHNNY *remains frozen in disbelief; he then moves slowly in awe to first chair, sits in it, and relishes the moment; music fades slowly out*)

I stayed first chair throughout my senior year. But the accomplishment, the triumph, was tarnished.

Mr. Garcia, that wonderful man, resigned in disgrace at the end of my junior year. From what we were told, he had violated – perhaps knowingly, perhaps not – Texas state competition rules for concert bands. He had used a few of the same musicians from the upper class band in the freshman band, something obviously not permitted.

Our junior year first-ratings sweepstakes was maintained by the state organization, but our school was disqualified from competition for one year – my senior year – as punishment. So, Mr. Garcia left. A new band director, fresh out of music school, was hired to take his place. And he was a disaster.

(*looking at second chair*)

Tammi Jo, who entered that year as second chair, after just one month, dropped out of band. She became disillusioned, as I did, with the new director. Instead, during that period she attended the local private Catholic college in the mornings so she could learn calculus.

(*rises*)

Our senior year band director was so bad that the parents mobilized to have him fired after just one semester. Several years later we would learn that – true story – he murdered his wife by hitting her over the head with a frying pan, stuffed her body in a garbage bag and hid it in the trunk of his car, and was eventually arrested at a local flea market selling their household possessions.

(*brief pause*)

No, really.

And Tammi Jo? I learned at our ten-year high school reunion back in 1982 that she had indeed attended medical school: Harvard – of course – and was now a psychiatrist in private practice.

(*pause; smiling, sincerely*)

Good for her.

(*sits in first chair*)

I'm too rooted in academia and too old now to learn how to act professionally in film, so it's most likely I will never, ever win the Academy Award for best actor.

(*looks at second chair*)

But Tammi Jo may earn that Nobel Prize for medicine yet.

(*JOHNNY squirms uncomfortably in first chair, as if fighting with unseen forces, then slides to second chair; pause*)

I'm still striving to be first chair in many ways. As an older, overweight, gay, Hispanic without a PhD, it's always feeling and sometimes being treated as lesser than, second best, like playing a cheap-ass plastic Bundy when you'd rather be playing an ebony wood Selmer with a glass mouthpiece.

(*looks at first chair*)

I'm always looking sideways to see who's sitting next to me, ahead of me, better than me, more privileged than me. It's true what they say,

very true: when you're not of the mainstream, you have to work twice as hard to be considered half as good. Competition is deeply embedded in American culture. And in Texas culture. And in male culture. And in academic culture, and in Hispanic culture, and in gay culture, and in high school culture, and in band culture. It's been taught, reinforced, and socially hardwired into me.
(*rises, lightening the mood*)
    Oh, I've had my moments of triumph now and then: a book publishing deal here, a research award there.
    In all honesty, those things are very important to me. First chair doesn't give me "meaning." First chair gives me *value*.
(*walks to first chair*)
First chair lets me know – that I'm not stupid. Though, admittedly, I still say and do some very stupid things now and then. Who doesn't?
(*paces, as if trying to figure it out*)
First chair lets me know ... not that I'm the "best" but that, quite simply ...
(*pause*)
that I'm OK – that things are all right. Do you know what I mean?
(*pause*)
    Mr. Garcia inspired me to consider becoming a music educator myself. Since I was first chair clarinetist in my high school band –
(*smiling, raising his finger and emphasizing to the audience*)
and don't you ever forget that – I was recruited by the University of Texas conductor to attend a high school day to practice with the prestigious university concert band.
(*sits in first chair, flips through sheet music*)
    I went, mostly out of pride at being invited, and I played with them. But sight reading some of the selections was just too difficult. One of them was *Flight of the Bumblebee*. I felt so intimidated by all the talent there, I just couldn't go on. So, being a theatre major became my choice. And I have no regrets, it's been good to me. Besides, because of band, music is still a very vital part of my life.
(*picks up McBeth CD case from the music stand*)
    And W. Francis McBeth?
(*brief pause*)
He was just an adolescent phase.
(*returns the McBeth CD case and shows a Glass CD case; rises;* Glass's Music in Twelve Parts, Part 2 *music up*)
Now, my musical hero is Philip Glass.
(*to an audience member who may be laughing or smirking at that*)
    No, really! *The Photographer. A Descent into the Maelström*,
(*in awe*)
Einstein on the Beach. His music is so different, so ...
(*at a loss for words. he moves kinesthetically to the music*)
It's got a pulse. It's got style.

(*returns the CD case to music stand; he looks at his fingers*)
>The mouthpiece of a clarinet hasn't touched my lips for 36 years.

(*he mimes playing chromatically on a clarinet from low E to high F*)
>But to this day, I still remember the fingering positions for every single note. And when I'm driving . . .

(*JOHNNY picks up second chair, brings it downstage center and sits; pause as he looks at first chair; he thinks better of it, returns second chair to its place, takes first chair to downstage center and sits*)
>when I'm driving,

(*holds his fingers up and spread open*)
>because of band, my ex-clarinetist fingertips still move – *joyfully* – to the music playing in my car!

(*Glass music rises; JOHNNY taps his foot, bobs his head to the beat, smiles, holds onto an imaginary steering wheel, and moves his fingertips joyfully to the music as if playing a clarinet; lights slowly fade to black*)

Playwright's Commentary and Reflections

Writing this autoethnodramatic monologue was admittedly quite easy. By this time in my career, developing an extended story for the stage is almost second nature to me. The biggest challenge was allaying typical actor's nervousness before and during the live performance of the work, and my greatest fear was forgetting my lines, which I and my acting colleagues found ironic. You would think that if a text is your own personal story, you would remember everything that needs to be said. But *Second Chair* was a piece dependent on carefully selected language and exact music cues, so there was little room, if any, for variation and improvisation during performance.

So many topics about the experience could be discussed, but I will focus on just a few salient matters in this article.

Writing the Play

Out of 12 years of music education experiences from elementary through secondary school, the achievement of first chair clarinetist in grade 11 was the most memorable to me. Hence, the subject matter of the commissioned piece related to a significant (albeit relatively small) epiphany from my high school band days. I did worry, though, about the content's originality for the professionals in the audience. I was familiar with narrative inquiry methods, but completely unacquainted with the narrative inquiry in music education literature. I wondered if conference participants would roll their eyes in boredom during the performance and think, "Oh, God – not *another* second-chair-to-first-chair story." That fear, apparently, was groundless. Rather than recycle what I presumed was a stale plot, I seemed to have unintentionally struck a chord with those who had experienced the same phenomenon of challenging for chair placement in band.

From a playwriting (as opposed to a prose narrative) perspective, this personal story had traditional if not "classic" action-oriented elements for a script: a protagonist with a clear objective, a linear story-line with a strong conflict, relevant and cumulative exposition, and tension that led to a climactic turning point. The theatricality of the ethnodrama called for music soundtracking, simple suggestive scenery with folding chairs and music stands, band artifacts as props (a baton, sheet music, etc.), and opportunities for extensive actor movement and vocal dynamics. This was a story not just to be told but *shown*.

One of my favorite playwriting devices (and note its parallel to music composition) is the use of motif. Throughout *Second Chair* there is conscious repetition of selected phrases to unify the piece. I liken my delight with this literary element to Philip Glass's repetitive style in some of my favorite works by him. Considering which specific W. Francis McBeth pieces to incorporate into the production was also a facet of playwriting. I have always found his music quite active and dramatic – "It had a pulse; it had style," as I say in the script. I noticed afterward that all of his pieces I chose for the script are accompanied in performance with physical stage action, not just background music for mood. If I tried to "act with my clarinet" in the past, perhaps today I am still trying to physicalize music, not just hear it.

One of my goals as an ethnodramatist is to inform audiences about the participant-character's cultural world and what it's like to live in it. Davis and Ellis (2008) explain that autoethnography (and thus an autoethnodrama) "is the study of a culture of which one is a part, integrated with one's relational and inward experiences. The author incorporates the 'I' into research and writing, yet analyzes him- or herself as if studying an 'other'" (p. 284).

Second Chair openly addresses my personal and multiple categories of cultural identity such as class, ethnicity, and sexual orientation. Discussion of their relevance during high school band days in the earlier portions of the play served primarily as contextual foregrounding for the thematic issues posed in the denouement. I needn't summarize them here, as my perspectives are unabashedly presented in the script. Interestingly, one audience member at NIME2 noted the sociopolitical undercurrents of my text and their critical pedagogical implications for music education. I find it ironic, in post-production reflection, that my struggles with status and equity during high school were quite minor compared to the discriminatory, prejudicial, and occasionally hateful encounters I've experienced as a middle-aged adult from faculty colleagues in a presumably liberal university environment. The autoethnodramatic format provides me with a forum for sharing messages of personal and vital importance to fellow artists and educators. If musicians can understand the feelings accorded to someone of "second chair" status, they can hopefully understand the feelings of the marginalized individual in a competitive mainstream society: "it's always feeling and sometimes being treated as lesser than, second best, like playing a cheap-ass plastic Bundy when you'd rather be playing an ebony wood Selmer with a glass mouthpiece."

Development of the play also led me to realize the underlying symbolic and metaphoric significance of first and second chair's status (discussed further below). I always try to extend beyond the particulars of a case study to transcend and transfer to the general. One of my pet peeves is a tendency for some authors of narrative inquiry to let their stories speak for themselves. I personally feel cheated unless the author has done some insightful analytic thinking for me. Thus, I felt the need to include what the story "means" to me, even though I admonish the elusive search for it myself ("First chair doesn't give me 'meaning.' First chair gives me *value*."). Two reviewers of my early play script drafts each expressed dissatisfaction with this thematic passage, noting that it needed to be "unpacked":

(*paces, as if trying to figure it out*)
First chair lets me know . . . not that I'm the "best" but that, quite simply . . .
(*pause*)
that I'm OK – that things are all right. Do you know what I mean?
(*pause*)

What may not come across in print was intentionally nuanced during performance. Particular gestures, vocal tones, facial expressions, and silences were deliberately made that suggested a sense of resolved peace, accompanied with an undercurrent of slight dissatisfaction at the loss for just the right words to say. Even now, I still feel I cannot clearly articulate what I really think first chair provides for me. The closest related words I can find in a thesaurus are: "stability," "security," "certainty," "self-confidence," and "faith in oneself." But weaving all of these words into one line of monologue would result in very bad playwriting. I myself may be guilty of the ambiguity I fault other narrative writers for, but at least there is some sense of resolution to proclaiming the intrinsic albeit elusive value of being first chair.

Do you know what I mean?

Rehearsing and Performing the Play

As a director, I am very attuned to how my stage productions both look and sound. I have been complimented for my "performative" lecture voice in the classroom, and my vocal techniques (pausing, parsing, inflection, rhythm, word stress, variety, etc.) are consciously and strategically chosen to achieve particular effects. I do indeed speak musically, and I attribute that skill partly to my music training and love of the art. Performing for an audience of music educators heightened my awareness even more of how this production would be heard by others.

Rehearsal is a period during which the actor hopefully makes insightful discoveries about the text and brings those nuances to performance. The most significant moment to me was rehearsing the climax: "*Johnny got first chair!*" Accompanied with McBeth's haunting and beautiful music from *Of Sailors and Whales*, I literally broke down crying each time I shouted that line in private.

The awareness and power of the moment – its personal meaning and importance – were laid bare and generated within me a psychological, crystallizing "click." This was personal catharsis, aesthetic absorption and flow, emotional recall so vivid that it led me to tears, and a deep understanding of the metaphors of what it means to be second and first chair.

I needn't elaborate on the latter theme; the play script reveals quite honestly what I think and how I feel. But the thing to note here is that that climactic moment of crying was never realized during the final dress rehearsal for my ethnotheatre class and the NIME2 performance. I was open to letting myself cry, but the emotional trigger didn't happen – perhaps because of my personal nervousness during performance and the unexpected applause reaction from the audience. Rather than perform a false emotion and risk an unbelievable moment, I instead reacted with my "gut" – stunned awe at the triumph. In retrospect, I am still amazed at the power of that discovery during rehearsal. Perhaps the intent was cathartic for me and no one else. Trite as it may sound, this is the therapeutic and healing power of art. (A month and a half after the performance, in the privacy of my office as I wrote this article, I played *Of Sailors and Whales* as I recited the climactic section of the play. Again, I cried.)

Performing my own story gave me deep ownership of it – deeper than if I had simply written it as a prose narrative in a journal to be silently read by others. *Second Chair* and its true personal impact can be experienced by no one but myself. But I hope the empathetic and sympathetic audience member during performance resonated with the piece. I am more firmly convinced of my assertion that you can't learn how to tell someone else's story until you first learn how to tell your own. Autoethnodramatic work has enhanced my abilities as a narrative inquirer and storyteller.

Conclusion

Post-performance audience response was quite favorable to *Second Chair*. The most frequent comment was from those (mostly former clarinetists themselves) sharing with me their own stories about band challenges and chair placements. NIME2 conference co-chair Sandra Stauffer, after reading the first draft of the play script, remarked that challenging and its effects on students in band was "the elephant in the room that nobody's talking about." From what I was told, the play generated rich and honest dialogue that day among conference participants. All theatre artists hope that their production work has some type of impact on audiences after the performance. So, it's my wish that this play script offers music educators an opportunity to share their personal responses of what "meanings" or value *Second Chair* holds for them and their students.

Acknowledgments

Thanks are extended to Sandra Stauffer who, by inviting me to present as a plenary speaker, commissioned the development of *Second Chair* for the second annual Narrative Inquiry in Music Education conference at Arizona State University in February 2008; to Amira De la Garza, Galen Shotts, and Thomas C. Turner for script revision recommendations; and to Molly Gittelman for sound board operation during performances of the play.

References

Cahnmann-Taylor, M., & Siegesmund, R. (Eds.). (2008). *Arts-based research in education: Foundations for practice*. New York: Routledge.

Davis, C. S., & Ellis, C. (2008). Emergent methods in autoethnographic research: Autoethnographic narrative and the multiethnographic turn. In S. N. Hesse-Biber & P. Leavy (Eds.), *Handbook of emergent methods* (pp. 283–302). New York: Guilford.

Knowles, J. G., & Cole, A. L. (Eds.). (2008). *Handbook of the arts in qualitative research: Perspectives, methodologies, examples, and issues*. Thousand Oaks, CA: Sage.

Saldaña, J. (1998). "Maybe someday, if I'm famous . . .": An ethnographic performance text. In J. Saxton & C. Miller (Eds.), *Drama and theatre in education: The research of practice, the practice of research* (pp. 89–109). Brisbane: IDEA Publications.

Saldaña, J. (2002). Finding my place: The Brad trilogy. In H. F. Wolcott (Ed.), *Sneaky kid and its aftermath: Ethics and intimacy in fieldwork* (pp. 167–210). Walnut Creek, CA: AltaMira Press.

Saldaña, J. (Ed.). (2005). *Ethnodrama: An anthology of reality theatre*. Walnut Creek, CA: AltaMira Press.

Saldaña, J. (2008a). The drama and poetry of qualitative method. In M. Cahnmann-Taylor & R. Siegesmund (Eds.), *Arts-based research in education: Foundations for practice* (pp. 220–227). New York: Routledge.

Saldaña, J. (2008b). Ethnodrama and ethnotheatre. In J. G. Knowles & A. L. Cole (Eds.), *Handbook of the arts in qualitative research: Perspectives, methodologies, examples, and Issues* (pp. 195–207). Thousand Oaks, CA: Sage.

Saldaña, J. (2009). *The coding manual for qualitative researchers*. London: Sage.

Saldaña, J., Finley, S., & Finley, M. (2005). Street rat. In J. Saldaña (Ed.), *Ethnodrama: An anthology of reality theatre* (pp. 139–179). Walnut Creek, CA: AltaMira Press.

Vanover, C., & Saldaña, J. (2005). Chalkboard concerto: Growing up as a teacher in the Chicago public schools. In J. Saldaña (Ed.), *Ethnodrama: An anthology of reality theatre* (pp. 62–77). Walnut Creek, CA: AltaMira Press.

THE DRAMA AND POETRY OF QUALITATIVE METHOD

As a theatre artist, I have been trained to find the drama of everyday life so that it may be faithfully reproduced on stage for realistic plays. As a playwright, I have also been trained to find the poetry in everyday language so that it may inspire the creation of evocative monologue and dialogue. This conditioning preceded my study of qualitative inquiry by almost 25 years and greatly influenced my introduction to the literature.

When I first read selections from the canon of educational research and ethnography, I encountered everything from sterile reports to emotion-laden narratives. Just as there are some storytellers who are more theatrical than others, there are a few writers who are more dramatic than others. Contemporary works in narrative inquiry, qualitative research, auto/ethnography, and investigative journalism have provided riveting and sometimes haunting stories (e.g., Barbara Ehrenreich's (2002) *Nickel and Dimed: On (Not) Getting By in America*; Jennifer Toth's (1993) *The Mole People: Life in the Tunnels Beneath New York City*). Yet for some reason, I found myself initially drawn to and engaged with the methods literature most of all. There was something about the "how to" that kept me enthralled. I was evolving into a "research geek" (my term), and I was literally fascinated with field-note protocol, coding schemes, and analytic procedures. Depending on the author, even seemingly mundane research methods books contained inspired writing.

Wolcott (1995), in *The Art of Fieldwork*, reflects on the parallels between art and ethnography:

> My purpose in this book is to examine how fieldwork not only invites but also requires something of an artistic approach.... [A]rt plays a significant role in my life, not merely in terms of what I enjoy and appreciate aesthetically, but as well in what I have been able to create, in spite of the absence of any recognizable talent. I like to think that there is something of the artist in me, some capacity not only for appreciating but for creating, just as I assume there is something of the artist in you, and in everyone.
>
> (p. 13)

When I read the works of Harry F. Wolcott during my qualitative research courses with Tom Barone and Mary Lee Smith at Arizona State University, it was in his articles and methods books that I found the drama and poetry of qualitative research. Wolcott's gift with language – even at the technical level – engaged me. And the series of articles dubbed "The Brad Trilogy" – an anthropological case study profiling Wolcott's relationship with a young man who eventually descended into paranoid schizophrenia – kept me in awe. "This is theatre,"

[Originally published as Chapter 17 in *Arts-Based Research in Education: Foundations for Practice*, edited by Melisa Cahnmann-Taylor and Richard Siegesmund, New York: Routledge, 2008, pp. 220–227; edited slightly for this publication.]

208 *Writing Ethnodrama*

I thought to myself, and it would eventually influence my ventures into arts-based research (see Saldaña, 2005, *Ethnodrama: An Anthology of Reality Theatre*).

Some writers in the social sciences have a flair for evocative writing, even if their works are academic in reportage. Their prose is vivid or conversational and "feels" like monologue or dialogue that can be directly transferred – even from a methods textbook – onto the stage.

Wolcott is one of those writers. Sentences from his texts found their way into our theatrical adaptation of *Finding My Place: The Brad Trilogy* (Saldaña, in Wolcott, 2002). When appropriate, insightful and even humorous passages from *Writing Up Qualitative Research* (1990), *Transforming Qualitative Data: Description, Analysis and Interpretation* (1994), *The Art of Fieldwork* (1995), and *Ethnography: A Way of Seeing* (1999) became part of his monologues.

The Art of Fieldwork was particularly rich with "one-liners." For example, in the Prologue of the play, Wolcott addresses the audience on his love for ethnography: "In fieldwork, you immerse yourself personally – with passion, without apology – for the purposes of research. Fieldwork beckons, even dares you, to become part of what you study" (Wolcott, 1995, p. 239–240; Saldaña, in Wolcott, 2002, p. 171). Later, Harry notes that Brad can make a valuable contribution to a commissioned report on education if he consents to be interviewed: "Like Blanche DuBois in *A Streetcar Named Desire*, fieldworkers must rely on the kindness of strangers to help get where they want to go" (Wolcott, 1995, p. 148; Saldaña, in Wolcott, 2002, p. 177). And when Brad catches Wolcott covertly writing field notes about his behavior, Harry notes to the audience in a tone reminiscent of Oscar Wilde, "We humans are not above making surreptitious observations, but we most certainly hate to get caught making them" (Wolcott, 1995, p. 152; Saldaña, in Wolcott, 2002, p. 185).

Wolcott's (2002) *Sneaky Kid and Its Aftermath: Ethics and Intimacy in Fieldwork* includes the original Brad Trilogy articles, additional information and reflections on the case, and the ethnodramatic adaptation of the story, *Finding My Place: The Brad Trilogy*. The title character is a young drifter whom Harry befriends, but whose unforeseen mental illness and destructive behavior wreaks havoc on Wolcott's professional and personal life. I have included excerpts below from the dramatization as a sample of ethnodramatic dialogue and monologue: the beginning of Scene One, and the Epilogue. The former was Harry's choice for inclusion in this chapter to introduce the work, and the selection demonstrates the dramatization of qualitative data (Saldaña, 2002, 2003). The latter was my choice to showcase the poetic cadences of method. As for what happens in between, read Wolcott's *Sneaky Kid* to find out.

Selections from *Finding My Place: The Brad Trilogy*

SCENE ONE: DESCRIPTION

(SLIDE: *Serendipity*)
HARRY: I first came to know Brad through what ethnographers sometimes refer to as serendipity.

(music up: "Heart of Glass" by Blondie)
(HARRY finds a bow saw on the ground, picks it up, looks at it curiously)
>Literally as well as figuratively, I discovered Brad in my own backyard, unannounced and uninvited.

(SLIDE: BRAD's cabin)
(BRAD enters, carrying a sapling, stops when he and HARRY see each other; BRAD sets the sapling down, shuts radio music off; they look at each other warily)
>A 19 year-old had managed to construct a crude but sturdy 10- by 12-foot cabin at a remote corner of my densely wooded, 20-acre home-site, which my partner Norman has shared with me since 1968. He didn't know on whose property he had built his cabin, perhaps hoping he had chosen public land next to mine.

(hands BRAD the saw, which he grabs)
BRAD: *(defensively, to HARRY)* Can I stay?
(SLIDE: Early Encounters)
HARRY: *(beat, as HARRY looks BRAD over; to audience)* I attach great importance to first impressions.
(HARRY stares at BRAD; BRAD starts packing up his tools)
>At the moment of our first and unexpected meeting, I felt hesitant about allowing him to remain on my land; yet I felt an even greater reluctance in insisting that he leave.

BRAD: *(to HARRY)* I needed some place to get out of the wind and keep dry. The rent ran out. I knew the rains would continue and I'd have to do something.
HARRY: *(to audience)* He had no money, no job, and no place to go. I couldn't see how I could claim to be any kind of humanitarian and throw him off my property.
(SLIDE: Courtesy and Common Sense)
(HARRY picks up the sapling and examines it; to BRAD)
>I guess if you're going to be here, I need to know something about you: Where you're from? What kind of trouble you're in?

BRAD: *(takes sapling, saws into it)* I'm not in any trouble. I'm not that stupid. I used to live at this end of town; my father still lives here but I never see him. And I've lived in a lot of different places, like California, Portland, out in the country; different places in town, like The Mission – you had to sing for Jesus before they'd feed you there – a halfway house, *(slightly mumbling)* reform school.
HARRY: Reform school?
BRAD: *(defensively)* Yeah, but it wasn't really my fault.
(SLIDE: Survival)
>I picked up my sleeping bag and the stuff I had and headed for the hills. I didn't know exactly what to do. I saw this piece of level ground and I set up a tarp for shelter. There were plenty of trees around. I decided to build a place for myself, because I wasn't doing anything anyway.

(SLIDE: BRAD's cabin)
(HARRY looks at the cabin as BRAD describes it)

I put up four posts and started dragging logs around till the walls were built. As I went along I just figured out what I would need. I got the stuff I needed – tools and nails – from new houses being built nearby. The roof's made of paneling that I carried up from some kid's tree fort. I knew about plaster because I had worked with it before, so I smeared some on the walls. So now, I've got this cabin. This is better than any apartment I've ever had, that's for sure. It really works good for me. Here I am.

(*beat; BRAD shrugs his shoulders*)

That's it.

(*SLIDE: Getting a Start and Building on Later*)

HARRY: It wasn't much of an introduction, but it marked the beginning of a dialogue that lasted almost two full years from that moment.

(*returns to his desk; BRAD turns on his radio to a loud volume and returns to fixing his bike; HARRY glares at him, goes to the radio and lowers the volume; HARRY sits on the lawn chair and watches BRAD work*)

(*music: "Jump" by the Pointer Sisters*)

I didn't expect him to stay. Norman has an aversion to people he identifies as "losers," and from the outset had as little to do with Brad as possible. But as time went on and Brad continued to make improvements, he gradually became as much a fixture about the place as was his cabin. We saw rather little of him at first, but I became *fascinated* with him and intrigued with his –

(*BRAD removes his shirt; HARRY stares at his muscled torso*)

chosen lifestyle. . . .

(Saldaña, in Wolcott, 2002, pp. 173–176)

★ ★ ★

EPILOGUE

(*SLIDE: Epilogue*)

(*HARRY picks up some of the index cards, sets the stage aright as best he can, puts away things in his desk*)

HARRY: In a professional lifetime devoted to teaching, research, and writing, I know little and understand even less about this case, the one that's affected me the most, and the one that continues to haunt me for answers I doubt I'll ever find.

(*SLIDE: Getting It Right*)

I felt I knew Brad so well, so intimately, that I would get a straight story – and get the story straight. I was reeling then, and continue to do so to this day, from realizing how little we ever know, heightened in this instance by the feeling that this time, in my own cultural milieu, my own language, and even in my own backyard, I had finally *gotten it right*.

(*getting angry, he slams the desk drawer shut*)

I just wish that it all might have turned out differently.

(*SLIDE: Meaning*)

What is this *really* a study of? The meaning of the story isn't precisely clear because meanings themselves aren't all that apparent or clear. We don't have neat findings, tidy hypotheses, conclusions that can be summarized or reduced to tables and charts. There are no guarantees, no umbrellas or safety nets, no foolproof scientific method to follow.

(*SLIDE: Validity*)

Fieldwork consists of more than collecting data, something that catapults it beyond simply being there. And whatever constitutes that elusive "more" makes all the difference. Regardless of outcome, I think the critical test is how deeply you've felt involved and affected personally. *Provocative*, not *persuasive*.

(*SLIDE: Understanding*)
(*HARRY is close to tears*)

After years of attending so singularly to the sanctity of methods, I finally realize that only *understanding* matters. We must not only transform our data, we must *transcend* them. *Insight* is our forte! The whole purpose of the enterprise is *revelation*! When you emphasize description, you want your audience to see what you saw. When you emphasize analysis, you want your audience to know what you know. When you emphasize interpretation, you want your audience to . . . understand what you think you yourself have understood.

(*pause*)
(*SLIDE: Last Words*)
(*he walks to the projection screen*)

In the end, we only abandon our studies; we never really complete them. The human condition doesn't remain static long enough for the work to be completed, even for an instant. You need to recognize when to keep reaching, when to focus, and when to stop.

(*SLIDE: face shot of BRAD*)

So. How *do* you "conclude" a qualitative study?

(*music up: "Father Figure" by George Michael; HARRY looks at slide of BRAD*)

You don't.

(*lights fade to black; SLIDE of BRAD fades to black as music rises*)

(Saldaña, in Wolcott, 2002, pp. 209–210)

References

Ehrenreich, B. (2002). *Nickel and dimed: On (not) getting by in America.* New York: Owl Books.

Saldaña, J. (2002). Finding my place: The Brad trilogy. In H. F. Wolcott (Ed.), *Sneaky kid and its aftermath: Ethics and intimacy in fieldwork* (pp. 167–210). Walnut Creek, CA: AltaMira Press.

Saldaña, J. (2003). Dramatizing data: A primer. *Qualitative Inquiry, 9*(2), 218–236.

Saldaña, J. (2005). *Ethnodrama: An anthology of reality theatre.* Walnut Creek, CA: AltaMira Press.

Toth, J. (1993). *The mole people: Life in the tunnels beneath New York City.* Chicago: Chicago Review Press.

Wolcott, H. F. (1990). *Writing up qualitative research*. Newbury Park, CA: Sage Publications.
Wolcott, H. F. (1994). *Transforming qualitative data: Description, analysis and interpretation*. Thousand Oaks, CA: Sage Publications.
Wolcott, H. F. (1995). *The art of fieldwork*. Walnut Creek, CA: AltaMira Press.
Wolcott, H. F. (1999). *Ethnography: A way of seeing*. Walnut Creek, CA: AltaMira Press.
Wolcott, H. F. (2002). *Sneaky kid and its aftermath: Ethics and intimacy in fieldwork*. Walnut Creek, CA: AltaMira Press.

STREET RAT

Johnny Saldaña, Susan Finley, and Macklin Finley

Production History

Street Rat premiered at Arizona State University (ASU) April 6–8, 2004. The production was staged and directed by Johnny Saldaña and featured the following cast: Chris Marley (Mack), David Ojala (Roach), Jess Sari (Tigger), Christine Klein (Quiz), Kate Haas (Jewel), Miranda Lilley (Genie), Adam Bauer, Daniel Charns, and Wilana Ortega (Adult Ensemble Members). Production Assistants: Amy Crater, Justin DeRo, and Laura Hutton. Production support was provided by the ASU Department of Theatre and Katherine K. Herberger College of Fine Arts (J. Robert Wills, Dean).

Characters

MACK: male, early 20s, a street poet
ROACH: male, 17, a street rat; spider web tattoo on half his face
TIGGER: male, 22, a street rat; ROACH's best friend
QUIZ: female, 16, a street rat
JEWEL: female, 17, a street rat
GENIE: female, 16, a 7-month pregnant street rat
THREE ADULT ENSEMBLE MEMBERS (two male, one female) to portray: Tourists, Waitress, Drug Dealer, Gay Leatherman, Business Man, Conventioneers, etc. When needed, they also assist with the staging of the production. One Male Adult Ensemble member is African American; all other characters are White.

Setting

The French Quarter and a homeless squat in New Orleans; a Friday in January, 1997

Dedication

To the street rats

Preshow

(*music: a collage of New Orleans Cajun and Zydeco;* ROACH, TIGGER, QUIZ, JEWEL, *and* GENIE *sit on the ground by the entrance to the theatre or house; the*

[Originally published in *Ethnodrama: An Anthology of Reality Theatre*, edited by Johnny Saldaña, Walnut Creek, CA: AltaMira Press, 2005, pp. 104–145; edited slightly for this publication.]

214   Writing Ethnodrama

STREET RATS *hold their hands out to audience members and ask as they enter,* "Spare change?" "Spare change for alcohol?"; *MACK is nearby reciting his street poetry; inside the theatre,* ADULT ENSEMBLE MEMBERS *in Mardi Gras masks offer beads and other Mardi Gras souvenirs to incoming audience members*)

SCENE 1: FREE LIVE POETRY

(*preshow music fades to low level as house lights fade and stage lights rise; the set includes various street signs from the New Orleans French Quarter and suggestions of a condemned yet lived-in property; trash is strewn throughout the set and audience seating area;* MACK, *dressed casually, enters; he sets a cigar box on the ground, pulls a one dollar bill from his pocket and drops it in the box; he stands on an upturned milk crate and shouts to two* TOURISTS *passing by, both wearing Mardi Gras necklaces*)

MACK: Free live poetry! All's you have to pay . . . is attention!
(*the* TOURISTS *stop to listen as* MACK *recites to them; music fades out;* MACK *speaks with an easy passion*)
I find my definition
in storm patterns —
A change of energy.
I can feel it underfoot —
The sky is flecked
light with grey,
I think I may
feel partly
cloudy.
Like a thunderclap
I am deafening in
fierce self-proclamations.
Like the sky I am poisoned
by industry; the city's smokestacks
choke me, and the five o'clock
traffic jam is burning
holes in me with its
bitter exhaust.
(*one of the* TOURISTS *raises her camera and takes a snapshot of* MACK)
I think I may —
I think I may —
feel partly cloudy.
(TOURISTS *smile at each other, shake their heads and walk off as one drops a coin in* MACK's *cigar box;* MACK *speaks to them as they exit*)
And I don't want to
be a rain of history
on your day-in-the-park parade —

but I'm vaporous, controlled by
the elements raining
heard words on deaf
ears –

(*Cajun/Zydeco music up; as MACK continues to recite, ROACH, a 17 year old street rat, enters, empties a milk crate full of trash, turns it over, sits on the crate and glances both ways for people; MACK looks at ROACH, then to the audience as he speaks*)
you're walking
down a street of gutter
punks, starving,
wise children,
coast to coast wanderers –
and all this petty extravagance
has been hung on poles of
degradation: for your benefit.
Somebody tell the children
with their fiddle stories
and longtime bad habits,
that these neon beer
gardens are cesspools
of wasted minds
and lives of no
reward.
I think I may –
I think I may –
feel partly cloudy.

(*through the rest of the play, MACK sits, leans, rises, and walks across the stage, as necessary, while commenting on the action; music out*)

SCENE 2: SPARE CHANGE?

(*BUSINESS WOMAN in a dress enters, walks by ROACH*)
ROACH: Spare change?
(*BUSINESS WOMAN catches a quick glimpse of ROACH then looks away, clutches her purse tightly and keeps walking until she exits; BUSINESS MAN in a blue suit and tie enters, carrying a briefcase, walks by ROACH*)
Spare change?
(*BUSINESS MAN does not acknowledge ROACH and keeps walking until he exits; ROACH shakes his head, says half to himself, half to BUSINESS MAN*)
Mr. Blue-suit-on-his-way-to-work-business-maaan never even look my way. You got money in your pocket, actin' like you don't see me. You see me, mother-fucker!
(*a GAY LEATHERMAN enters, walks toward ROACH*)
Spare change?

(*GAY LEATHERMAN stops, glares at ROACH, reaches into his jeans, pulls out three pennies, drops them one at a time at ROACH's feet, then walks off; ROACH mutters to himself*)
Gay-yuppie asshole.
(*he picks up the pennies and pockets them; MACK looks at ROACH, speaks to him and to audience*)
MACK Three pennies
fall like
rain in
the thunderous
silence after.
Remorse is
a court word
holding no
tender in the
lives of men.
(*as MACK continues, TIGGER, a 22 year-old street rat and ROACH's best friend, enters and crosses to ROACH, sits close to him; ROACH mimes talking to TIGGER about the GAY LEATHERMAN who gave him the coins*)
As one
more chokes
into the
nameless
void and
one more
skirts
St. Claude
outside the
street light.
Eyes not
guilty,
but
free will
be blessed
with the
splendor
of another
southern
dawn.

ROACH: People try and trick with me for money all the time. I just say, "Fuck off, I'm not a whore." People figure that if you're in the gay district, you *are*. I'm not going to sell my ass.

TIGGER: I know plenty of fucking straight up prostitutes. They're cool as hell, but that's not something I'm going to do.

ROACH: It makes you compromise yourself. People who do it have to be comfortable with doing it. Sometimes people get caught up in it, when they aren't comfortable doing it, but they do it anyway. That causes so many problems.

TIGGER: That, and the simple fact that people who hustle – not the people who hustle, but the people who hustle them – it's like, the only reason why these rich fuckin' guys are doing this shit, lots of times, the simple fact is they know they can grab a guy off the street and just say, "Come home and fuck me!", "Come home, do this with me," and just take control. I don't know, it's just fucked up.

ROACH: And then they act all disgusted when you tell them, "No." Like you're nothing if you don't do something like that to earn money.

TIGGER: Like you don't have any choice in the matter.

(*a WAITRESS on her way to work passes by*)

ROACH: Spare change?

TIGGER: Spare change?

WAITRESS: (*smiles at them, pulls a coin from her apron pocket, and puts it in ROACH's outstretched hand*) There you go. (*exits*)

ROACH: Thanks.

TIGGER: Thanks.

(*ROACH and TIGGER leer at the WAITRESS as she leaves*)

ROACH: Now, if a woman wanted to pay me to have sex with her, I would.

TIGGER: Well, depends on the woman.

ROACH: Yeah. If it's some Nancy Reagan-looking woman, then no.

(*a GAY TOURIST enters, wearing Mardi Gras necklaces and with a clear plastic cup of beer in hand, walks past the boys*)

ROACH AND TIGGER: Spare change?

(*the TOURIST glances quickly at ROACH, shakes his head "no," and sets his half-empty cup on the sidewalk by a trash can; exits; TIGGER goes for the beer*)

ROACH: Fuck him. Sneakin' peaks at my facial tat.

(*as TIGGER gets the beer, ROACH smiles and starts a private joke between them*) Just say "No!"

TIGGER: No! (*he drinks from the cup, offers ROACH the last swig*)

MACK: We stand
on the
corner
amidst
the buzz
the flow
their cash
inextricable.
The flow
on which
we prey

which
invariably
covers us in
a film
of spilled
broken
bottles.

TIGGER: (*rooting through the trash can for food*) We better make quick work of the schwillies, man. We gotta sp'ange enough for all weekend today; it's gonna rain tomorrow.

ROACH: How do you know that? Are you a weather man now?

TIGGER: I read it in the paper. Town is gonna be packed and we can make bank. The Clover has a sign welcoming some conference, so there's plenty of green around. We just gotta get it while the weather holds.

ROACH: (*looks down the street*) I've gotta meet that guy in a couple hours.

(*pulls out some partially-smoked cigarettes from his pocket, gives one to TIGGER; they both light up*)

TIGGER: (*worriedly*) Right. I don't buy it. I don't trust him, Roach.

ROACH: (*tries to reassure TIGGER but sounds doubtful*) I'm not going to have anything on me. The guy holds the stuff. I just go find customers. I take them to him and he gives me a runner's fee. I'm not going to have the stuff on me.

TIGGER: Never in my life have I fucked with the needle.

ROACH: (*insistent*) I'm not using it, Tigger. I'm just running it.

TIGGER: You've done it before, now you'll want to do it again.

ROACH: No! It's only a job. I'm going to get money so we can get a place and we can eat. (*TIGGER does not look at him; impatiently as he sits*) I'm a fuckin' slinger, man. I sell drugs on occasion.

TIGGER: Being around the needle, talking about the needle, makes me very uncomfortable. Fucks with my head. But if someone's gonna do it, they're gonna do it. I've seen it – friends dead.

ROACH: You snort coke with me, but if I try heroin with the guy I'm going to sell it for, that makes it wrong? You're such a fucking hypocrite!

TIGGER: No I'm not! You know what I think's going to happen? You're going to start slammin' it again.

ROACH: (*singing the end of Neil Young's song to TIGGER*) "I've seen the needle and the damage done, a little part of it in everyone, but every junkie's like a setting sun." (*laughs; pulls TIGGER by the arm*) C'mon, let's get outta here.

TIGGER: (*yanks his arm away from ROACH's grip*) You do what you gotta do, I'll catch ya later.

ROACH: Tigger, . . .

TIGGER: (*as he exits*) I'll be on the Square. Hook up with me when you're through.

ROACH: Tigger! Damn. (*shouts after TIGGER*) I hate it when we fight! We fight just like a couple of fucking married people!

MACK: The heat
 has descended.
 Surely another
 night will
 follow, long,
 sleepless,
 dusty.
(ROACH *pulls a flask from his pants pocket, takes a swig*)
 How many
 have been
 lost?
 How many
 mothers'
 sons
 choke
 gasp
 and
 die
 as
 three pennies
 fall like
 rain in
 the thunderous
 silence
 after?
(ROACH *exits; MACK recites to audience; transition music rises*)
 We walk
 a fine
 line
 down
 Rampart's median,
 unwanted
 on either
 side.
 Nothing can
 be done
 as
 three pennies
 fall like
 rain in
 the thunderous
 silence
 after.
(lights fade on scene)

SCENE 3: THE FORTRESS

(lights rise and music fades as JEWEL and QUIZ enter, escorting GENIE, about 7 months pregnant and a worn tote bag strapped on her shoulder; they are orienting her to the life of a street rat at The Fortress, their squat)

JEWEL: Sometimes it takes a while before you find a squat.

QUIZ: You'll look around and find a place, and then find out that somebody's already squatting there.

JEWEL: Either that, or a place will be really dirty and you have to clean an area, pull all the trash.

QUIZ: Try to find a squat where there are already other squatters and then stay, because it's safer, as long as there aren't too many people.

GENIE: *(sitting and looking at the property)* The first place I stayed was this cool old house. It was abandoned. We slept in the attic.

JEWEL: This complex is condemned. The city is supposed to tear it down eventually.

QUIZ: Roach decides who can live here.

JEWEL: That means he can decide what'll happen to you. He kicked his girl-friend out during a raid, and she was afraid she would run out there and get arrested.

QUIZ: Most people don't give a fuck what Roach does. For one thing, he won't even hit girls. If he just dislikes you, he doesn't care if you stay here, but if you do something to piss him off, you don't even *want* to stay here. Roach and Tigger had to chase three people out last week. They beat Scooby up a couple of days before that. *(showing GENIE)* All these holes in the wall? They put his head through it.

JEWEL: Roach owns The Fortress. But you *want* some protection, some kind of squat boss. Every single room is open – take your pick. We call the court-yard the pit. If you're going to fight, you take it to the pit.

(TIGGER enters)

Tigger! This is Genie.

TIGGER: *(beat; smiles at GENIE)* Hi.

GENIE: *(smiling back)* Hi.

(ROACH enters and all stare at him; uncomfortable pause as he glares at GENIE)

QUIZ: *(half defiant, half pleading)* She wanted to know where she could stay.

GENIE: *(rising; as if anticipating his concern)* The cops ask me my name. I have a clear name so they just let me go.

ROACH: *(staring at GENIE's pregnant stomach)* Fuckin' cops out here are fuckin' evil. *(beat)* You can stay with us. *(ROACH approaches GENIE and speaks roughly)* I'm not a squat Nazi or anything like that. But I like my home to be peaceful and relaxing. When people fuck with my shit or fuck with me, I consider it disrespectful and I'll fight over it. We protect ourselves, and we try to protect our stuff. We try to make sure we're all safe and nobody's going to get us all busted. Some people think they can do whatever they want. *(shakes his head "no")* We go down. We'll bust your ass.

(*ROACH exits, motioning for TIGGER to join him; TIGGER follows, but looks back at GENIE*)

JEWEL: (*calling after ROACH*) You fucker!

GENIE: (*shaken, sits, starts crying; the girls go to GENIE*) This is Boy Scout's fault. When I met him, he was a squatter. He had a tattoo on his cheek and a carving out of one of his ears. I used to let him come to my house and take showers. I tried to convince my aunt to let him stay, that he needed a place for the night. My aunt was, "No!" So, I just said, "Fine, I'm going to spend the night with him." First night, we slept on this guy's porch.

(*looks at her stomach*)

QUIZ: When I went home for Christmas, my mom beat the shit out of me and told me I couldn't come back to her house anymore. It ended up with me in a hospital and yelling at my mom that she was a fucking bitch because I nearly had a heart attack because of crack cocaine. (*to JEWEL*) Remember when I had stitches on my chin? I couldn't fight back because I was too high; I couldn't really stand up.

JEWEL: (*to GENIE*) I ran away from home when I was 12. Came back, got put into rehab, got out, ran away again, came back about three months later. (*gets a paper bag from the floor*) I've been in and out of 11 rehab centers from the time I was 11 years old. (*pulls a pint of vodka out of the bag*) That was a big mistake on my parents' part.

QUIZ: (*to GENIE*) Have you danced?

GENIE: Huh?

QUIZ: You can make good money dancing. I know a girl who does private parties.

GENIE: Yeah?

QUIZ: (*touching GENIE's stomach*) Well, she's pregnant.

JEWEL: That's a fetish. Turns some guys on – you know, dancing pregnant.

GENIE: Makes a lot, huh?

JEWEL: Every month more pregnant, the price goes up. These guys like it best when they're ready to deliver.

QUIZ: One girl who did it has her own apartment now. She's already got her kid, but she never quit doing drugs so he looks a little strange. Seems a little slow. I'm careful. I'm not having kids until I can take care of them.

(*takes a drink of vodka*)

GENIE: My sister has a friend who went to cosmetology school. She made a lot of money as a beautician. You have to get your own chair, though. Otherwise, it's minimum and by the hour. Without a degree I couldn't get a job or an apartment and stuff. Just the fact that I'm young, and I don't have anywhere to go.

(*ROACH and TIGGER enter, listen to the GIRLS*)

JEWEL: I made close to 35 dollars last night and plan on making more tonight. I figure I'll make twice what I made last night because it's Friday and everyone will be getting their pay checks and getting drunk off their asses.

ROACH: (*to GENIE*) "Nawlins" is a good city to panhandle in. You can make 40 to 50 bucks a day. It's variable; it doesn't always work, but you can make that much. Weekends are good when there's no rain. Conferences make weekdays feel like weekends.
TIGGER: (*sitting by GENIE*) Roach has been making tons every night. It seems like I only make money when I'm with Roach.
ROACH: We sp'ange in the gay district. Guys can make money down there.
TIGGER: Yeah, but the bigwigs in the gay community wants us to get the fuck out of there. They say we scare tourists.
JEWEL: (*to GENIE*) Work closer to the bars. A good spot is next to The Bourbon Bar.
(*ROACH starts walking off*)
TIGGER: Where y' goin'?
ROACH: (*a lie*) I'm . . . gonna go hustle at the market, find a truck to unload 'til I got enough to make schwillies. If ya wanna job, sometimes ya gotta take care of the nasty shit. (*exits*)
QUIZ: (*to TIGGER*) I hear Roach is slingin'.
TIGGER: (*picking up a book to read*) I don't care, so long as he fucking stays clean, doesn't fucking rob anybody.
(*lights fade and transition music rises*)

SCENE 4: NEEDLES IN VEINS

(*lights up; as MACK recites, the DEALER, a short nervous Jamaican, about 30 and going bald, enters and waits nervously; ROACH enters; they meet covertly and mime talking to each other; music fades out*)
MACK: Lobotomizing without tools,
tubes in noses,
paper on tongues –
Constant escape,
circular streets
around and down,
scraping gutters,
sleeping in abandoned homes
watchful of peripheral motion –
Always taking chances
With motions like
a train.
(*the DEALER passes ROACH a baggie of heroin packets, a cell phone, and a piece of paper with phone numbers written on it and mimes talking the directions for hook-ups*)
Needles in veins
Needles in veins
Needles in veins.
Pink blood, diluted

blood, blocking the
works blood, cramming the
artery blood. Metallic tastes
numb tongues, prickly eyes
watery walls –
unaware a thousand
tomorrows rusty machines
around like turnstile justice.
(*the DEALER pulls out a joint from his pocket and lights it, drags, passes it to ROACH who also takes a hit*)
Like a train rhythm – money
burning – like a train rhythm –
bondsmen and pushers
bondsmen and pushers
bondsmen and pushers –
Insane on floors –
Spinning – Hot hairy Middle-
Aged hands – Gotta pay somehow –
like a train rhythm:
Shaking at dawn
for another,
another,
another.

DEALER: (*keeps and continues to drag on the joint*) For every hook-up you make with a customer, you take a 10 dollar cut, whatever size the sale.

ROACH: Thas' OK. There's nobody lookin' to me for more than an evening's entertainment anyways.

DEALER: You use?

ROACH: No. Well, I have. I don't anymore, not now. (*laughs*) Tell you the truth, I'm back on that shit all the time.

DEALER: (*reaches in his coat pocket, pulls out a packet of heroin and places it in ROACH's hand*) That one's on the house. Gift to newcomers from your Neighborhood Club. (*he laughs through his cough and flicks the joint down on the ground*) Meet me here tomorrow night. Same time, same place. We'll settle accounts then. (*he turns and walks away briskly, exits*)

(*as MACK recites, ROACH looks at the heroin, slips it in his pocket, picks up the joint the DEALER flicked to the ground, snuffs it out to save for later*)

MACK: In and out
dusty phone booths
dying young with bad lookin'
yellow, inflated corpses.
Dusty back-alleys
risks like a train rhythm,
needles in veins
needles in veins

224 *Writing Ethnodrama*

    needles in veins
    blood wash spoon
    nicotine
    chasers
    there will be a change.
(ROACH *dials a phone number written on the piece of paper on the cell phone, mimes talking as he looks about nervously*)
    Gotta pay – born in debt – hot
    hairy – Clorox clean-up
    committee – phone call
    to Jimi/Janis – shot up –
    Put down – hung on last
    generation's sellout
    ambitions – song of
    somebody else –
    Phone call to Walt Whitman –
    Unlisted – sanity – sobriety –
    Change – will there be –
    Is there an I – change –
    Sanity – train rhythm –
    Ran risk stop sign –
    Clean-up committee –
    Zero tolerance –
    Heard words – symphony.
    Phone call to William
    Shakespeare – heard words –
    Othello blackface comedy –
    downstairs train rhythm –
(ROACH *hangs up on the phone, stuffs it in his jacket, and thinks deeply*)
    It's very drug culture –
    I don't know if I can
    hang with all the smoke
    up in here.

SCENE 5: DOC HOLLIDAY

(*lights suggest an isolation from real time and "reality"; MACK stands on a milk crate*)
MACK: (*to ROACH*) Free live poetry! All's you have to pay . . . is attention!
(ROACH *takes a swig from his flask, walks toward MACK and stops to listen as he recites*)
    Doc Holliday
    spat a little
    shriveled lung in
    his kerchief,
    straightened

his hat —
found the next
whiskey —
savored the irony.
His boots
were always
shined to
a bright
black glow —
matching
his eyes.
He was a
wizard
of a kind.
He was a
wizard
way ahead
of his time.
Doc Holliday
was wise
to the
plans of
the other man —
Doc Holliday
was wise
to the
deck in
hand —
Doc Holliday
was wise
to the
street
before there
was a
street to
be wise
to.

(*pause; MACK smiles at ROACH, they give each other a quick friendly nod; ROACH reaches in his pocket, pulls out a coin and flips it to MACK; MACK steps off the milk crate and makes a gesture as if to suggest they trade places; they do so; MACK listens as ROACH speaks and takes an occasional swig from his flask*)

ROACH: I started drinking in 7th grade. That was the only reason to go to school — drugs and alcohol. Pot, cocaine, heroin. I dropped out in 7th grade, never been to high school. Teachers don't care, but they were nothing like the kids. I lived in a trailer park in Texas; it was the worst. I was kind of small. Kids who didn't live in the trailer park used to chase me home. If I made it to our trailer, I wouldn't get beat up. A lot of the time, I didn't make it and they'd beat the shit outta me. I missed school whenever I could.

MACK: *(walks to a second crate)* Doc Holliday
stood – thin –
shakin' in the
too hot sun –
He was dying
and he knew
it didn't
matter –
the country was
growing –
modernizing.
He would be
an anecdote –
if he made
it that
far –

(MACK sits on the crate, ROACH steps off his crate and crosses to MACK)

ROACH: I pretty much taught myself. I listen. I watch. I've got a lot of time under my belt, a lot of experience. I didn't read about survival of the fittest and say, "Wow, that's cool; that'll be me." I've just lived it. But I've still got a lot to learn, just like everybody does. Learning is a life-long process, whether you're in school or not. I have ADD, so I didn't pay any attention at school, I didn't do my homework. My mom would tell me something and I would forget it two minutes later. I've pretty much fixed that. I haven't completely grown out of it, I'm still ADD and all that, but I've learned how to focus when I need to focus.

(MACK rises, stands on his crate)

MACK: The sun
formed
slow
bubbles in
his eyes.
A fifteen year old
kid stood a
hundred paces downwind –
A drunken bet
was the cause.
Draw Squeeze –
One shot
a body falls
A boy died

in the street.
It did not
matter.
Doc Holliday's
next drink's
free –

(*MACK steps off his crate as the two circle each other, scoping each other out*)

ROACH: The first time I was on my own, I ran away to Dallas when I was thirteen, didn't come home for a long while. I spent a year on the streets selling cocaine. Had a cocaine habit. (*stands on a crate*) Fuckin' slammin'. Needle in the vein, man.

MACK: the fever
worse – he sweats
through his sportcoat –
Saw white horses
ridin' high in
strange black
streets – eerie humming
glowing signs
in impossible
windows.

(*ROACH remains on the crate while MACK sits on the ground*)

ROACH: I don't really blame my mom. She didn't kick me out. I sort of left, and when I tried to come back, she'd already had enough watching me go down hill and knowing what I was doing and knowing I was lying in her face. Being apart from my mom for so long – having me go out into the world and learn things – helped my relationship with her. I've become more independent. I'm not so needy all the time. I had the problem when I was younger. I always needed her attention and stuff, although I didn't play it off like I wanted her. Deep down I really did. But I'm not like that anymore. My mom and I are good now. I mean, we smoke pot and drink together, because she realizes that I've been on my own for, what, six years in January. She's realized that I take care of myself, that, "Hey, you're still alive. You're an adult." I go there sometimes and I get a job to support myself while I'm living there, because they don't have the money to support me. They don't have the money to support themselves. You know what I mean? To me, it's just a visit. One day I get up and I leave.

(*he steps off the crate; MACK rises and crosses to him; ROACH stares at MACK, as if hypnotized*)

MACK: Children squatting
on stone walks
near the black
patch –

ROACH: their
hands out,

        their eyes
        dead –
MACK AND ROACH: odd
        bruises, scabs
        tracing their
        veins thumping
        in unison –
(*beat; MACK gives ROACH a slight push to bring him to*)
MACK: Cough shakes
        him to –
(*MACK sits*)
ROACH: Sometimes I think about my family, my mom and my little brother. I give them a call and I keep in touch. My brother just had his thirteenth birthday. Sometimes it makes me kind of sad, that I can't visit with them. I can; I can go and visit with them. It's just that it's far and it's cold. My mom lives in Maryland now.
(*BUSINESS MAN from Scene 2 passes by*)
        Spare change?
(*BUSINESS MAN looks straight ahead and does not acknowledge ROACH, exits; ROACH runs after him and shouts*)
        Mr. Corporate Man! White collared mother-fucker wearing a suit and tie, look me in the face! Remember me? Wouldn't give me spare change. Shoot you in the head – boom, boom!
MACK: Praised be the
        vision of our murderous
        Father, Doc Holliday!
(*ROACH, angry, crosses to MACK*)
ROACH: Fuck you! Every square dad and Arab between here and there gonna look me up and down, hate me, throw me away with their eyes. I don't waste my time on smellin' nice or livin' a lie. I'm not a bad guy, but I'm looked on as a piece of shit, and that's just totally wrong! I don't want to be part of a society that hates me, and wants to assimilate me, that won't allow me the chance to do the things that I want to do, and allow me to live the way I want to live. I have the right, just like any other human being, to do anything I want to do as long as I'm not hurting anybody.
(*ROACH sits on a crate, dejected, looking away from MACK; MACK rises and pushes the other crate with his foot in increments toward ROACH's*)
MACK: There's a
        kid down the
        way
        with a finger
        in every pie –
        He's got
        old style
        hustle

with his
hat on.
Majesty
is nothin' but
practice for
comfort;
the boy's
a king of
unthinkable
consequence
makin' it
work –
(*ROACH pulls out from his pocket the packet of heroin and stares at it*)
Night to
night, day
to day.
He's gotta
take care of
the
(*MACK shoves the crate forcefully against the one ROACH is sitting on, startling him*)
shit
that gotta
be taken
care of –
(*MACK sits on the crates, smirking*)
ROACH: We have an animal instinct for survival. If you had my reality for 24 hours, your view would change forever.
(*grabs MACK by the shirt; MACK grabs ROACH by the shoulders*)
On the street, if all shit hit the fan, the Yuppies wouldn't survive.
(*they let each other loose*)
So where do I fit? Right here, in my heart. That's where I fit. I'm planning on staying in New Orleans another day, maybe another twenty minutes, maybe a year from now. (*ROACH starts walking off*)
MACK: (*standing on a crate*) So when
a boy dies
on the
paved streets
of modern day
America –
Everyone knows
it does not
matter.
ROACH: *Fuck you!* (*exits*)
MACK: Boy/king
'round the

corner
lights a
candle
on the
altar for
every soul
he brings down
in grim street
light.

SCENE 6: FUGUE

(lights rise back to "reality" level; as MACK calls out, a CONVENTIONEER with a name badge and convention program book passes by and stops to listen)
MACK: Free live poetry! All's you have to pay . . . is attention!
(MACK's recitation varies in energy, passion, and anger)
    Young and poor –
    No god to pray to –
    No luck to pray for –
    Nothin' but life chokin'
    on life.
    So whatcha in for?
    Call it "Public drunk," not
    doin' a damn thing. Jus'
    walkin', but th' cop go's
    me figured on a diff 'rent
    score –
    Who ain't in the central
    for jus' bein' bo'n?
    Who ain't?
    Some try to sleep it off
    in the late-night
    holding cells,
    no relatives to call,
    no bail to be posted.
    Some stand and pace,
    bitter stomachs
    and torn minds
    toiling against broken
    stamina.
    What next? What next?
    Bullshit tournaments in
    the corner –
    Who's the baddest?
    In this last-stop

dead-end cell he
with loudest voice
is booming his
notorious command –
"You be my bitch in the house!"
And it's misplaced anger
for that last five minutes
of out time
that went so
wrong.
There will be a change.
(*a second CONVENTIONEER with a name badge and convention program book passes by and stops to listen*)
Nights that plague
reality, poking holes
in it, setting it
to purple flames
of delusion –
Mystified, pinned
on walls in pale
street lights –
passing smiles in
choking voiceless
rooms and unconscious
connections
forming lines
at money burners
Begging for a little
escape
(fast set down
fast money
for fast connections),
Itching at the corners:
Escape! Escape!
Making kissing noises
at the passing faces –
Gotta pay somehow –
need a ride –
need a bed –
need a hot, hairy, middle-aged
hand on your thigh –
"Cause you look a little
cold, and I could use a
little company."
That little wedding ring

don't mean a damn thing 'cause
I can buy out the sentiment
behind it.
Besides, if it's not you it's
some other beer-starved
mouth.
You need the fix,
po' white trash, nigga,
spic, queer, li'l boy with
no one to talk with, and
no bed to sleep in, never
mind your confused sexuality –
I got a big green paper
dick for you to suck on –
and once you have, you can
get high.
Won't that be nice?
Wake up, middle-aged
whore monger,
there will be a great day
of reckoning.

(*a third* CONVENTIONEER *with a name badge and convention program book passes by and stops to listen*)

Living on broken bread-crust
promises –
Telling her I'll be
fine.
Struggling to get a
foothold outta bed –
Bleak – slow – blurry –
No comfort – itching
at the corners –
Struggling for control
of the headboard –
You can't have it
'till you cut me –
Red/brown bed sheets,
grinding – in/out
sweating/reeling/
needing/releasing
gentle song
neighbors complaining
springs –
Needing – itching at
the corners – confusing

desires – wanting – metallic
tastes.
(*TIGGER, GENIE, JEWEL, and QUIZ enter and stop to listen with the crowd*)
Needing
Needing
Needing
Hot Hairy Middle-Aged
Hands
Gotta pay –
Gotta pay somehow –
Is there an "I" –
Am I all that I am?
I want to keep the promises,
but, y'see there's this
train rhythm.
(*one CONVENTIONEER looks at his watch, leaves the crowd*)
So, who am I?
is there an "I" that stands
out as more than a cog
in this rusty old machine?
Who Am I –
Who Am I –
Who Am I?
Am I the junk in veins –
The wine in skin –
An inebriate forming
consciousness cocktails –
scotch and soda handcuffs?
Happy Hour
Happy Hour –
3 for 1 Happy Hour –
Who wants sanity –
Who wants sobriety?
(*a second CONVENTIONEER leaves the crowd as she reads her convention program*)
Neon-rendered
Uncle Sam points
fingers at fine
foreign slaughters
and I know –
I know who
doesn't.
Corporation
America with its
indirect democracy
has bred a

quarter generation
of dead-end
addicts;
the children beg
your spare
change for
alcohol – spare
change for
alcohol.

(the third CONVENTIONEER leaves the crowd; the four STREET RATS listen)

Give this generation
An uncoated tongue.
We will do what the
hippies sold out on.
Give this generation
one night, one night
to come up sober,
and we will change
these things that
have been done.
Hey, mid-line easy
solution conservatives,
it's time to
light another flare
of audacious contempt,
honesty is for those
too weak to invent
a history of
victory:

(MACK becomes passionately angry)

Fall into goose-step
formation
Horatio Alger.
These porch-step
children
starve for your
legacy,
and those in
steadfastly
full states and
sensible
shoes bypass with
biting
remarks.
Emotion is for the gays,

The artists, and other
enemies of the state.
Callous is the
call to arms for anybody
with anything to
speak of.
And poverty?
"Poverty
is the rising tide of laziness."
So rise to the
occasion
heads of state,
there's a new generation
to screw over,
and they're too
atrophied to resist.
All it should take
is the offer of
a Big Mac to pull
them into line.
Or a simple co-optation
of their heroes,
maybe.
Bend this generation
and
pump them
hard with their MTV
reality.
There is no
movement,
just look how
hard
you banged the baby
boomers
with theirs!
(*pause; MACK breathes heavily, exhausted; he and the STREET RATS stare at each other in silence as lights fade; transition Cajun music up softly*)

SCENE 7: THIS COUNTRY IS FUCKED UP

(*lights rise, music out; back at The Fortress, QUIZ is looking carefully through GENIE's hair; JEWEL is drinking from a pint of vodka; GENIE is writing a poem in a worn spiral notebook with a blunt pencil*)

QUIZ: I think Ferret was the only squatter I ever knew who was clean. His name was Ferret, and he had a ferret named "Human." Everyone – except

> one or two of us – in this squat has head and body lice, plus scabies. Thank God, I don't.
>
> GENIE: I had body lice, once.
>
> QUIZ: I would have, but they sprayed me down when they arrested me for loitering. After I went to jail I got an apartment. I went in with this girl. I even paid the rent for that month, but then after two weeks, I just thought: I don't want to live in a house.
>
> GENIE: I'd like to be set up in an apartment somewhere.
>
> JEWEL: I could go to Covenant House, but they'd make me come in every night at nine. I couldn't do that. And while I was in jail, some stupid asshole gave The Blitz away. A lonely girl without her doggie is all I am now. But, alcohol's treating me good. (*cheering the GIRLS with her pint*) Smile. It's good for you, too.
>
> QUIZ: (*jokingly admonishing*) Just say "No!"
>
> JEWEL: No! (*takes a swig from her pint; QUIZ crosses to join her*) I love to drink, but not so much that I'll have no liver in three years. (*QUIZ takes a drink; to GENIE*) We've gotta teach you a game! Ever hear of the Straight Edge Band? Every time the lyrics say "drink,"
>
> JEWEL AND QUIZ: you gotta drink!
>
> (*ROACH and TIGGER enter, in the middle of an argument*)
>
> TIGGER: I believe in monogamy because I have respect for people! Personally, I haven't gotten laid in two months or so. And if I don't have sex for the next five months or so, oh fuckin' well.
>
> (*crossing to GENIE*)
>
> I want to have someone who I can wake up to and rub her hair and hold her and all that.
>
> ROACH: I'm seventeen, man. I go through that shit for about two days and then I get sick of the bitch. I'm a beer slut and proud of it.
>
> TIGGER: Yeah, but you'd never force anyone.
>
> ROACH: No, I wouldn't force her. No way, but I'd make her want to. (*intimidating, to GENIE*) And I'd *fuck* the hell out of her. (*exits*)
>
> TIGGER: (*to GENIE, almost apologizing*) I'd never force anyone. We're not rapists.
>
> GENIE: (*smiling, but nervous*) Yeah, go to jail for a long time for that.
>
> (*TIGGER sits and talks with GENIE as MACK recites; JEWEL and QUIZ speak on their own and start playing a card game; GENIE sets her spiral notebook and pencil by her side*)
>
> MACK: I was just
> too shy
> to ever
> do or
> say the
> right thing.
> So a timid
> virgin went
> down in flames

while being
chased by
a deep brown,
Mexican
horse –
She didn't
scream or
fight, and
ten stories
were more
than plenty
to render
her limp and
lifeless.

GENIE: (*as if continuing a conversation*) I'm willing to deal with society. Society is just a group of people interacting with each other. I live in a society. We have our own society.

TIGGER: I'm not anti-society, I just don't consider myself part of society at all. I've just been in jail – 30 days for sleeping in Jackson Square. Little Hitler, this beat cop who gets his kicks from arresting people for not really doing anything at all, that's who got me.

GENIE: I don't think America works as it should, but it's not like I can say, *this* is the way it's going to work.

TIGGER: This country is fucked up.

GENIE: There's too many people trying to run it; too many people trying to say, "You have to do this," "You have to do that."

(*ROACH enters and listens to the conversation*)

TIGGER: I think you have to fight for what you believe in.

GENIE: I'm a pacifist.

TIGGER: I don't believe pacifism works. I'm willing to die for my convictions.

ROACH: Ah, beat me! Pacifism subjects you to a lot more abuse than anyone needs to take. (*mimes masturbating*) Yeah, I "pass a fist" all the time.

TIGGER: (*pointing to ROACH, as if it's hard to believe*) This guy's my best friend.

ROACH: (*grabs and holds onto TIGGER from behind*) Doesn't matter who's around, doesn't matter what's going on, doesn't matter what or where. Whatever's goin' down, Tigger is always Tigger and he'll always be my brother.

TIGGER: He's my fuckin' best friend.

ROACH: Patience and tolerance is what it takes to get along. We fight like we're fuckin' married, people say, we've been together so long.

(*they wrestle on the floor*)

TIGGER: We've been hanging out long enough that we have the right to fight like a married couple.

ROACH: He's my family. We're fucking married!

TIGGER: And I'd better never catch anybody fucking with him. I'd fucking kill 'em. Straight out just kill 'em. I'd take a knife and just stab 'em through the eye!

238   Writing Ethnodrama

(ROACH *and* TIGGER *howl and give each other five;* ROACH *sits with* JEWEL *and* QUIZ *and drinks;* TIGGER *and* GENIE *continue their conversation;* TIGGER *picks up* GENIE's *spiral notebook and pencil and starts sketching*)

MACK: Timid, little
tough girl
struggles
for the
love of
a barred-in
street king,
and I guide
her to the
bottle-gets-
y'to-the-
backroom
bars –
Talking
of bail,
she goes
down on
Hope,
and I am just
too shy
to tell
her that
Hope is
for Hollywood.

TIGGER: (*as if continuing a conversation*) My dad kicked me out when I was just 17. When I graduated from high school, he said "Congratulations." Then he gave me two weeks to get out. That was six years ago. When I first left home, I lived in Chicago, in the subway. I did what I had to do to survive. It's all about survival. You either survive or you die. (*he tries erasing his drawing error, but there's no eraser on the pencil; he turns to a new page in the spiral notebook and starts sketching again*) People who live here, the professionals, the fucking little yuppie people, they don't even see this side of life. They don't see it, they're blind to it. That's why they ignore me when I ask them for change. But how am I going to stay fed, other than asking people for money? I hate it. I'm free, but things aren't free. I need things so I have to get money. I want a regular job. (*stands*) When I go job hunting I dress smart, wear button downs most of the time. If I had a tie, I'd wear it. But, I mean, just look. Who the fuck is going to want some nasty lookin', dirty lookin', someone who hasn't taken a shower in God knows how long, handling their food, or ringing them up on a cash register, or whatever? I've got over a hundred goddamn applications out in this city. I've got a voice mail number. Nobody ever calls. I make plans, but anytime I make plans they always fall through. (*sits*) So, I take things day by day, don't make plans too far in the future. Every minute of my life is another minute of my life. (*he messes up his drawing again, rips the page angrily from the notebook, crumples it and throws it; pause; he looks at the next page of the notebook curiously*)

GENIE: Oh. I write poetry. Would you like to hear some?

(*TIGGER shrugs; GENIE takes the spiral notebook and reads aloud*)

Once in a while I awaken, asking myself "what am I doing?"
    Am I going to live my life like this forever?
Have the streets really become my home,
    a permanent way of life?
Is this what I have chosen, or can I not do better?
    For I am finding myself truly unhappy.
Spare change, leftovers, or just anything
    to survive on a daily basis.
Day by day. One day at a time.
    Not knowing where my next meal will come from.
Wishing for a better life.
    Not knowing where to start.

(*pause*)

ROACH: (*sarcastically*) Aw, poor little runaway! (*cruelly*) We're not your fuckin' counselors.

(*JEWEL angrily moves away from ROACH and gets a chess set, joins TIGGER and GENIE; ROACH laughs and holds onto QUIZ, looking uncomfortable; JEWEL arranges pieces on the chess set; GENIE looks forlorn, closes her spiral notebook; TIGGER tries to comfort her but she pulls away and exits by the end of MACK's poem*)

MACK: The only
    one that
    ever mattered
    waits,
    protruding;
    a baby
    breathes
    between
    her belly
    and her lap –
    And I
    tell her
    we can
    do it,
    together,
    but every
    face informed
    shakes –
    And I am

not a
father
figure –
How well
we know
the words,
but settling
into a
room rendered
gray and
smoky
by too
many
hangers-on,
I am just
too shy.

(*TIGGER and JEWEL start their game of chess*)

ROACH: (*rises*) C'mon, Tigger, it's almost 10 o'clock. Let's go.

TIGGER: (*glares at ROACH, then moves one of his chess pieces; JEWEL moves a chess piece*) I want to stay and play chess, man.

ROACH: No, have to panhandle, Tigger.

TIGGER: (*moving a piece*) I want to stay and play chess.

ROACH: (*moving closer to TIGGER*) No! We gotta get out and make money. You're forgetting the time factor, man. It's Friday night.

TIGGER: (*getting angry*) I know what fucking night it is. I don't want to make money. Right now I want to fucking play chess!

ROACH: You have to get out there! It's just like fucking Christmas, man. I want to do this so we're going to do this.

(*grabs TIGGER'S arm, TIGGER yanks away*)

TIGGER: (*looking at ROACH; pointedly*) No, it's not like Christmas!

(*TIGGER turns his attention back to the chess board; ROACH kicks the chess set*)

ROACH: We fight like we're fucking married!

(*ROACH goes to QUIZ, who now has an empty liquor bottle, and takes her by the arm*)

I've got enough for another pint. Whaddya say?

QUIZ: (*hesitantly*) OK.

(*QUIZ rises and walks off with ROACH, who glares at TIGGER*)

JEWEL: (*once ROACH is out of earshot*) That fucker!

(*lights fade; transition music into next scene: slow Cajun dance music; TIGGER and JEWEL exit during transition*)

SCENE 8: WHY DO YOU WANT TO BEAT ME UP?

(*lights up at low level; music fades to low volume and continues; a ROMANTIC COUPLE wearing Mardi Gras masks and necklaces strolls slowly past MACK; the COUPLE slow dances and exits by the end of his poem*)

MACK: Does my name
sound different
on your lips
now that I'm
not with you?
Does the water
miss the sun
it has reflected
when it passes
underground?
(ROACH and QUIZ enter, giggling, laughing, both drinking from ROACH's flask; they fall to the ground and stare into each other's eyes; ROACH strokes QUIZ's arm, they kiss in-between drinks, become physically passionate)
Do the voices
of happy people
fill you with
shame for all
the time we
wasted pretending
to be like
them?
I've never loved,
only feared loneliness.
I sit in crowded places
alone
until they empty
and I must
accept the
solitary state.
I don't mind it
as much
now that I
have the
comparison
of your
company.
The lessons of
silence are
now open
to me.
(music fades out, segues into distant thunder through the remainder of the play; the BUSINESS MAN from Scenes 2 and 5, now drunk and holding a plastic cup of beer in one hand and briefcase in the other, enters, mumbles softly, walks unsteadily, stopping now and then to collect himself; ROACH and QUIZ stare at him; ROACH smiles and whispers to QUIZ)
ROACH: Let's roll 'im. Knock six kinds of shit outta him.

(QUIZ *giggles; they sneak toward the* BUSINESS MAN; ROACH *blocks his way while* QUIZ *stands behind the* MAN)
   Hey, man – spare change?
BUSINESS MAN: (*stares blankly, shakes his head*) No.
(*beat*)
ROACH: Hey. I know you. Mr. Corporate Man!
(ROACH *knocks the beer cup out of the* MAN's *hand*)
   Got some spare change for me now, mother-fucker?
(*the* MAN *shields himself with his briefcase as* ROACH *pounds on it*)
QUIZ: Spare change, mister?
(*she reaches into his coat and pants pockets searching for money; the three physically struggle with the characters overlapping their lines and improvising during the roll,* ROACH *pounds repeatedly on the* MAN's *briefcase*)
BUSINESS MAN: No. Leave me alone. Don't hurt me! Please!
ROACH: C'mon, asshole, give it up. Think you're better than me? Think 'cause you wear a fancy fuckin' suit you're better than me?
QUIZ: Where do you keep your wallet, mister? Got some spare change for me? Spare change?
(*suddenly the* MAN *screams and throws his briefcase to the ground*)
BUSINESS MAN: *I don't have any spare change!* (ROACH *and* QUIZ *back away, startled*) I lost my job today! (*pause; the* MAN *crumples to the ground sobbing*) Why do you want to beat me up? Why? Why?
(ROACH *and* QUIZ *stare at him in stunned silence;* ROACH *looks around as if disoriented, trying to figure out what to do next; he grabs* QUIZ *by the arm and they run off stage; the* MAN *rises and tries to collect himself as* MACK *recites*)
MACK: Another head splits
   under the thrust
   of a billy club,
   another wrong-looker
   goes down for this or
   that – and a right-looking
   wrongdoer violates
   the trusting nature
   of a street rat,
   'round the corner,
   knowin' he doesn't
   have a thing to
   fear.
(*the* BUSINESS MAN *stumbles offstage*)
   I've spent six years
   pouring sand
   into a coffee cup,
   watching it overflow
   and add character
   to otherwise sterile

free verse.
In an induced dream
I was kept at the
bottom of a well
that filled in
icy purity around
me – and all the
while, mice died
in the bare lightbulbs
miles overhead.
(*lights fade; distant church bells chime three o'clock*)

SCENE 9: I *AM* HOME

(*lights rise to low level; ROACH enters the squat, staggering, drunk, and crashing from a heroin hit; as he walks he knocks over empty beer cans on the floor with his feet; QUIZ, JEWEL, and GENIE are asleep but do not hear the noise; TIGGER, aroused from sleep, sits up; both young men stare at each other*)

TIGGER: You OK?

(*ROACH shows TIGGER an empty heroin packet and drops it to the floor; he takes a swig from his flask*)

ROACH: I'm drinking cognac right now. (*thrusting the flask to TIGGER*)

TIGGER: I don't like cognac.

ROACH: You're drinking it anyway.

TIGGER: (*rising, taking the flask*) No, I'm not a slave to alcohol. I know all twelve steps.

ROACH: Just say "No."

(*looks at TIGGER for the traditional response but gets none; TIGGER drops the flask on the floor; ROACH angrily grabs TIGGER*)
You know, you're my best friend and you're my brother and all, but I can still whup your ass. You know I can whup . . . your . . . (*he collapses*)

TIGGER: Roach!

(*TIGGER catches him and helps him to the floor; QUIZ, JEWEL, and GENIE wake up and stare at the boys; ROACH yanks away and pulls his jacket tighter around his chest*)

ROACH: This city's always cold for mornin'. No matter how hot the day, cold for mornin'. All I gotta do is walk through it. (*beat*) I wish I could go home. (*looks at TIGGER*) I can go home. (*beat; to himself*) I *am* home.

(*ROACH lies down and mumbles softly; the girls go back to sleep; TIGGER pulls a blanket over ROACH's shoulders, sits next to him, cries softly, and watches ROACH drift to sleep; MACK walks to them, strokes ROACH's hair and speaks softly*)

MACK: Above it all,
there's this
beautiful sky.

I pray you listen,
as I call:
I'm caught,
brother,
I'm hung down.
Chained. Owned.
My voice doesn't
reach far,
and I can't speak
too long.
But our four
hands together
could break two
chains this strong.
No generals are
needed to strike up
a march.
Just us,
just us, going the same
way.
Let's just move with
a wink, and a nod.
Let's see who winds
up on top, when we
pull the top down.

SCENE 10: THERE WILL BE

(lights dim on TIGGER and ROACH; MACK rises, speaks to the audience, his anger rising)

MACK: There will be a change –
It'll take time –
It took 220 years for one nation to
fall this far.
There will be a
great day of reckoning.
It won't be biblical in nature.
It will be fueled
on street rat blood.
We will roll down
the gutters and
paint your uptown
condos red.
There will be
as little mercy

as possible.
Your Romanesque
capitols and monuments
will fall about
your presidential
myths
like the levied
pound of flesh.
(*lights focus intensely on MACK*)
There will be
a great day of
reckoning.
Caste-system
education
will burn
and tumble
on pretty
blonde pep rallies –
dunce cap
wrong trackside
bag search children
will wipe
their names
from the board –
education – humiliation
forced into dropout
situation –
(*beat*)
All's you have to pay . . . is – attention.
(*lights fade to black; music up: the Cajun* Les Flammes d'en Fer *– "The Flames of Hell"; lights up for curtain call tableaux; lights fade and actors exit; house lights up for audience exit as music continues; the STREET RATS sit outside the theatre and ask audience members as they pass by, "Spare change?" "Spare change for alcohol?"; MACK angrily recites his street poetry to the crowd*)

12 Writing in Role

Character in Qualitative Inquiry

Writing in role is a drama education technique in which students compose such forms as diary entries, personal letters, original poetry, and other written materials from a particular character's point of view. For example, students might role play and dialogically improvise as immigrants arriving in a new land. To strengthen characterization and immersion in the drama, the facilitator asks each student to write a letter to family members still living in their homeland. In role and if truly engaged with the imaginary circumstances of the drama, students will compose heartfelt and poignant messages to loved ones about the hardships of arriving in a strange country. This is the power of writing in role: thinking and feeling like a character, and articulating what's in the character's mind through written form.

Writing in role for the qualitative researcher can be employed as a technique for gaining deeper insight into the participants we study. Perhaps you've been observing a case during a day's fieldwork and, in addition to your own field note entries, you compose a section of your notes from the *participant's* point of view. Writing in role can cultivate your empathetic abilities and provide richer understanding of the lived experiences of other people.

Writing in role can also be employed for qualitative write-ups and presentations. The technique gives you permission to assume a persona that can tell the research story better than your own academic voice. Two examples are included in this final chapter. The first, "All I Really Need to Know About Qualitative Research I Learned in High School: The 2016 Qualitative High Graduation Commencement Address," was presented at the May 2016 International Congress of Qualitative Inquiry conference and included as the Coda in *Qualitative Inquiry in Neoliberal Times* (Denzin & Giardina, 2017). The title and theme were inspired by Robert Fulghum's (1988) classic essay, "All I Really Need to Know I Learned in Kindergarten." I composed and presented this monologic, performative keynote in role as a high school valedictorian. Conference attendees were dropped into role as graduating seniors of the fictitious Qualitative High School, joined by their faculty, family, and friends.

Months before the keynote, I struggled with how to deliver the address – that is, the specific character I was to portray. I envisioned people I actually knew during my high school days and tried to replicate their gestural mannerisms and vocal tones in rehearsal, but couldn't find the right persona for the piece. It wasn't until the address actually began that a stunning realization occurred to me on stage: I'm not supposed to be playing a character; I'm supposed to be playing an *age*. My presentation went forward with me in role as an exuberant 18-year-old filled with optimism and hope for a bright future after graduation.

Also notice that the script includes five short video clips from popular films about high school life related to the subtopics of the presentation, plus an array of PowerPoint image and title slides. I attempt to be as visual and even as audience participatory as I can in my keynote addresses. Most conference attendees appreciate the visual variety of a briskly moving multi-slide presentation, and the unexpected insertion of media can delight the senses and keep audiences engaged.

The second piece, "Blue-Collar Qualitative Research: A Rant" from *Qualitative Inquiry*, is my only published work that many readers have felt motivated to e-mail me with their praise and thanks. It also motivated a follow-up commentary article from Graham Francis Badley (2015). This is a piece written out of anger (a powerful stimulus for writing, by the way) at the scholarly pretentiousness I observed at professional research gatherings. I grew up poor and surrounded by Texans with a down-to-earth sensibility. As an adult, I live simply and humbly and learned that people appreciate my "realness" when we speak to each other. I also enjoy the self-proclaimed redneck humor of comedians such as Ron White and Trae Crowder. Their ability to hone in on the foibles of politicians, big business, and the wealthy through rambunctious comedy stimulated me to apply that same approach to comment on what I privately thought to myself were "tight-assed, shit-for-brains" researchers.

"Blue-Collar Qualitative Research: A Rant" is written in role as an angry redneck. The character I took on permitted me to write in an informal rural dialect, laced with colloquialisms and profanities, about the scholarly pretense some researchers assume. Though the article is brief, it took over four years to crystallize. I had a character but not the script. I had the rage but not the voice. I had the feelings but no form. Writing this piece was an on-again-off-again venture. It wasn't until I could set aside my anger and think about the article's structure that an idea finally emerged – an idea that was so obvious it should have been apparent from the very beginning: write as a stand-up comedian performing at a comedy club. Each section of the article is a comedic "set" for an audience of qualitative researchers, ending with a litany that pays homage to Jeff Foxworthy's signature "You might be a redneck" one-liners.

In everyday life, my conversations with close male friends are laced with obscenities. I read on a Facebook news story that highly intelligent people tend to curse more often, which I arrogantly took as validation of my propensity for profanity. "Blue-Collar Qualitative Research: A Rant" permitted me to say what I've always wanted to say directly to the faces of "highfalutin'" scholars but couldn't. Writing in role gave me the opportunity for cathartic release after a professional lifetime of feeling "lesser than." It is the one journal article from my entire body of published work I wish to be associated with and remembered for creating.

References

Badley, G. F. (2015). Qualitative ranting? *Qualitative Inquiry, 21*(9), 759–765.
Denzin, N. K., & Giardina, M. D. (Eds.). (2017) *Qualitative inquiry in neoliberal times*. New York: Routledge.
Fulghum, R. (1988). *All I really need to know I learned in kindergarten: Uncommon thoughts on common things*. New York: Random House.

ALL I REALLY NEED TO KNOW ABOUT QUALITATIVE RESEARCH I LEARNED IN HIGH SCHOOL: THE 2016 QUALITATIVE HIGH GRADUATION COMMENCEMENT ADDRESS

Alma Mater

(the Valedictorian of Qualitative High School, dressed in a black graduation gown and cap, steps to the podium; he addresses the audience)
VALEDICTORIAN: Could we all please rise, as you're able, for the singing of our school's alma mater. We all know the melody, right? I'll warm up to get us started; join in when you catch on.
(the Valedictorian leads the audience as they hum through the melody of "Daisy")
Everyone, now:
(slides: song lyrics; the audience sings to the tune of "Daisy")
Qual High, Qual High,
Oh, what a lovely name!
Life is our lab,
Researching is our game.
Whether narrative, codes, or theory,
We love to do inquiry.
And how we write
Into the night.
Hail to thee, hallowed school,
Qual High!
(*Valedictorian shouts:* Second verse!)
Qual High, Qual High,
Loyal are we to you.
We're word crazy,
Some of the chosen few.
We don't really crunch statistics,
We're more about heuristics.
And we'll not rest
Until we're the best.
Hail to thee, hallowed school,
Qual High!
(applause and cheers)
Thank you. Please be seated.

Welcome

(slide: graduation cap and diploma)

Principal Denzin, distinguished faculty and staff, parents, family members, friends, and students of Qualitative High: Welcome, and thank you for the

[Originally published in *Qualitative Inquiry in Neoliberal Times*, edited by Norman K. Denzin and Michael D. Giardina, New York: Routledge, 2017, pp. 179–189.]

honor of selecting me as valedictorian for Qual High's 2016 graduation commencement address.

Curriculum

We've all worked hard for our high school degrees by studying lots of different subjects in qualitative inquiry. We had a great curriculum and set of classes at Qual High with some really outstanding teachers. Just in my senior year alone, I took:

(*slides: class titles*)

Period 1, Grounded Theory, with that teacher that everybody loves, Ms. Charmaz.
Period 2, Phenomenology, with the mellow and laid back Mr. Vagle.
Period 3, Ethnography, with Qual High's sweetheart of a teacher, Ms. Tracy.
Period 4, Case Studies, with my soulful mentor, Ms. De la Garza.
Then Lunch, which usually consisted of either barbeque or fried chicken.
Period 5, Autoethnography, with that rockin' dude, Mr. Poulos.
Period 6, CAQDAS Computer Lab, with my gal-pal Ms. Jackson.
Period 7, Ont-Ep, or Ontologies and Epistemologies, with the brilliant Ms. Mirka.
And Period 8, with Mr. Creswell, AP Mixed Methods – or, as we jokingly liked to call it, the "mixed meth lab."

(*slide: dancers on stage*)

We had great after school extracurricular activities, too, like Poetic Inquiry and Arts-Based Research. These programs were after school for no credit because, you know, they're frills. But our award-winning Qual High drama club did put on some pretty outstanding play productions this year, like:

(*slides: play productions*)

A Datum in the Sun, Category on a Hot Tin Roof, To Code a Mockingbird, the children's theatre touring show of *The Wizard of Observation,* and the club's annual musicals: *The Phenomenology of the Opera* and *Fieldwork on the Roof.*

(*slides: high school proms*)

But at Qual High it wasn't all work. We also had fun, like at the school's annual proms with our wonderful themes: "Enchanted Ethnography," "A Million Case Studies," and "Grounded Theory Under the Sea."

Now, you may think that there's more to learn after we receive our diplomas today. But, in a way, all we really need to know about qualitative research we learned in high school.

Cliques

(slides: high school cliques)

For example, at Qual High we learned that there are cliques – social groups of like-minded tribes who cluster into categories of affinity such as the arts-based researchers, the autoethnographers, the mixed methods researchers, the grounded theorists, and the poststructuralists.

(video clip: the cliques and cafeteria scene from Mean Girls: www.youtube.com/watch?v=IVhfrUkH5JY)
(slides: high school cliques)

Cliques usually sat together at their respective lunchroom tables and shop-talked passionately about what they shared in common. We naturally gravitate to those with whom we share a common interest. And, it made us feel as if we belonged to a little community. But remember at lunch how, in our cliques, we sometimes talked smack about others sitting at different tables? Ethnographers would glance toward the phenomenologists and think, "I wonder what it is they do, exactly." Poststructuralists would sneer at the grounded theorists and think, "Losers!" Mixed-methods researchers would glance suspiciously at the arts-based inquiry table and whisper among themselves, "Well, yeah, but it's not *real* research."

What we learned is that Qual High, like life, has cliques. And though some of us crossed borders now and then because of our different interests, there seems to be a tightly controlled mind-set in some of these camps, with their leaders or big dogs who set the tone for the rest of the group. There'll be people in your clique who'll be your best friends forever and ever, and others from different cliques who'll think that they're just too cool for you. We were told by our teachers that we're one big global community and that we should all learn to get along with each other. But at Qual High, we've been taught to compete with our raging hormones of professional disagreement, fighting in the parking lot or locker room over who's got the biggest paradigm.

Rivalry

(slide: high school football players)

Now, sometimes competition can be a good thing. We had great team rivalry with the alternative school, Post-Qual High, with their post-football games at their post-stadium, watching their post-students in the post-stands post-applauding their post-marching band making post-formations on the post-field, with their post-cheerleaders and post-pep squad excitedly waving their post-pom-poms, rallying around the post-football team's post-quarterback making post-touchdowns at the post-goal posts.

252   *Writing in Role*

(*slide: math Olympics winners*)

We had great team rivalry with Quant High, too, even though they always kicked our butts at science fairs and math Olympics. After all, their school motto was (*slide*), "*Gloria in numero*" – "Strength in Numbers." But let's not forget our school motto (*slide*): "*Ut intellegas omnia*" – "To Understand Is Everything." Yeah, Quant High may calculate the mean, but at Qual High *we* calculate *meaning*.

Literature

(*slides: libraries and book covers*)

In literature classes, we read the great masterworks of the field, like *The Presentation of Self in Everyday Life*, *The Discovery of Grounded Theory*, and *Naturalistic Inquiry*. In secret, a few of us even snuck off and delved into the banned books section to get off on such titles as *Sick Societies* and *Tearoom Trade*. We learned a lot from our teachers about the classics. They felt it was important to know our literary history, our scholarly roots.

Admittedly, I originally thought that these moldy-oldies wouldn't have anything to say to me now. But after reading books by Ina Corinne Brown, Clifford Geertz, and Elliot Liebow – not just reading *about* them in a research handbook but reading what *they themselves* actually wrote – it made me realize how rich our field is, how insightful our ancestors were, and how our own work today is truly built on their foundations. And just because we can Amazon.com or Wikipedia our way through a literature review these days, doesn't mean we should ignore the genius of what's already been discovered and written about social life. I encourage my incoming and current classmates: Don't just stick to what's been published in the last five to ten years. Pick up a 20th-century classic now and then. Read it. Learn for yourself why it's considered a masterpiece.

Composition

Now, reading was hard but writing was harder – even the faculty admitted how tough it was to write qualitatively.

(*video clip: the writer's struggle scene from* Hamlet 2: www.youtube.com/watch?v=hg10aV0uPQk)
(*slides: people writing*)

Rivalry wasn't just with other schools, it was even amongst ourselves. Sometimes we felt bullied when a senior mocked us because we couldn't grasp an ontology, or when we hadn't read the latest journal issue, or if we hadn't cited their work in our most recent report. Manuscript submissions were the worst – when our articles that we worked so hard on were ripped apart by badass peer reviewers who tore down our self-esteem. It was qualitative hazing, of sorts – a ritual we had to go through to be accepted into the publications club. But many of us will never forget that day when we finally made it into the journal of life!

(*slide: the journal cover for* "Qualitative Inquiry")

Teachers kept telling us to "find" our voice. And, that journey took a bit of time. But what I eventually learned at Qual High was that I didn't need to "find" my voice – all I needed to do was to *trust* it.

CAQDAS Lab

(*slides: CAQDAS screenshots*)

I did OK in reading and writing qualitatively, but math and science were not my strong suit. That's probably why I flunked CAQDAS computer lab and had to retake the course – twice. I remember going up to Ms. Jackson one day after my program crashed and whining, "Ms. Jackson – digital tools are, like, *hard!*" She looked me straight in the eye and said, "Johnny, it's not the software that's holding you back; it's your fear." Nevertheless, she placed me in the freshman remedial CAQDAS class. But even there, I had a very hard time trying to figure things out, even after learning that stupid "Qualitative Software Song" – remember it? Sing along with me, if you do:

(*slides: song lyrics; sung to the tune of* "The ABC Song")

AnSWR, AQUAD, Qualrus, CAT,
ATLAS.ti, Dedoose, INTERACT,
Transana, NVivo,
V-Note, WordStat, Quirkos, oh,
MAXQDA, DiscoverText,
HyperRESEARCH, none of these complex.

(*slides: CAQDAS screenshots*)

But they *were* complex – to me, at least. Some students aced these courses: tech-head whiz kids who got it and knew all the right functions to click while I was still struggling to learn the difference between a code and a node. But I didn't give up, and I came out with an A-minus – the qual nerd's "F." I'll admit there's still a lot more to learn, and you're never too old to learn, right? Like Ms. Jackson said – it's not the software that's holding us back; it's our fear.

Driving

(*slides: high school drivers*)

Speaking of fear, high school was also the time we learned how to drive. It was a major achievement to get that license from the PhD-DMV. In dissertation driving class, we were scared, at first, to get behind that wheel, armed only with our master's learning permit and a committee chair yelling at us, "You're going too fast! Slow down, slow down, *slow down!*" But we paid careful attention to the road as we sped down Seminar Street and Doctoral Drive, following the rules and braking quickly when danger lay ahead. We'd steer and swerve and not accidentally step on the fast-track gas pedal and run head on into committee members standing on a sidewalk, even though there were times when some of us really, really wanted to. Oh, but what an achievement, to finally get that license from the PhD-DMV! Yeah, there are student car loan payments to make for what seems like an eternity, but now, we can go anywhere we want.

Detention

Admittedly, a few of us did spend a little time in in-school and after-school detention.

(*video clip: the detention monitor's opening instructions scene in* The Breakfast Club: www.youtube.com/watch?v=Z2WZrxuwDhs)
(*slides: high school detention*)

Detention wasn't all that bad, though. It was a time and place to reflect, to reflex, to refract. A time when the suspension monitor forced us to write analytic memos on our deviant actions and what they all mean. The bad boys and bad girls of Qual High who refused, rejected, avoided, and failed, who wouldn't put up with anyone's othering or interactional BS, critically theorized about the oppressive panopticons of power and the stigma of our presentations of self in this total institutional asylum of a school.

The badasses of Qual High even had a nickname for their gang – the Outliers. The police would sometimes catch them spray painting graffiti on school walls such as (*slides*): "POWER TO THE PARTICIPANTS," "N = *ME*!", and "FOUCAULT? FOUC YOU!"

Deviance, though, can sometimes be a good thing. It means you're straying away from the norm, challenging the status quo, and presenting an alternative perspective on life. The time it becomes a problem, however, is when resistance transforms into intellectual obstruction. It becomes a problem when ontological defiance transforms into epistemological bullying and axiological manipulation. Walk your own path, but don't peer-pressure or kidnap others along the way. Butting heads with someone may get yours bitten off. As we were taught in our Ethics class (*slide*): "Do no harm, but take no shit."

(*aside*)

Sorry, Principal Denzin.

Teachers

Us students had a tough time at Qual High, but we also know our teachers did, too.

(*video clip: the literature class scene from* 10 Things I Hate About You: www.youtube.com/watch?v=H_3eOtD_0GA)
(*slides: high school teachers interacting with students*)

Sometimes when I passed by the faculty lounge, I heard teachers saying things behind the door such as, "I can't teach my students how to think," or "He wouldn't know a paradigm if it fell on his head," and "What do those kids expect me to do, pull a grounded theory out of my butt?" Some teachers made darn sure that when it came to research methods, it was either their way or the highway, while others nurtured and encouraged us to find our own ways of working.

Perhaps you're hoping some of us will become the next Arlie Russell Hochschild or the next Erving Goffman. But maybe, just maybe, I want to be the next Barbara Ehrenreich or the next Dwight Conquergood. Or maybe I just want to be the *first* Johnny Saldaña. After we leave Qual High, the methodological decisions are up to us.

Teachers: We appreciate what you did for us, shaping, sharpening, and challenging our minds. We know that qualitative teachers work hard, put in long hours, and you're grossly underpaid. But we'll never forget what you did for us. You taught us how to look at life in new and different ways. You taught us how to think for ourselves, to not be swept away by what's trendy in the field. And you taught us to strive for rigor, credibility, and trustworthiness in everything we do. You have influenced and affected our lives for the better, and we are eternally grateful to you.

Sex

All we really need to know about qualitative research we learned in high school. For example, we learned about sex.

(*video clip: the fake bedroom sex scene from* Easy A: www.youtube.com/watch?v=QGIQQBEj9uU)

Oh yeah, our classes in qualitative health care taught us about the biological and reproductive aspects of being human, but the teenagers in us fooled around. We even had labels for it, too

(*slides*):

1st base: Codes
2nd base: Categories
3rd base: Theories

It was a time to naturally experiment, to discover what turned us on. I'm not ashamed to admit it, we all did it. When we should have been constructing matrices, flow charts, and diagrams for mixed-methods class, sometimes I was locked away in my bedroom under the covers – writing autoethnography.

(*slides: terms*)

But, I mean, let's face it – in high school, sex was all around us: gender studies, women's studies, masculinity studies, feminist theory, queer theory, trans studies – it seemed as if every course in junior year was about sex, sex, sex. I mean, come on, the terms our teachers used: *raw data, horizontalization, probing, oral history, thick description*. Some days I didn't know the difference between an IRB and an STD.

Qual High was a magical period, though, for first-time experiences: Losing our virginity on the first day of fieldwork; that awkward moment of silence during our first formal interview; and the heartbreaking crush of our first journal article rejection letter.

Yet through it all, we were taught to analyze responsibly in ethics class, to practice safe research. And we learned that no matter what our methodological preference or orientation – qualitative, quantitative, or mixed – we are all loved. We are OK, just as we are.

The Real World

(*slides: people in despair*)

People say that high school prepares you for the real world. And, unfortunately, the real world waiting for us consists of bad things like government accountability, massive cuts to higher education, restricted or conditional funds for our research, unsolved social problems all around us, and some really, really stupid people with way too much money and power.

(*slide: "Hope"*)

But we're a resourceful graduating class – we have to be. We have skills that can change the world. We have knowledge about the way things work that can make a significant impact on others.

Life Learnings

All we really need to know about qualitative research we learned in high school. But like they taught me in Constructivism class, I acknowledge that my perspective is not the only one that exists. So, I asked my Facebook friends from our graduating class what *they* learned at Qual High, and this is what they told me:

(*slides: high school yearbook photos from the 1950s to today*)

Being a researcher means to find your passion and follow it. Getting involved in projects you love makes life worth living. If you have an interest in a research topic, it's up to you, and only you, to pursue it. You can let research happen to you, or you can make research happen. Other scholars may come and go and be supportive or not, but it's your responsibility to be in the world, so it's your responsibility to know the world.

Research isn't always as hard as we make it out to be. Maybe you don't want people to know how dumb you *think* you are, or how smart you *really* are. Nobody, not even you, will remember in a few short years the stupid things you said in a seminar that made you feel like hiding away forever. And even if you're a senior researcher with a kick-ass publications record, you're not entitled to anything; if it's worth having, then it's worth working for. Teachers aren't always right; sometimes students are.

Yeah, there were some mean bullies at Qual High who shoved us into methodological lockers. It made us want to build walls to protect ourselves. But we survived. Life goes on after we graduate from Qual High. There are many more great inquiries ahead. Life isn't always fair, but *you* can be. Put good into the world every day. Despite what our teachers told us, these weren't "the best years of our lives," because it gets *better*.

If you're new to Qual High, not fitting in is OK; everyone's insecure. Find a paradigmatic place where you can be who *you* need to be. If you get tired of grounded theory, then write an autoethnography. If you're bored with generating codes and categories, then write a data poem. Reinvent yourself.

Good research colleagues, good friends, are the most important thing. Don't put your heroes on pedestals, though, because it'll hurt really bad when they come crashing down. It's better to be you than someone else. Like our teachers taught us in Autoethnography class: "You can't learn how to tell someone else's story until you first learn how to tell your own."

The Future

High school is the time for the search for our identities. And some of us have already found a focus as grounded theorists, arts-based researchers, mixed methodologists, and so on. But you know what? That may change in the future. We are adolescents – or dare I say, young adults – with a lot more growing up to do. There are many opportunities ahead of us, and we need to be ready for them in any way we can.

(*slide: forks in the road*)

Like baseball great Yogi Berra said, "When you come to a fork in the road, take it!" We need to keep ourselves open to *all* quests for knowledge. We'll interview when we need to, we'll observe when we need to. We'll crunch numbers when we need to, we'll think with theory when we need to. We'll write a poem when we need to, we'll compose an autoethnography when we need to. We'll code when we need to, we'll categorize when we need to, we'll use a CAQDAS software program when we need to. We need to know how to do it *all* – because we never know what our futures hold.

Farewell

(*slide: Qual High motto*)

"*Ut intellegas omnia*" – "To Understand Is Everything."

(*slide: graduation cap and diploma*)

Qual High class of 2016, we did it! We've gotten through, and we've received our diplomas. We're research geeks, and damn proud of it. So let's go out there, raise some qualitative hell, and change the world! Thank you, and *congratulations*!

(*recessional music: Elgar's* "Pomp and Circumstance": www.youtube.com/watch?v=Q0PHWKRFgZ0)

BLUE-COLLAR QUALITATIVE RESEARCH: A RANT

Abstract

This here's a kick-ass article 'bout a pissed off qualitative researcher who feels that some of you higher ed profs out there got a lotta attitude and need to be brought down a notch. I speak my mind in this piece 'bout a lotta stuff, like me, positionality, voice, labels, method, theory, ethics, and other crap like that. I write like a redneck 'cause that's what's in my blue-collar soul. I keep it real. Take it or leave it.

Keywords

blue-collar, qualitative research, rant

Hey, y'all. This here's an article 'bout gittin' real with what we do. Of course, I want ever'body doin' qualitative research to read it, but I know that ain't gonna happen. So, if you like this piece, tell your friends. If you don't like this piece, tell 'em that, too. I'd appreciate the word-of-mouth, regardless. Like that playwriter Oscar Wilde said, "The only thing worse than bein' talked about, is *not* bein' talked about."

Grad students: This is an article some of your tight-ass professors may not want you to read – which is exactly why you *should* read it, OK?

So, loosen your tie, uncinch your belt a notch, kick your shoes off, and read on …

My Position

The only reason I'm writin' 'bout this is 'cause some people seem to put a lotta stock in "positionality." Me: I can take it or leave it. But in case ya need to know, here goes:

My position? I'm right here in front of you. Look at me: I'm a 63-year-old man with a white beard. Gay leather bear, Hispanic, a touch of Cajun (in spirit, not by blood), with a little bit of bad-ass biker in me, and a proud dash of redneck-wannabe. Overweight, asthmatic, a little arthritis; I don't complain much, I git by. There's other weird shit, but you really don't wanna know 'bout that. None of your business anyways. I worry 'bout a secure retirement; who doesn't at my age in these times? No PhD here. I got a MFA in theatre, though. Some people look down on that. I used to care but don't anymore. I got street cred now. I know people, and they know me.

I grew up poor, too. That's prob'ly the most important thing ya need to know 'cause that's what really matters in this piece. My mama and daddy, God

[Originally published in *Qualitative Inquiry*, vol. 20, no. 8, 2014, pp. 976–980; doi 10.1177/1077800413513739; edited slightly for this publication.]

rest their souls, worked hard to raise five kids and send me to college – the first one in my family. I'm middle class now; doin' good, got a nice suburban roof over my head, worked hard for it. But there's a sayin' from one of my cultures: "A Mexican may git rich, but he'll still drink in the cantina." (If you need someone to explain to you what that means, then maybe a lotta this article's gonna be over your head.) I can have a real good time talkin' to a trucker, construction worker, day laborer, server, janitor, any minimum-wage earner, and show him or her the respect that is their due. But I can't always say the same for some of the so-called "doctors" I talk to at professional conferences, though.

In the early American plays, the common workin' man characters was the heroes and called the "blue shirt" roles – prob'ly 'cause they was traditionally dressed up in blue shirts, and maybe where the term "blue-collar" comes from. This everyday man was prized over the rich, elite, snobbish characters in the plays who was always made fun of for their highfalutin' ways and who always got their comeuppance in the end.

I wrote this piece 'cause a coupla years ago I got really pissed off at some of the highbrow attitude I heard at a research conference. It offended me that some people – some very smart but, in my opinion, very misguided people – talk like that, *think* like that. My lower-class roots got gnarled up tight at the indignity of their pretension, their assumptions of authority, their "I know the truth and you don't" arrogance. People like that prob'ly won't read what I have to write anyways. No matter. The important part is that this is in print somewhere for others who care.

So, where and what is my position? It is smack dab in the middle of my blue-collar universe, and smack dab in the middle of your face.

Where I'm Comin' From

OK. Now . . . you see . . . this is another one of those things that some people seem to put a lotta stock in: "conceptual framework," "theoretical perspective," "epistemological foundations," "methodological premises" – whatever. How 'bout me just sayin' what it really is and what I really mean: *This is where I'm comin' from.*

First point: Jim Goad's *The Redneck Manifesto: How Hillbillies, Hicks, and White Trash Became America's Scapegoats* is a bitter but kick-ass rant. Sure, you gotta take some of what Goad writes with a grain of salt – he's an angry white man, after all. But I learned more 'bout what it feels like and what it means to be a white man in today's society from his manifesto, more than from any of my scholarly multicultural education textbooks and journals. Go figger. But the reason I'm pointin' this book out is 'cause this article is *my* redneck manifesto – my pissed-off, blue-collar perspective on where some crazy qualitative researchers is goin'. It kinda adopts Goad's writin' style, too. I'm givin' him credit for that.

Second point: Jeff Foxworthy of the Blue-Collar Comedy Tour humorously defines a redneck as anyone with "a total lack of sophistication." Him and his buddies Bill Engvall, Ron White, and Larry the Cable Guy are seen by many as the blue-collar heroes of today – men who ain't afraid to speak their minds and point out all the weird and stupid stuff we do. Are their routines racist? Yeah. Sexist? Yeah. Homophobic? Yeah. Funny? Hell yeah. What these guys did was make bein' a redneck acceptable – fashionable, even. Trendy redneck-wannabes, like me, are *knowin'ly and tongue-in-cheekly performin'* their total lack of sophistication. But there's a pride 'bout it, too. To be a redneck, to be blue-collar, is to be real – to have your feet on the ground and not your nose up in the air.

Third point: Norm Denzin and Yvonna Lincoln (God love 'em, they're good people) wrote 'bout "moments" in the history of qualitative research. Sometimes, I shake my head at the off-the-wall talk flyin' 'round at conferences today and think, "Well, we must be in the *'bullshit moment'* now!" Some of the things I've been hearin' at these meetin's make me madder than a grounded theorist without a core category.

My Blue-Collar Voice

Most people say that each person's voice is important – but sometimes we don't always wanna hear what some folks gotta say, right? Be honest. There's others out there who want desperately to understand other people through their research, but some scholarly types don't always make the effort to *listen*. Sometimes, I have to say what I feel needs to be said two times before people are actually listenin'. Sometimes, I have to say what I feel needs to be said two times before people are actually listenin'. You wanna know who I am, what I think, and how I feel? Then just *listen*. Really *listen*. Shut the fuck up, and *listen*.

Now, what's with all the cussin', you're prob'ly thinkin'. Well, the blue-collar voice can be a profane voice. Obscenities are said not just out of a total lack of sophistication, but to make a point, or because we're pissed off, or sometimes just 'cause it's dirty fun. Throughout this article, you'll read the occasional "goddamn" and "fuck you" and other choice cuss words. They're not always meant to shock, but to make a point, or because I'm angry, or to keep you awake.

Profanity is subjective, anyways. What's profane to me is not someone who says "fuck." What's profane to me is what happened to the people trapped in the World Trade Center on 9/11. What's profane to me is big business CEOs makin' millions of dollars in salary perks while their minimum wage workers is livin' off food stamps. What's profane to me is all the racist, sexist, legislative bullshit happenin' in states like Arizona, North Carolina, and Texas. Profanity, to me, is not what someone says. Profanity is what people *do* to each other that hurts or kills. I really doubt that me sayin' one "goddamn" is as profane or offensive as the thousands if not millions of folks in Africa dyin' from AIDS right now. So, keep my cussin' in perspective, OK? If you got problems with my profane voice, then *fuck you* – go read somethin' else. Let the people with balls on 'em keep readin'.

(Granted, "fuck you" is not the most sophisticated of retorts, but when it's said by me, at least you know it's heartfelt and sincere.)

Labels

Labels can be very deceivin'. For example, the label "conservative" makes me think, "Why don't you just call yourself what you really are – a tight-assed, hateful, holier-than-thou bigot." (But that's just me thinkin' out loud.) I can understand the need for labels to identify who you are; I use 'em all the time. Sometimes I'm a "pragmatist." Sometimes I'm a "bear." And sometimes I'm a "vindictive little bitch." It all depends on where I am, who I'm with, and what the occasion calls for as the need arises.

Some people proudly call themselves a "post-structuralist" or "critical theorist" or some other fancy five-dollar term. And you can certainly make a life's work out of studyin' that stuff. But if that's all you do, it kinda limits who you are and what you can accomplish. Every time I hear or read that someone's followin' the "hermeneutic circle," I keep thinkin' of some dumb ol' hound dog chasin' its own tail 'round and 'round and 'round. It *looks* like fun, but he ain't really gittin' anywhere, is he?

Me, I keep myself open to bein' and doin' what needs to be done. I'll be a grounded theorist when I need to be. I'll be a statistician and crunch some numbers when I need to. And I'll be a poet or playwright or artist when the occasion calls for it. It's all 'bout findin' the right tool for the right job. There's somethin' to be said 'bout that. Blue-collar folks are good craftspeople – they know their tools. They work hard and they sweat harder. Sweatin' analysis is gittin' your hands dirty in the data. It's muscle work, and you git stronger and smarter with each project. Nothin' wrong with the craftspersonship of it. An honest day's qualitative work for an honest day's quantitative pay.

I used to think that the "intellectual elite" attack was the narrow-minded conservatives' slam-dunk at things they didn't understand. But after hearin' some of them "intellectual elites" at research conferences, maybe they got a point. After all, I think that post-structuralists are the Republicans of qualitative inquiry – they's firmly convinced that they's always right and everybody else should think the same way. *Fuck that.* There's been this talk in our field 'bout the "crisis of representation." Well, lemme tell you: Some of us *are* the "crisis of representation"'cause a coupla people out there are representin' themselves as real elitist assholes.

Post-positivist, post-modernist, post-colonial, post-structuralist – aw, post-, my ass. Post *this*. . . .

Method

A teacher by the name of Dorothy Heathcote once told me, "You don't go 'back to basics,' you go *forward* to basics once you've figured out what those new basics are." The problem with our field is that there's some kinda general understandin' 'bout what's what, but no real tried-and-true "how to." Seems like ever'body's got their own way of doin' things – which is good, in a way.

It's kinda like puttin' your ironin' brand or personal signature on what you did and wrote. Yeah, I got my own ways of workin'; I never met a code I didn't like. Qualitative research is kinda like meat loaf: ever'body's got their own way of makin' it. But if we're all doin' stuff our own way, then how do we know if we hit the nail on the head? Some folks call it "credibility" or "trustworthiness." I just call it "the real thing." When I'm talkin' 'bout my findin's, and I see other people's heads noddin' or – even better – hearin' 'em say out loud, "That's right!" then I know I got the bull by the horns and caught the real thing.

Theory

OK . . . here's where I got *real* problems. Maybe it's just me, but those folks who promote and teach a lot 'bout theory and feel that it's the be-all-and-end-all of research are a lotta times those who rarely come up with any original theories of their own. A teachin' buddy of mine with a doctoral degree herself once told me, "PhDs are paid to think of a lotta useless stuff." Some theory is good and has its place; it helps us in day-to-day life. But git to the point already. If it's a theory, say it's a theory. Don't make me go huntin' for it through 30-some-odd pages of manuscript. Italicize it, bold it, put it in a box, hold it up to my hairy face and say, "Here's my theory!" – and fill in the blank.

And while we're at it, to be "critical" doesn't mean to bitch and whine 'bout it. It means to take somethin' apart, to show where all the warts are, and to right the wrongs. If you really wanna know what's wrong with the world, then git your ass out to the 'hood, walk 'round and talk to people. *Listen* to what they have to say.

And one more thing: Blue-collar qualitative researchers don't give a god-damn fuck 'bout what Foucault says.

Questions and Answers

If alls there is these days is ambiguity, uncertainty, unresolved complexity, and unanswered questions, then Jesus Christ, what's it all for? Let's just pack up and go home.

There's some misguided people out there who think that alls they gotta do is come up with a smart question and their job's done. Well, fuck that noise. I want answers. I *need* answers. Some folks will say, "Well, it's not that simple," to which I usually reply, "It's prob'ly not that complicated, either." Straight talk – sometimes the most profound thoughts are said usin' the simplest of words. The steelworker from Studs Terkel's *Working* said, "It isn't that the average working guy is dumb. He's tired, that's all." Wow. . . .

Try to put the complexity of what you need to say into as simple a language as possible. Now *that's* the sign of a true data analyst and a true thinker. Find the essence, the essentials, the elegance. If you're lookin' for answers, then find out what drives people to do the crazy shit that they do. It's usually out of love, duty, hatred, anger, ambition, boredom, jealousy, desperation, revenge, hunger, thirst, sleepiness, horniness – your basic emotional and physical food groups.

I got a lotta problems with highbrows who just wanna mentally masturbate and think up a lotta questions and not even bother answerin' 'em. Ask me a question if you want me to think, but at least give it a shot yourself. Stop wastin' paper or conference time or digital space if you don't have any answers yourself to the questions you ask. *Do your goddamn job as a researcher and answer the goddamn questions you pose.* If you don't have an answer – even your best guess – then don't bother askin' *me* the question, OK? It's not the questions that are interestin'. It's the answers that are interestin'. It's the answers that are profound. "Is there a God?" won't be half as excitin' as a definitive "Yes," "No," or "It's somethin' different all together." So if you ask tough questions, you better damn well come up with some tough answers.

On Bein' Ethical

I usually avoid goin' to any conference session that has the word "ethics" or "ethical" in the title. Those gigs are usually a lotta frettin' and angstin' and hand wringin' and a lotta – yeah – unanswered questions. Some folks seem to make a life's work out of studyin' the subject. I got no problem with that, I know it's important. But I do slyly remember an old folk sayin' that goes, "We teach what we wanna learn."

Now, I ain't gonna pass myself off as some high and mighty saint when it comes to research ethics. I've made my fair share of mistakes in the field, and fucked up pretty bad on two occasions with my work. Both times, it was one of those I-didn't-see-it-comin' moments. I learned from that and moved on and vowed to keep my eyes wide open so it hopefully never happens again. But there comes a time when you just gotta git to the bottom line, and to those who just go on and on and on 'bout ethics, I really wanna ask, "What part of 'But first, do no harm' do you not understand?"

Respect

I don't always dis' those with a doctoral degree. Ain't got one myself, but I know some of you worked real hard for one. And I won't deny that some people are very smart, but when you lord it over me, you just lost favor in my eyes. Then what happens is that people like me start resentin' and makin' fun of people like you. And when you become somebody else's satire, then you really gotta take a good hard look at yourself, you know?

I like that sayin', "You're entitled to your own opinions, but not your own facts." So, state your opinions, but not so forcefully or arrogantly that they seem like gospel truth. It's just one person's opinion. Tell me what you think – I'll listen. I may agree, I may disagree. I may think it's insightful, I may think it's total bullshit. But at least I'll listen. Just extend me the same courtesy, OK? You can even feel free to think that what I say is bullshit, too. But if the reason is 'cause you feel you're just smarter than me, then what you're really sayin' is you think

I'm dumber than you. No need to tell me, "You're wrong." That assumes you automatically got the right answer. Just tell me, "I got a different way of lookin' at it," and tell me what's goin' through your head. But don't try to persuade me or make me change my mind. That's my job, not yours.

Now, there's some folks out there who's never gonna change no matter what. I guess they learned that bein' a professor means bein' super smart and thinkin' you got the inside edge on the rest of us. Well, I don't hang out with "those kind of people" – admittedly, maybe that's why I don't understand 'em, right? (C'mon – tell the truth and shame the devil!) Well, human nature, I guess, that some of us is just plain folks and others is ambitious folks. The newer generation should honor the older generation for their contributions to the field. Show 'em the respect which is their due. But the newer generation also needs to cut through some of the older crap that's out there and say, "Thanks, but, we'll take it from here." Lead the charge. Raise some qualitative hell.

Blue-collar researchers got a secret handshake, of sorts – a smile and head nod to a stranger as you're approachin' each other. It's a small action but says so much. It says, "I see you as a fellow human bein' and worthy of respect. You ain't got a corner on the truth and neither do I. But together, I bet we can figger it out." Remember that the original meanin' of datum is "somethin' given." Data is a gift, so be thankful for it when it's given to you and treat it with respect.

You Need to Bring It Down a Notch

Just like the Blue-Collar Comedy guys got their signature lines – "You might be a redneck," "Here's your sign," and "Git 'er done" – I got mine: "You need to bring it down a notch." That means that if your head's floatin' off into some outer space dimension, or if your hoity-toity attitude's pissin' some people off, then you need to git back in touch with reality. "You need to bring it down a notch" is a little more civil than "Take the stick outta your ass, you shit-for-brains," but it means the same thing. For example, if you don't like the food at Cracker Barrel, you need to bring it down a notch. If you would never dream of stayin' a night at a Motel 6, you need to bring it down a notch. Here's my list for my qualitative research buddies:

- If you feel you *gotta* cite Foucault, Derrida, Deleuze, or Habermas in any of your work, you need to bring it down a notch.
- If you put prefixes in parentheses, like (re)search or (de)construction, or separate 'em with slashes like un/conditional or mis/appropriation, you need to bring it down a notch.
- If you use any combination of the words *body, bodies, bodied, bodying, embodied, embodying,* or *embodiment* more than five times in one paragraph, you need to bring it down a notch.
- If you say you're usin' grounded theory, but don't have a core category, you need to bring it down a notch.

- If you teach a lot 'bout theory, but haven't come up with any original theories of your own, you need to bring it down a notch.
- If you think that anythin' is "undertheorized," you need to bring it down a notch.
- If you call yourself a "post-*anything*," you need to bring it down a notch.
- If you're making any money offa your research with people who make less money than you, you need to bring it down a notch.
- If your conference session don't make people take notes, or if your book don't make people highlight passages in yellow pen, or if people ain't motivated to download your article after readin' the abstract, you need to bring it down a notch.
- If you worship the *APA Manual* like a bible, you need to bring it down a notch.
- If you call your work a "performance," but alls you're really doin' is just sittin' on your ass behind a table readin' aloud from a paper – and poorly, at that – you need to bring it down a notch.
- If ever'body on your five-member conference session panel is white, you need to bring it down a notch.
- If you'd feel uncomfortable interviewin' a homeless person, a gay transsexual with HIV, or a Mexican immigrant, you need to bring it down a notch.
- If you're a professor and really don't want your students to read this article, you need to bring it down a notch.
- If you're thinkin' this article is a "performance," *fuck you* and you need to bring it down a notch.
- If you're pissed as hell after readin' this article – well, that's actually a good thing, but still – you need to bring it down a notch.

See Ya – Bye

To those of you who still feel the blue-collar qualitative research perspective is total bullshit, thanks for kickin' my hairy brown ass and makin' me write this piece. It's people like you who make people like me wanna be a better researcher. And, it felt good to git this offa my chest.

To those of you who laughed out loud or even shouted "Fuck yeah!" as you read any of this stuff, hook up with me at the next research conference and let's go out for a beer. The drinks are on me, buddy.

Notes

Ain't got none.

References

Ain't got none of these, neither.

Author Biography

Johnny Saldaña is a worn-down, burnt-out prof who's retired from Arizona State University and just spendin' the rest of his years writin' books and messin' on the Interweb. He wrote *The Coding Manual for Qualitative Researchers* (Sage Publications) and he's pretty goddamn proud of that.

Index

action research 5, 10, 29–30, 123, 138, 158, 163; evaluation of 43–47
Adams, Tony E. 156
Alexander, Bryant Keith 144, 157
Allen, Mitch/Mitchell 6, 21, 101
analysis 8, 10, 11, 13, 16, 29, 87, 102, 116, 119, 120–121, 127–128, 130–138, 142, 146–147, 176–177, 211
Angrosino, Michael V. 49
arts-based research 10, 23, 24, 25, 109, 143, 145, 147, 176, 192–193
assertion heuristics 5, 34
autoethnodrama 5, 186–188, 192–194, 203, 205; *see also* ethnodrama/ethnotheatre
autoethnography 5, 24, 116, 118, 120, 156–158, 177, 186, 203

Badley, Graham Francis 247
Barone, Thomas E./Tom 3, 87, 207
Boal, Augusto 3, 30, 31, 46, 47, 50, 52, 54, 55, 72–73, 75, 136
Bram, Joseph 17
Brindle, Patrick 6–7
Brown, Brené 114
Brown, Ina Corinne 252

case study 5, 9–10, 18–19, 23, 49–50, 52, 70, 82, 85–86, 88, 93, 102, 116, 138, 156, 186, 204
"Chalkboard Concerto" (Vanover and Saldaña) 19
Chekhov, Anton 113, 173
Clark-Ibáñez, Marisol 49
coding 5, 6–7, 106, 127, 130, 132, 137–138, 172, 207; attribute 133; axial, selective 137; codeweaving 13; dramaturgical 193; focused 133, 136; *in vivo* 13–16, 33–34, 87, 89, 121, 124–125, 133, 136; magnitude 133; motif 167, 193; open,

initial 136; pattern 130, 133; theoretical 137; values 133; verbal exchange 102, 104–106, 109, 117
Coding Manual for Qualitative Researchers, The (Saldaña) 6–7, 102, 104, 128, 167, 193, 267
Conquergood, Dwight 144, 255
conversation analysis 5, 102, 104–106, 108–109, 116, 117
creative nonfiction 10, 113
critical pedagogy 5, 34, 69–70
cummings, e. e. 12

De la Garza, Amira 3, 102, 206
Denzin, Norman K. 3, 17, 85, 88, 144
dialogue 10, 31, 50, 87, 101, 104–105, 109, 116–119, 124, 177, 186, 187, 208
"Dick and Jane and Johnny: A Childhood Primer" 24–25
Dickinson, Emily 12, 170–171
Donmoyer, Robert 143
duoethnography 118–119

Ehrenreich, Barbara 207, 255
Eisner, Elliot 87
elements 8–10, 25, 112, 114, 124, 165, 171, 193–194, 203
emotional intelligence 70, 79, 153
ethics 19, 81–83, 93–99, 138, 264
ethnodrama/ethnotheatre 5, 17–20, 84–86, 87, 92, 98–99, 109, 117–118, 138, 143–144, 146, 186–189, 192–194; *see also* autoethnodrama; performance text
Ethnodrama: An Anthology of Reality Theatre (Saldaña) 6, 189, 208
ethnography 5, 28–29, 104, 106, 156, 207
Ethnotheatre: Research from Page to Stage (Saldaña) 6, 144

field experiment 32
fieldwork 28–30
film 128, 137–138
Finding My Place: The Brad Trilogy (Saldaña) 18–19, 188, 207–212
Finley, Macklin 12, 19–20, 188–189, 213
Finley, Susan 19–20, 188–189, 213
Foxworthy, Jeff 247, 260
Freire, Paulo 70, 73
Frost, Robert 12
Fulghum, Robert 246
Fundamentals of Qualitative Research (Saldaña) 7, 9

Geertz, Clifford 28, 165, 252
genres 8–9, 10, 25, 109, 112–113, 114, 124, 138, 178
Goffman, Erving 50, 53, 65, 66, 144, 255
Goldstein, Tara 143
Goodall, H. L. 102, 104–106, 109
grounded theory 5, 121, 134, 136–137

Hanauer, David Ian 176
Handke, Peter 177
Hawthorne, Nathaniel 113, 168
Hochschild, Arlie Russell 255

influences and affects 1, 31, 33, 43–44, 127, 138
interview/interviewing 5, 13, 114, 116, 117, 119–121, 123, 124, 128, 138, 145–146, 176, 186

Janesick, Valerie 143
Judge Judy (television series) 3–4

Kozol, Jonathan 69, 87

Leavy, Patricia 7, 143
Liebow, Elliot 252
Lincoln, Yvonna S. 143
Longitudinal Qualitative Research: Analyzing Change through Time (Saldaña) 6
longitudinal research/study 5, 82, 84, 85, 138, 158, 165

Martínez, Alejandra 156
"*Maybe someday, if I'm famous . . .*" (Saldaña) 18, 87–88, 98–99
McCammon, Laura A. 144, 148
Melville, Herman 168
memory work 158, 163, 164, 165, 167, 168
Mienczakowski, Jim 144

mixed methods 5, 138, 141, 165
Molière 12, 177
moment/moments 50, 55, 69–70, 104, 105, 115, 117, 119, 121, 187, 204–205, 261
monologue 10, 18–20, 49–50, 55, 58, 87, 89, 113–116, 119, 124, 146, 186–188, 192, 207–208
motif 165, 167, 171, 174, 187, 194, 203
multicultural education 5, 6, 69, 70, 72, 78–79

narrative inquiry 109, 111–114, 192, 204
Nordmarken, Sonny 156
Norris, Joe 144

Omasta, Matt 8, 145

Pascoe, C. J. 69
performance/performing 2, 11, 17, 19, 20, 83, 85, 89, 93, 94, 97–99, 104–105, 140–142, 143–147, 177–178, 186–189, 204–205, 266
performance text 5, 17, 84–86, 88, 89, 93–99, 177–178; *see also* ethnodrama/ethnotheatre
Peshkin, Alan 115
phenomenology 5, 121, 138
playwright/playwriting 12, 17, 21, 86, 89, 93, 95, 146, 176, 177, 186, 187, 202–204, 207; *see also* writing, dramatic
poetic/poetry 10, 12–13, 16–17, 20, 119–121, 147, 169, 170–171, 176–178, 188, 193, 207–208
Prendergast, Monica 144, 177
proverbs 121–124, 125, 128, 156, 157
purpose statement 1, 5, 113

Qualitative Data Analysis: A Methods Sourcebook (Miles, Huberman and Saldaña) 7
Qualitative Research: Analyzing Life (Saldaña and Omasta) 8
quantitative research 1, 5, 113

reader's theatre 86, 141–142, 143–147
Robinson, Edward Arlington 171–172

Salmon, Helen 7
Sandburg, Carl 12
Schechner, Richard 144
"Science Fiction of Qualitative Inquiries, The" 24
Sexton, Anne 12

Shakespeare 12, 123, 166, 177
significant trivia 28, 50
Smith, Anna Deavere 13, 119, 176
Smith, Mary Lee 3, 87, 88, 207
Stake, Robert E. 102
Steinbeck, John 165
stigma/stigmatized 4, 37, 50, 52–57, 65–67, 72, 75–77, 113
Street Rat (Saldaña, Finley, and Finley) 19–20, 188–189
style/styles 8–10, 20, 25, 81, 112–114, 124, 173
survey 5, 138, 141, 145, 146

taxonomy 34–35
teaching 2–4, 8, 11, 25, 78–79, 101–103, 119, 127–129, 155, 157–158, 161
Terkel, Studs 263
Tharp, Twyla 1
theatre for social change 5, 30, 70
Theatre of the Oppressed 30, 31–32, 46, 50, 52, 70, 72; dynamizing 37, 40, 58; Forum Theatre 31, 33, 37, 41–43, 52, 54–55, 60–63, 65–66, 72; games 31, 37–40, 47, 52, 54, 73; Image Theatre 31, 37, 40–41, 52, 54, 64; joker 42, 47, 54–55, 66, 73, 76–77
thick description 28, 256
Thinking Qualitatively: Methods of Mind (Saldaña) 7, 102–103
Thomas, Dylan 12

Tracy, Sarah J. 3
Turner, Victor 17, 144

unity 9, 10, 20, 127

Van Maanen, John 8, 81, 82
Vanover, Charles 19
vignette 9, 50, 90, 109, 112, 157–158
Vine, Chris 64

Ward, Daryl 113
Weems, Mary E. 12, 178
Whitehouse, Ann 2, 157–158
Whitman, Walt 12, 165, 169, 171
Wilde, Oscar 165, 208, 259
Wolcott, Harry F. 1, 18–19, 24, 49, 81, 82, 92, 188, 207–208
writing: analytic and formal 9, 10, 81, 112; collaborative or polyvocal 10, 81; confessional 10, 18, 28, 81–83, 84, 116; critical or advocacy 10, 81, 116; descriptive and realistic 10, 81, 113; dramatic 10, 17–20, 111, 118, 177, 178, 186–187 (*see also* playwright/playwriting); impressionist 10, 81, 116; interpretive 10, 81; literary narrative 9–10, 111–114; poetic *see* poetic/poetry; presentations 140–141; prosaic 10–12, 111, 117–118, 187; in role 246–248; technical 20–23, 207